# The
# BASQUE
# HISTORY of
# WORLD the

## Also by Mark Kurlansky

**COD**
A Biography of the Fish That Changed the World

**A CHOSEN FEW**
The Resurrection of European Jewry

**A CONTINENT OF ISLANDS**
Searching for the Caribbean Destiny

# The
# BASQUE
# HISTORY of
# WORLD the

*Mark Kurlansky*

WALKER & COMPANY ✻ NEW YORK

*Copyright © 1999 by Mark Kurlansky*

*All rights reserved.*
*No part of this book may be reproduced or transmitted*
*in any form or by any means, electronic or mechanical,*
*including photocopying, recording, or by*
*any information storage and retrieval system,*
*without permission in writing from the Publisher.*

*First published in the United States of America in 1999 by*
*Walker Publishing Company, Inc.*

*Illustrations on pages 17, 44, 46, 105, 106, 109, 115,*
*133, 265, and 305 by the author; illustrations on pages 7, 20, 40,*
*55, 83, 86, 130, 150, 310, and 348 from the author's collection.*

*Library of Congress Cataloging-in-Publication Data*
*Kurlansky, Mark.*
*The Basque history of the world/Mark Kurlansky.*
*p.    cm.*
*Includes index*
*ISBN 0-8027-1349-1*
*1. País Vasco (Spain) 2. Pays Basque (France) 3. Basques.*
*I. Title.*
*DP302.B46K85    1999*
*946'.6—DC21       99-26808*
*CIP*

*Book design by Krystyna Skalski*

*Printed in the United States of America*
*2 4 6 8 10 9 7 5 3 1*

*To Marian,*
*who makes life sparkle*

# Contents

*vii*

## *Part Three*
## EUSKADI ASKATUTA

# Maps

# The
# BASQUE
# HISTORY of
# WORLD the

SEVEN PROVINCES OF BASQUELAND

*Bay of Biscay*
Landes
FRANCE
San Sebastian
(Donostia)
Bayonne
Bilbao
Bermeo
Irún
Adour R.
BÉARN
LABOURD
Guernica
Bidasoa R.
BASSE
NAVARRE
SOULE
VISCAYA
GUIPÚZCOA
ASTURIAS
Toloso
Pamplona (Iruña)
Vitoria (Gastoiz)
ALAVA
Ebro R.
NAVARRA
*Rioja Alta*
Logroño
*Rioja Baja*
*Bardenas
Reales*
ARAGÓN
CASTILLA
Tudela
Ebro R.
SPAIN
©1999 Jeffrey L. Ward

*Atlantic
Ocean*
FRANCE
Lyon
Bordeaux
Bilbao
Marseilles
SPAIN
PORT.
Madrid
Barcelona

# Introduction: The Island and the World

*The Basques are one of the unique people-islands to be found on the face of the earth, completely different in every sense from the peoples around them, and their language, surrounded by Aryan languages, forms an island somehow comparable to those peaks which still surface above the water in a flood zone.*
*—Lewy D'Abartiague,* On the Origin of Basques, *1896*
*(A study made at the request of the London Geographic Congress of 1895)*

*"These Basques are swell people," Bill said.*
*—Ernest Hemingway,* The Sun Also Rises, *1926*

THE FIRST TIME I heard the secret tongue, the ancient and forbidden language of the Basques, was in the Hotel Eskualduna in St.-Jean-de-Luz. It was the early 1970s, and Franco still ruled Spain like a 1930s dictator. I was interested in the Basques because I was a journalist and they were the only story, the only Spaniards visibly resisting Franco. But if they still spoke their language, they didn't do it in front of me in Spanish Basqueland, where a few phrases of Basque could lead to an arrest. In the French part of Basqueland, in St.-Jean-de-Luz, people spoke Basque only in private, or whispered it, as though, only a few miles from the border, they feared it would be heard on the other side.

Much of St.-Jean-de-Luz, but especially the Hotel Eskualduna, seemed to function as a safe house for Basques from the other side. Spanish was almost as commonly heard as French. But at the little café on the ground floor of my hotel, the elderly hotel owner and her aging daughter whispered in Basque.

*1*

When I walked into the room, they would smile pleasantly, offer me a suggestion for a restaurant or a scenic walk, and then resume talking in full voice in Spanish or French. As I opened the big glass-and-iron door to the street, I could hear them once again whispering in Basque.

The first time I went to St.-Jean-de-Luz, I arrived by train and was carrying heavy bags. I chose the Eskualduna because it was close to the train station. It was also inexpensive and housed in a fine, historic, stone building with a Basque flag over the doorway and antique wooden Basque furniture inside. I kept returning there because it seemed that something interesting was going on, though I never found out what. For that matter, it was years before I realized that the hotel had been a center for the Resistance during World War II and that my helpful, smiling hosts were decorated heroes who had been the bravest of people at one of mankind's worst moments.

Everything seemed a little exciting and mysterious in Basqueland. With so much painful and dramatic history surrounding these people, I could never be sure who anyone was, and many Basques told astonishing stories about their experiences during the Spanish Civil War, World War II, and the Franco dictatorship. The silhouette of a long high mountain crest rises up behind St.-Jean-de-Luz where the sun sets, and this mountain, looking too rough to be French, is in Spain. I wrote in my notebook that the mountain, this Spanish border, looked like a "vaguely dangerous mystery."

I don't feel that way about Spain anymore. I now know that mountain as a benign nature preserve in Navarra near the border. And I have come to realize that the Basque survival in France is, in its way, as impressive an accomplishment as Basque survival in Spain.

In 1975, I stood in the Plaza de Oriente to hear Franco's last speech. I witnessed "the transition" after his death when freedom and democracy and Western ideals were supposed to be established, and Basque violence was supposed to disappear, because it would be unnecessary and irrelevant. But with Franco's men still in powerful positions and no one daring to remove them, the new Spain fell far short of the open democracy so many had hoped for, though it turned out considerably better than the enduring Francoism many had feared.

But the Basques were a surprise. Had I known more about Basque history, I would have expected this, but I had no idea that their language and literature and music and traditions would burst out like a flower after rain. Nor did I realize that neither Spanish democracy nor European integration would pacify the Basque longing.

FEW PEOPLE KNOW the Basques. What they do know is that Basques are tenacious. In Cervantes's sixteenth-century *Don Quixote de la Mancha*, the Basque, the "Vizcayan," can barely speak Spanish, has a large sword, and tiresomely insists on fighting. "Me kill you or me no Vizcayan," he says.

Four hundred years later, Anaïs Nin, in her erotic short story cycle, *Delta of Venus,* created a character simply called "the Basque." She wrote, "The Basque suddenly opened the door. He bowed and said, 'You wanted a man and here I am.' He threw off his clothes."

Derogatory like Cervantes, laudatory like Hemingway, or a little of each like Nin, in most of literature and films "the Basque" has always been the same character—persevering and rugged and not even intimating the rare and complex culture, nor the sophisticated and evolved calculations behind this seemingly primitive determination to preserve the tribe.

The singular remarkable fact about the Basques is that they still exist. In 1896, Lewy D'Abartiague observed in his study of their origins:

*This people is perhaps the only one in the world, at the least, the only one in Europe, whose origin remains absolutely unknown. It is strange to think at the end of the 19th century, which has been so fertile on the subject of origins, that these few people still remain a mystery.*

If it was strange a century ago, after Darwin, it seems even more unlikely today with our knowledge of DNA and genetic testing. But the Basques remain a mystery. Even more improbable—something few except Basques would have predicted—is that the mysterious Basques enter the twenty-first century as strong as, in some ways stronger than, they entered the twentieth century. This has been accomplished with more than simple tenacity and unshakable courage, though it has required that as well.

ACCORDING TO A popular Bilbao joke, a Bilbaino walks into a store and asks for "a world map of Bilbao." The shop owner unflinchingly answers, "Left bank or right?"

This is *The Basque History of the World* because Basques at times think they are the world. They feel inexplicably secure about their place among nations. But more important, Basques, while they are protecting their unique and separate identity, always endeavor to be in the world. No word less describes Basques than the term *separatist*, a term they refuse to use. If they are an island, it is an island where bridges are constantly being built to the mainland. Considering how small a group the Basques are, they have made remarkable contributions to world history. In the Age of Exploration they were the explorers who connected Europe to North America, South America, Africa, and Asia. At the dawn of capitalism they were among the first capitalists, experimenting with tariff-free international trade and the use of competitive pricing to break monopolies. Early in the industrial revolution they became leading industrialists: ship-builders, steelmakers, and manufacturers. Today, in the global age, even while clinging to their ancient tribal identity, they are ready for a borderless world.

WHEN CAPITALISM was new and New England traders were beginning to change the world, Boston enjoyed a flourishing trade with Bilbao. John Adams ascribed the prosperity of the Basques to their love of freedom. In 1794, he wrote of the Basques, "While their neighbors have long since resigned all their pretensions into the hands of Kings and priests, this extraordinary people have preserved their ancient language, genius, laws, government and manners, without innovation, longer than any other nation of Europe."

This is a people who have stubbornly fought for their unique concept of a nation without ever having a country of their own. To observe the Basques is to ask the question: What is a nation? The entire history of the world and especially of Europe has been one of redefining the nation. From pre-Indo-European tribes—all of whom have disappeared, except the Basques—Europe shifted to kingdoms, empires, republics, nation-states. Now there is to be a united Europe, touted as a new kind of entity, a new relationship between nations—though the sad appearance of a European flag and a European national anthem suggests that this new Europe could turn out to be just a larger nineteenth-century nation-state.

Europeans learned in the twentieth century to fear themselves and their passions. They distrust nationalism and religious belief because pride in nationality leads to dictatorship, war, disaster, and religion leads to fanaticism. Europe has become the most secular continent.

An anomaly in Europe, the Basques remain deeply religious and unabashedly nationalistic. But they are ready to join this united Europe, to seize its opportunities and work within it, just as they saw advantages to the Roman Empire, Ferdinand's consolidation of Spain, and the French Revolution.

We live in an age of vanishing cultures, perhaps even vanishing nations. To be a Frenchman, to be an American, is a limited notion. Educated people do not practice local customs or eat local food. Products are flown around the world. We are losing diversity but gaining harmony. Those who resist this will be left behind by history, we are told.

But the Basques are determined to lose nothing that is theirs, while still embracing the times, cyberspace included. They have never been a quaint people and have managed to be neither backward nor assimilated. Their food, that great window into cultures, shows this. With an acknowledged genius for cooking, they pioneered the use of products from other parts of the world. But they always adapted them, made them Basque.

A central concept in Basque identity is belonging, not only to the Basque people but to a house, known in the Basque language as *etxea*. Etxea or *echea* is one of the most common roots of Basque surnames. *Etxaberria* means "new house," *Etxazarra* means "old house," *Etxaguren* is "the far side of the house," *Etxarren* means "stone house." There are dozens of these last names referring to ancestral rural houses. The name Javier comes from Xavier or Xabier, short for Etxaberria.

A house stands for a clan. Though most societies at some phase had clans, the Basques have preserved this notion because the Basques preserve almost everything. Each house has a tomb for the members of the house and an *etxekandere*, a spiritual head of the house, a woman who looks after blessings and prayers for all house members wherever they are, living or dead.

These houses, often facing east to greet the rising sun, with Basque symbols and the name of the house's founder carved over the doorway, always have names, because the Basques be-

Etxea—a typical Basque farmhouse.

lieve that naming something proves its existence. *Izena duen guzia omen da.* That which has a name exists.

Even today, some Basques recall their origins by introducing themselves to a compatriot from the same region not by their family name, but by the name of their house, a building which may have vanished centuries ago. The founders may have vanished, the family name may disappear, but the name of the house endures. "But the house of my father will endure," wrote the twentieth-century poet Gabriel Aresti.

And this contradiction—preserving the house while pursuing the world—may ensure their survival long after France and Spain have faded.

Historian Simon Schama wrote that when Chinese premier Zhou En-lai was asked to assess the importance of the French Revolution, he answered, "It's too soon to tell." Like Chinese history, the Basque history of the world is far older than the history of France. The few hundred years of European nation-states are only a small part of the Basque story. There may not be a France or a Spain in 1,000 years or even 500 years, but there will still be Basques.

| | |
|---|---|
| Nire aitaren etxea | I shall defend |
| defendituko dut, | the house of my father, |
| Otsoen kontra, | against wolves, |
| sikatearen kontra, | against draught, |
| lukurreriaren kontra, | against usury, |
| justiziaren kontra, | against the law, |
| defenditu | I shall defend |
| eginen dut | the house of my father. |
| nire aitaren etxea. | I shall lose |
| Galduko ditut | cattle, |
| aziendak, | orchards, |
| soloak, | pine groves; |
| pinudiak; | I shall lose |
| galduko ditut | interest |
| korrituak | income |
| errentak | dividends |
| interesak | but I shall defend the |
| baina nire aitaren etxea defendituko dut. | house of my father. |
| Harmak kenduko dizkidate, | They will take my weapons, |
| eta eskuarekin defendituko dut | and with my hands I shall defend |
| nire aitaren etxea; | the house of my father; |
| eskuak ebakiko dizkidate | they will cut off my hands, |
| eta besoarekin defendituko dut | and with my arms I will defend |
| nire aitaren etxea; | the house of my father; |
| besorik gabe | They will leave me armless, |
| sorbaldik gabe, | without shoulders, |
| bularrik gabe | without chest, |
| utziko naute, | and with my soul I shall defend |
| eta arimarekin defendituko dut | the house of my father. |
| nire aitaren etxea. | I shall die, |
| Ni hilen naiz, | my soul will be lost, |
| nire arima galduko da, | my descendants will be lost; |
| nire askazia galduko da, | but the house of my father |
| baina nire aitaren etxeak | will endure |
| iraunen du | on its feet. |
| zutik. | |

—Gabriel Aresti

*Part One*

# THE SURVIVAL OF EUSKAL HERRIA

*Nomansland, the territory of the Basques, is in a region called Cornucopia, where the vines are tied up with sausages. And in those parts there was a mountain made entirely of grated Parmesan cheese on whose slopes there were people who spent their whole time making macaroni and ravioli, which they cooked in chicken broth and then cast it to the four winds, and the faster you could pick it up, the more you got of it.*
—*Giovanni Boccaccio*, THE DECAMERON, *1352*

# The Basque Cake

*The truth is that the Basque distrusts a stranger much too much to invite someone into his home who doesn't speak his language.*
—LES GUIDES BLEUS PAYS BASQUE FRANÇAIS ET ESPAGNOL, *1954*

THE GAME THE rest of the world knows as jai alai was invented in the French Basque town of St.-Pée-sur-Nivelle. St. Pée, like most of the towns in the area, holds little more than one curving street against a steep-pastured slope. The houses are whitewashed, with either red or green shutters and trim. Originally the whitewash was made of chalk. The traditional dark red color, known in French as *rouge Basque,* Basque red, was originally made from cattle blood. Espelette, Ascain, and other towns in the valley look almost identical. A fronton court—a single wall with bleachers to the left—is always in the center of town.

While the French were developing tennis, the Basques, as they often did, went in a completely different direction. The French ball was called a *pelote,* a French word derived from a verb for winding string. These pelotes were made of wool or cotton string wrapped into a ball and covered with leather. The Basques were the first Europeans to use a rubber ball, a discovery from the Americas, and the added bounce of wrapping rubber rather than string—the *pelote Basque,* as it was originally called—led them to play the ball off walls, a game which became known also as *pelote* or, in Spanish and English, *pelota.* A number of configurations of walls as well as a range of racquets, paddles, and barehanded variations began to develop. *Jai alai,* an Euskera phrase meaning "happy game," originally referred to a pelota game with an additional long left-hand wall. Then in

1857, a young farm worker in St. Pée named Gantxiki Harotcha, scooping up potatoes into a basket, got the idea of propelling the ball even faster with a long, scoop-shaped basket strapped to one hand. The idea quickly spread throughout the Nivelle Valley and in the twentieth century, throughout the Americas, back to where the rubber ball had begun.

St. Pée seems to be a quiet town. But it hasn't always been so. During World War II the Basques, working with the French underground, moved British and American fliers and fleeing Jews on the route up the valley from St.-Jean-de-Luz to Sare and across the mountain pass to Spain.

The Gestapo was based in the big house next to the *fronton*, the pelota court. Jeanine Pereuil, working in her family's pastry shop across the street, remembers refugees whisked past the gaze of the Germans. The Basques are said to be a secretive people. It is largely a myth—one of many. But in 1943, the Basques of the Nivelle Valley kept secrets very well. Jeanine Pereuil has many stories about the Germans and the refugees. She married a refugee from Paris.

The only change Jeanine made in the shop in her generation was to add a few figurines on a shelf. Before the Basques embraced Christianity with a legendary passion, they had other beliefs, and many of these have survived. Jeanine goes to her shelf and lovingly picks out the small figurine of a joaldun, a man clad in sheepskin with bells on his back. "Can you imagine," she says, "at my age buying such things. This is my favorite," she says, picking out a figure from the ezpata dantza, the sword dance performed on the Spanish side especially for the Catholic holiday of Corpus Christi. The dancer is wearing white with a red sash, one leg kicked out straight and high and the arms stretched out palms open.

Born in 1926, Jeanine is the fourth generation to make *gâteau Basque* and sell it in this shop. Her daughter is the fifth generation. The Pereuils all speak Basque as their first language and make the exact same cake. She is not sure when her great grandfather, Jacques Pereuil, started the shop, but she knows her grandfather, Jacques's son, was born in the shop in 1871.

Jacques Pereuil and his son in front of their pastry shop at the turn of the century. (Courtesy of Jeanine Pereuil)

Gâteau Basque, like the Basques themselves, has an uncertain origin. It appears to date from the eighteenth century and may have originally been called *bistochak*. While today's gâteau Basque is a cake filled with either cherry jam or pastry cream, the original bistochak was not a gâteau but a bread. The cherry filling predates the cream one. The cake appears to have originated in the valley of the winding Nivelle River, which includes the town of Itxassou, famous for its black cherries, a Basque variety called *xapata*.

Basques invented their own language and their own shoes, *espadrilles*. They also created numerous sports including not only pelota but wagon-lifting contests called *orgo joko*, and sheep fighting known as *aharitalka*. They developed their own farm tools such as the two-pronged hoe called a *laia*, their own breed of cow known as the blond cow, their own sheep called the whitehead sheep, and their own breed of pig, which was only recently rescued from extinction.

And so they also have their own black cherry, the xapata from Itxassou, which only bears fruit for a few weeks in June but is so productive during those weeks that a large surplus is saved in the form of preserves. The cherry preserve-filled cakes were sold in the market in Bayonne, a city celebrated for its chocolate makers, who eventually started buying Itxassou black cherries to dip in chocolate.

Today in most of France and Spain a gâteau Basque is cream filled, but the closer to the valley of the Nivelle, the more likely it is to be cherry filled.

Jeanine, whose shop makes nothing besides one kind of bread, the two varieties of gâteau Basque, and a cookie based on the gâteau Basque dough, finds it hard to believe that her specialty originated as cherry bread. Just as the shop's furniture has never been changed, the recipe has never changed. The Pereuils have always made it as cake, not bread, and, she insists, have always made both the cream and cherry fillings. Cream is overwhelmingly the favorite. The mailman, given a little two-inch cake every morning when he brings the mail, always chooses cream.

Maison Pereuil may not be old enough for the earlier bistochak cherry bread recipe, but the Pereuil cake is not like the modern buttery gâteau Basque either. Jeanine's tawny, elastic confection is a softer, more floury version of the sugar-and-egg-white macaroon offered to Louis XIV and his young bride, the Spanish princess María Theresa, on their wedding day, May 8, 1660, in St.-Jean-de-Luz. Ever since, the macaroon has been a specialty of that Basque port at the mouth of the Nivelle.

When asked for the antique recipe for her family's gâteau Basque, Jeanine Pereuil smiled bashfully and said, "You know, people keep offering me a lot of money for this recipe."

How much do they offer?

"I don't know. I'm not going to bargain. I will never give out the recipe. If I sold the recipe, the house would vanish. And this is the house of my father and his father. I am keeping their house. And I hope my daughter will do the same for me."

Itxassou cherries

# 1: The Basque Myth

*The Basques share with the Celts the privilege of indulging
in unrivaled extravagance on the subject of themselves.*
—Miguel de Unamuno quoting Ampère,
HISTORY OF FRENCH LITERATURE BEFORE
THE TWELFTH CENTURY, *1884*

THE BASQUES SEEM to be a mythical people, almost an imagined people. Their ancient culture is filled with undated legends and customs. Their land itself, a world of red-roofed, whitewashed towns, tough green mountains, rocky crests, a cobalt sea that turns charcoal in stormy weather, a strange language, and big berets, exists on no maps except their own.

Basqueland begins at the Adour River with its mouth at Bayonne—the river that separates the Basques from the French pine forest swampland of Landes—and ends at the Ebro River, whose rich valley separates the dry red Spanish earth of Rioja from Basqueland. Basqueland looks too green to be Spain and too rugged to be France. The entire area is only 8,218 square miles, which is slightly smaller than New Hampshire.

Within this small space are seven Basque provinces. Four provinces are in Spain and have Basque and Spanish names: Nafaroa or Navarra, Gipuzkoa or Guipúzcoa, Bizkaia or Vizcaya, and Araba or Alava. Three are in France and have Basque and French names: Lapurdi or Labourd, Benafaroa or Basse Navarre, and Zuberoa or Soule. An old form of Basque nationalist graffiti is "4 + 3 = 1."

As with most everything pertaining to Basques, the provinces are defined by language. There are seven dialects of the Basque language, though there are sub-dialects within some of the provinces.

In the Basque language, which is called Euskera, there is no word for Basque. The only word to identify a member of their group is *Euskaldun*—Euskera speaker. Their land is called *Euskal Herria*—the land of Euskera speakers. It is language that defines a Basque.

THE CENTRAL MYSTERY IS: Who are the Basques? The early Basques left no written records, and the first accounts of them, two centuries after the Romans arrived in 218 B.C., give the impression that they were already an ancient—or at least not a new—people. Artifacts predating this time that have been found in the area—a few tools, drawings in caves, and the rudiments of ruins—cannot be proved to have been made by Basques, though it is supposed that at least some of them were.

Ample evidence exists that the Basques are a physically distinct group. There is a Basque type with a long straight nose, thick eyebrows, strong chin, and long earlobes. Even today, sitting in a bar in a mountainous river valley town like Tolosa, watching men play *mus,* the popular card game, one can see a similarity in the faces, despite considerable intermarriage. Personalities, of course, carve very different visages, but over and over again, from behind a hand of cards, the same eyebrows, chin, and nose can be seen. The identical dark navy wool berets so many men wear—each in a slightly different manner—seem to showcase the long Basque ears sticking out on the sides. In past eras, when Spaniards and French were typically fairly small people, Basque men were characteristically larger, thick chested, broad shouldered, and burly. Because these were also characteristics of Cro-Magnons, Basques are often thought to be direct descendants of this man who lived 40,000 years ago.

Less subjective physical evidence of an ancient and distinct group has also surfaced. In the beginning of the twentieth century, it was discovered that all blood was one of three types: A, B, or O. Basques have the highest concentration of type O in the

Tolosa, typical of Basque towns, was connected to its valley and the seacoast by a river but isolated from the rest of the area by mountains.

world—more than 50 percent of the population—with an even higher percentage in remote areas where the language is best preserved, such as Soule. Most of the rest are type A. Type B is extremely rare among Basques. With the finding that Irish, Scots, Corsicans, and Cretans also have an unusually high incidence of type O, speculation ran wild that these peoples were somehow related to Basques. But then, in 1937, came the discovery of the rhesus factor, more commonly known as Rh positive or Rh negative. Basques were found to have the highest incidence of Rh negative blood of any people in the world, significantly higher than the rest of Europe, even significantly higher than neighboring regions of France and Spain. Cro-Magnon theorists point out that other places known to have been occupied by Cro-Magnon man, such as the Atlas Mountains of Morocco and the Canary Islands, also have been found to have a high incidence of Rh negative.

Twenty-seven percent of Basques have O Rh negative blood. Rh negative blood in a pregnant woman can fatally poison a fetus that has positive blood. Since World War II, intervention techniques to save the fetus have been developed, but it is probable that throughout history, the rate of miscarriage and stillborn births among the Basques was extremely high, which may be one of the reasons they remained a small population on a limited amount of land while other populations, especially in Iberia, grew rapidly.

Before Basque blood was studied as a key to their origins, several attempts were made to analyze the structure of Basque skulls. At the beginning of the nineteenth century, a researcher reported, "Someone gave me a Basque body and I dissected it and I assert that the head was not built like that of other men."

Studies of Basque skulls in the nineteenth century concluded, depending on whose study is believed, that Basques were either Turks, Tartars, Magyars, Germans, Laplanders, or the descendants of Cro-Magnon man either originating in Basqueland or coming from the Berbers of North Africa.

Or do clothes hold the secret to Basque origins? A twelfth-century writer, Aimeric de Picaud, considered not skulls but skirts, concluding after seeing Basque men in short ones that they were clearly descendants of Scots.

The most useful artifact left behind by the ancient Basques is their language. Linguists find that while the language has adopted foreign words, the grammar has proved resistant to change, so that modern Euskera is thought to be far closer to its ancient form than modern Greek is to ancient Greek. Euskera has extremely complex verbs and twelve cases, few forms of politeness, a limited number of abstractions, a rich vocabulary for natural phenomena, and no prepositions or articles.

*Etxea* is the word for a house or home. "At home" is *etxean*. "To the house" is *etxera*. "From home" is *etxetik*. Concepts are formed by adding more and more suffixes, which is what is known as an agglutinating language. This agglutinating language only has about 200,000 words, but its vocabulary is greatly extended by almost 200 standard suffixes. In contrast, the *Oxford English Dictionary* was compiled from a data base of 60 million words, but English is a language with an unusually large vocabulary. It is sometimes said that Euskera includes just nouns, verbs, and suffixes, but relatively simple concepts can become words of formidable size. *Iparsortalderatu* is a verb meaning "to head in a northeasterly direction."

Euskera has often been dismissed as an impossible language. Arturo Campión, a nineteenth-century Basque writer from Navarra, complained that the dictionary of the Royal Spanish Academy defined Euskera as "the Basque language, so confusing and obscure that it can hardly be understood." It is obscure but not especially confusing. The language seems more difficult than it is because it is so unfamiliar, so different from other languages. Its profusion of *k*s and *x*s looks intimidating on the page, but the language is largely phonetic with some minor pitfalls, such as a very soft *b* and an aspirated *h* as in English, which is difficult for French and Spanish speakers to pronounce. The *x* is pronounced "ch." *Etxea* is pronounced "et-CHAY-a." For centuries Spanish speakers made Euskera seem friendlier to them by changing *x*s to *ch*s as in echea, and *k*s, which do not exist in Latin languages, to *c*s, as in *Euscera*. To English speakers, Basque spellings are often more phonetic than Spanish equivalents. The town the Spanish call Guernica is pronounced the way the Basques write it—Gernika.

The structure of the language—roots and suffixes—offers important clues about Basque origins. The modern words *aitzur*, meaning "hoe," *aizkora*, meaning "axe," *aizto*, meaning "knife," plus various words for digging and cutting, all come from the word *haitz* or the older *aitz*, which means "stone." Such etymology seems to indicate a very old language, indeed from the Stone Age. Even though the language has acquired newer words, notably Latin from the Romans and the Church, and Spanish, such words are used in a manner unique to this ancestral language. *Ezpata,* like the Spanish word *espada,* means "sword." But *ezpatakada* means "the blow from a sword," *ezpata-joka* means "fencing," and *espatadantzari* is a "sword dancer."

Though numerous attempts have been made, no one has ever found a linguistic relative of Euskera. It is an orphan language that does not even belong to the Indo-European family of languages. This is a remarkable fact because once the Indo-Europeans began their Bronze Age sweep from the Asian subcontinent across Europe, virtually no group, no matter how isolated, was left untouched. Even Celtic is Indo-European. Finnish, Estonian, and Hungarian are the only other living European languages that are not related to the Indo-European group. Inevitably there have been theories linking Finnish and Euskera or Hungarian and Euskera. Did the Basques immigrate from Lapland? Hungarian, it has been pointed out, is also an agglutinating language. But no other connection has been found between the Basque language and its fellow agglutinators.

A brief attempt to tie the Basques to the Picts, ancient occupants of Britain who spoke a language thought to be pre-Indo-European, fell apart when it was discovered the Picts weren't non-Indo-European at all, but were Celtic.

If, as appears to be the case, the Basque language predates the Indo-European invasion, if it is an early or even pre-Bronze Age tongue, it is very likely the oldest living European language.

If Euskera is the oldest living European language, are Basques the oldest European culture? For centuries that question has driven both Basques and non-Basques on the quest to find the Basque origin. Miguel de Unamuno, one of the best-known Basque writers, devoted his earliest work, written in 1884 when he was still a student, to the question. "I am Basque," he began, "and so I arrive with suspicion and caution at this little and poorly garnered subject."

As Unamuno pointed out, and this is still true today, many researchers have not hesitated to employ a liberal dose of imagination. One theory not only has Adam and Eve speaking Euskera but has the language predating their expulsion from the Garden of Eden. The name Eve, according to this theory, comes from *ez-bai*, "no-yes" in Euskera. The walls of Jericho crumbled, it was also discovered, when trumpets blasted a Basque hymn.

The vagaries of fact and fiction were encouraged by the fact that the Basques were so late to document their language. The first book entirely in Euskera was not published until 1545. No Basques had attempted to study their own history or origins until the sixteenth-century Guipúzcoan Esteban de Garibay. Spanish historians of the time had already claimed that Iberia was populated by descendants of Tubal, Noah's grandson, who went to Iberia thirty-five years after the Flood subsided. Garibay observed that Basque place-names bore a resemblance to those in Armenia where the ark landed, and therefore it was specifically the Basques who descended from Tubal. Was not Mount Gorbeya in southern Vizcaya named after Mount Gordeya in Armenia? Garibay traced Euskera to the Tower of Babel.

In 1729, when Manuel de Larramendi wrote the first book of Basque grammar ever published, he asserted that Euskera was one of seventy-five languages to have developed out of the confusion at the Tower of Babel. According to Juan Bautista de Erro, whose *The Primitive World or a Philosophical Examination of Antiquity and Culture of the Basque Nation* was published in Madrid in 1815, Euskera is the world's oldest language, having been devised by God as the language of Adam's Paradise, preserved in the Tower of Babel, surviving the Flood because Noah spoke the language, and brought to present-day Basque country by Tubal.

In one popular legend, the first Basque was Aïtor, one of a few remarkable men who survived the Flood without Noah's ark, by leaping from stone to stone. However, Aïtor, still recognized by some as the father of all Basques, was invented in 1848 by the French Basque writer Augustin Chaho. After Chaho's article on Aïtor was translated into Spanish in 1878, the legend grew and became a mainstay of Basque culture. Some who said Aïtor was mere fiction went on to hypothesize that the real father of all Basques was Tubal.

Since then, links have been conjectured with languages of the Caucasus, Africa, Siberia, and Japan. One nineteenth-century researcher concluded that Basques were a Celtic tribe, another that they were Etruscans. And inevitably it has been discovered that the Basques, like so many other peoples, were actually the lost thirteenth tribe of Israel. Just as inescapably, others have concluded that the Basques are, in reality, the survivors of Atlantis.

A case for the Basques really being Jews was carefully made by a French clergyman, the abbot J. Espagnolle, in a 1900 book titled *L'Origine des Basques* (The Origin of the Basques). For this theory to work, the reader first had to realize that the people of ancient Sparta were Jewish. To support this claim, Espagnolle quotes a historian of ancient Greece who wrote, "Love of money is a Spartan characteristic." If this was not proof enough, he also argues that Sparta, like Judea, had a lack of artisans. The wearing of hats and respect for elders were among further evidence offered. From there, it was simply a matter of asserting, as ancient Greek historians had, he said, that the Spartans colonized northern Spain. And of course these Spartan colonists who later became Basques were Jewish.

With issues of nationhood at stake, such seemingly desperate hypotheses may not be devoid of political motives. "Indigenous" is a powerful notion to both the French and Spanish states. Both define their history as the struggle of their people, the rightful indigenous occupants, to defend their land against the Moors, invaders from another place, of another race, and of another religion. In Europe, this heroic struggle has long been an essential underpinning of both nationalism and racism. The idea that Basques were in their European mountains, speaking their own indigenous European language, long before the French and the Spanish, is disturbing to French and Spanish nationalists. Unless the Basques can be shown to be from somewhere else, the Spanish and French are transformed into the Moorish role— outside invaders imposing an alien culture. From the sixteenth century on, historians receiving government salaries in Madrid wrote histories that deliberately minimized the possibility of indigenous Basques.

But the Basques like the idea, which most evidence supports, that they are the original Europeans, predating all others. If true, it must have been an isolating experience, belonging to this ancient people whose culture had little in common with any of its neighbors. It was written over and over in the records of those who observed the Basques that they spoke a strange language that kept them apart from others. But it is also what kept them together as a people, uniting them to withstand Europe's great invasions.

# 2: The Basque Problem

*There lived many brave men before Agamemnon, but all are overwhelmed in unending night, unmourned and unknown, because they lack a poet to give them immortality.*
*—Horace,* ODES, *23 B.C.*

WHEN BASQUES FIRST began appearing on the stage of recorded history, even before there was a name for them, they were observed acting like Basques, playing out the same roles that they have been playing ever since: defending their land and culture, making complex choices about the degree of independence that was needed to preserve their way of life, while looking to the rest of the world for commercial opportunities to ensure their prosperity.

Long before the Romans gave the Basques a name, a great many people attempted to invade the mountains of what is now Basqueland, and they all met with fierce resistance. The invaders were Indo-Europeans intending to move into the Iberian peninsula. It seems to have been acceptable to the indigenous people that these invaders pass through on their path to the conquest of Iberia. But if they tried to settle in these northern mountains, they would encounter a ferocious enemy.

The rulers of Carthage, a Phoenician colony built on a choice harbor in present-day Tunisia, seem to have been the first to learn how to befriend these people. Carthage began about 800 B.C. as a port city. As its commercial power expanded in the Mediterranean, this city-state with elected leaders and only a small population increasingly relied on mercenaries to defend its interests. By the third century B.C., the Carthaginians had made their way up Iberia to Basque country, but they did not try to settle, colonize, or subjugate the inhabitants. Instead, they paid them.

By this time the Basques were the veterans of centuries of war and were valued as mercenaries throughout the Mediterranean. They had fought in Greece in the fourth century B.C. In 240 B.C., a conflict first over Sicily and then over Iberia led to a series of bitter wars between Carthage and Rome. Basque mercenaries fought for Carthage, the losing side, and are thought to have been part of Hannibal's legendary invasion of Italy in 216 B.C. The Basques knew Carthage when it was the greatest commercial center in the world, a city of imposing wooden houses on a hillside facing a prosperous harbor. And they saw Carthage after Rome destroyed it in 146 B.C., when the city was nothing but the blackened stone foundations of burned buildings, the once green hillside sowed with salt to kill agriculture. This taught the Basques to underestimate neither the power nor the ruthlessness of Rome.

ACCORDING TO POPULAR MYTH, their rugged, mountainous terrain made the Basques unconquerable, but it is also possible that few coveted this land. Many passed through, disproving the assumption that their mountains were impenetrable. They are small, but their steepness, the jagged protrusion of rocks above the rich green velvet beauty of sloped pastures, gives them false importance, making them appear far higher than the mere foothills of the Pyrenees and minor ranges of the Cantabrian Sierra that they are. In a harsh winter the peaks are powdered with snow, giving them the illusion of alpine scale. But most of the passes, which appear at regular intervals throughout the Basque Pyrenees, are usable year round. In French, the passes of the region are called *ports*, meaning "safe harbors" or possibly even "gateways." The Basse Navarre village of St.-Jean-Pied-de-Port, on the Nive River, is surrounded by imposing peaks. Its name comes from being the rest-and-supply stop before the pass, what seems a thrilling climb up to the clouds. Yet the altitude of the peaks is not quite 5,000 feet, not as high as the tallest of New York's Adirondacks, and the highest point in the pass below is a mere 3,500 feet at the heights of Ibañeta, before dropping down to Roncesvalles in Spanish Navarra. The other high pass, the Port de Larrau between Soule and Navarra, climbs through rocky peaks so bald it seems to be above the timberline. But it is only 5,200 feet high, and the Port de Lizarrieta, near the Nivelle Valley, has an altitude of less than 1,700 feet, an easy crossing for Celts, Romans, or World War II underground refugees. The central Pyrenees, to the east of Basqueland, have peaks twice the altitude of the highest Basque mountains.

It was not the foothills of the Pyrenees with their brilliant green, steeply inclined pastures, or the cloud-capped rocky out-croppings of Guipúzcoa, nor the majestic columns of gray rock towering above the Vizcayan countryside near Durango, nor the

BASQUE BORDER PASSES

©1999 Jeffrey L. Ward

Cantabrian Sierra with its thrilling views of the wide Ebro Valley below, that conquerors coveted. Instead, invaders wanted the great valley of the Ebro where now lie the vegetable gardens of Logroño and the vineyards of Rioja, or the rich lands beyond in Spain, or they wanted the plains of France north of the Adour.

It is uncertain how large an area belonged to the pre-Roman Basques. The fact that their currently known borders are edged by lands considered more valuable suggests that the Basques were pressed into this smaller, less desirable mountainous region, that they live in what was left for them.

The perennial issue of Basque history—who is or is not a Basque—obscures the boundaries of pre-Roman Basqueland. The Romans referred to a people whom they called Vascones, from which comes the Spanish word *Vascos* and the French word *Basques*. The earliest surviving account of these Vascones is from the Greek historian Strabo, who lived from 64 B.C. to A.D. 24, which was after the Roman conquest of Iberia. But the Latin word *Vascones* is also the origin of *Gascognes*, the French word for the Basques' neighbors in the French southwest. It is not always clear when Roman accounts are referring to Basques and when they are referring to other people in the region. Or were Gascognes originally Basques who became Romanized?

A forceful Roman presence first appeared on the Iberian peninsula in 218 B.C., during the wars against Carthage. In the rest of Iberia, the local population was first crushed, then Romanized, but Basqueland was more difficult to conquer. Rebellions continually broke out in Vasconia, not only by Vascones, but also by the previous invader, the Celts. The Romans sent in additional legions, and in 194 B.C. the Celts, who had never been able to conquer the Basques, were decisively defeated by the Romans. Soon after, the Romans defeated the Basques as well.

Their defeat by the Romans marks the beginning of the first known instance of Basques tolerating occupation without armed resistance. But the reason appears to be that the Romans, intent on more fertile parts of Iberia, learned to coexist with the Basques, and the Basques came to learn that Roman occupation did not threaten their language, culture, or legal traditions. The Romans came to understand that the Basques could be pacified by special conditions of autonomy. The Basques paid no tribute and had no military occupation. Most important of all, they were not ruled directly by a Roman code of law but were allowed to govern themselves under their own tradition-based system of law. The Romans asked little more from Basques than free passage between southern Gaul and the lands beyond the Ebro.

The Basques were left to their beloved sense of themselves, surrounded by an empire to which they didn't belong, speaking a language that none of their neighbors understood.

Crowded into steep, narrow valleys, their society was organized around control of the limited workable land. The needs of this cramped agricultural existence made Basque social structures different from those of societies that lived in ample expanses. The bottomland by the river was usually owned communally. Rights to grazing on the good slopes were administered by local Basque rule.

Leaving the Basques content in their mountains, the Romans conquered the Ebro and fought with each other over it. In 82 B.C., two Roman factions began a ten-year war for control of the Ebro. Sertorius, a battle-scarred warrior, proud of having lost one eye in combat, seized the valley with some local support. In a previous campaign against the Celts, Sertorius had learned enough Celtic to pass himself off in the enemy camp, and he boasted of his ability to penetrate local cultures. But in 75 B.C., the handsome and elegant Pompey, a favorite of Rome and commander of the forces loyal to the emperor, retook the Ebro and founded a town on a tributary, the River Arga. It was to be a strategic fortress, controlling both the plains south to the Ebro and important passes to the north through the Pyrenees. The town, which Pompey, with unflinching immodesty, named Pompaelo, also was intended to be a great outpost of Roman civilization. Later it became known in Spanish as Pamplona.

The few surviving fragments of Pompaelo do not suggest great Roman architecture, but even if it was only a provincial town of the empire, marble-pillared villas, temples, and baths built by the Romans must have been dazzling to the wild mountain Vascones.

At the time of Christ, Strabo wrote of three cities: Pamplona; Calahorra, which Pompey captured from the Celts the year he founded Pamplona; and Oiasona, of unknown origin and today called Oiartzun, a town located between San Sebastián and the French border. To the north, a military base called Lapurdum, thought to have been at the present-day site of Bayonne, began to grow into an urban center.

Roman cities became important to the Basques because the Romans also built an excellent road system connecting all of Vasconia, so that farmers and shepherds could bring their goods to the Roman-built cities to be sold. The Vascones learned to grow Roman crops such as grapes and olives for the Roman market. Rural Basque communities started decorating their villages with Roman mosaics and Roman-style monuments.

Basque mercenaries defended the far borders of the Roman Empire. Basques who fought well for the empire were offered Roman citizenship, a rare distinction until Caracalla, Roman emperor in 211, granted it to all the Empire. A Basque unit served in England, based in present-day Northumberland, and Basques helped defend Hadrian's Wall, which stretched across northern England to keep the Picts and other Celts out. Plutarch wrote that Gaius Marius, the antipatrician commander in whose name the one-eyed Sertorius had taken the Ebro, freed enslaved prisoners of war and made them his personal, fiercely loyal bodyguard. This force was composed of several thousand liberated Varduli, a Basque tribe from Guipúzcoa, whom he took with him when he was exiled to Africa. When he was able to return to Rome, he brought them to frighten his patrician Roman adversaries. The Varduli ran wild in the imperial city and, in fact, frightened almost everyone in Rome. They attacked patricians and raped their wives. Finally, Marius's ally Sertorius ordered his troops to their camp, where he had the Varduli Basques killed with javelins.

A tour of duty in the empire was twenty-five years, and so Basques saw the empire and its inventions. They were at peace with Rome. There is no record of a conflict between Basques and Romans from 20 B.C. for the next four centuries until the fall of Rome. This may have been the longest period of peace in Basque history.

As they learned of new ideas, they expressed them in Euskera with Latin words. Olive is *oliba*; statue is *estatu*, which also means "state"; statesman is *estatari*.

If a new idea offered commercial opportunities, the Basques embraced it—a characteristic that would remain with them throughout history. Through their mountain passes, they traded the olive oil they had learned about from the Romans, just as they did the wheat and iron they had learned of from the Celts. The iron and wheat trades continued long after the Celts had left, and the trade in Roman products long survived that empire as well.

But though Basques learned from both the Celts and the Romans, they did not assimilate with either one. All of Iberia except Vasconia was speaking a Latin language, living under Roman legal institutions, and practicing the Roman religion, which by the fourth century was Christianity. South of the Ebro in present-day Castile, north of the Adour in present-day Aquitaine, and to the east in present-day Aragón, all areas the Romans preferred to Basqueland, the people were assimilated. They spoke a Latin dialect and acquired the Christian religion.

But only a few Basque areas left any records of Christianity during Roman rule. By modern times these same places had completely lost their Basque identity. Calahorra, the Roman city on the Ebro, where stories of early Basque Christian martyrs have been preserved, today is no longer Basque. Today, the closer in Basqueland one is to the Ebro, the more Roman influence can be felt. The part of Basqueland with the fewest Euskera speakers is southern Navarra and Alava, the part the Romans wanted. The olive groves and vineyards that the Romans introduced in these areas flourish. Pre-Roman Basques probably cooked with animal fats and drank fermented apple cider, but modern Basques cook almost exclusively with olive oil and reserve the butter that they produce in their northern mountain pastures only for baking. And they are wine drinkers. Only occasionally do they consume cider made, during the winter, from the apples that prosper in Guipúzcoa.

But in the mountains on both sides of the Pyrenees, the Basque language and culture have remained strong. The borders of cultural zones remain much the way the Romans left them 1,600 years ago. The Romans were clearly the most effective assimilators the Basques ever encountered. Given enough time, they might have swallowed up the remaining Basques as they did most of the cultures in the empire. But before that could happen, the Roman Empire fell.

IN THE LONG Basque memory, the Roman Empire is considered a good period. In the context of Basque history a good period was one with a reasonable invader, an intruder with whom you could do business. Today, Basques still refer to this time as an example of how they would like to peacefully coexist with larger powers.

In the unstable atmosphere of power vacuums left by the decline of Rome, several groups moved into Iberia. These so-called barbarians—Vandals, Suevi, and Alans—easily passed the

Basque ports of the Pyrenees, overran Pamplona, took the Ebro, and passed on to control most of the peninsula without ever bothering with most of Vasconia.

By the year 400, the disintegrating Roman Empire turned to the Visigoths, who had helped the Romans control Gaul, to do the same in Iberia. From that moment on, chronicles of the life of Visigoth monarchs end with two words: *Domuit Vascones*. All the rulers of the peninsula to follow down to the present-day Spanish government have had the same thought: "We must control the Basques."

The Visigoths were romanized central Europeans who had moved west from the Danube Valley. Like most of the peoples in the area at the time, they professed a self-styled variation of Christianity. Establishing a capital in what is now the southern French city of Toulouse, these one-time allies of Rome became competitors. In A.D. 410 they overran Rome itself.

In 415, they entered Iberia, not from Vasconia but from Catalonia on the other end of the Pyrenees. From there they moved up the Ebro, from its mouth at the Mediterranean near the Catalonia-Valencia border. Eventually they gained control of all of Iberia and held on to it for 250 years. Until 507 they ruled from Toulouse, and then, after they lost southern France to the Franks, Toledo became their capital.

During the century of Toulouse-based rule, Basqueland was the crossroads of Europe. Again, as long as populations, merchants, soldiers were just passing through on their way to Iberia, the Basques accepted them. But Visigoth rule was not to be like Roman rule. The Visigoths wanted to conquer and control the Basque mountains. And so the Basques fought them in campaign after campaign, swooping down from their mountains to attack the new rulers on the plains.

In two and a half centuries, the Visigoths mounted twenty campaigns against the Basques. The Basques won battles and they lost battles, but for the 200,000 Visigoth soldiers attempting to hold all of Iberia, the Basques were always an insurmountable problem.

In hindsight, the Visigoths were one of many misfortunes of history that helped preserve the Basques. The constant warfare united a people who had previously remained separate mountain tribes. The Romans had written of the Caristos, Vardulos, and Autrigones—distinct tribes of Vascones who may have been Alavans, Guipúzcoans, and Vizcayans. The Visigoths found no such people, only a single group of ferocious enemies throughout Vasconia—the Vascones whom they could not control.

The Basques always resisted not only militarily but culturally. They kept their language and religion. Only after the fall of the Visigoths did Christianity slowly penetrate Basque culture, and even then, Basque religious beliefs coexisted with Christianity for centuries. Some still survive.

FOR SEVERAL CENTURIES, while everyone around them spoke Latin languages, the Basques spoke Euskera. While neighboring cultures followed the male line, the female line of Basques inherited property and titles because women did the farm work, while men went off to war. While everyone else was Christian, the Basques worshiped the sun and moon and a pantheon of nature spirits. Surrounded by the cult of Jesus Christ and the apostles, they had Baxajaun, the hairy lord of the forest, and Mari, who dwelled in caves and assumed many forms. And while all the people around them had learned from the Romans to live by a legal code, Basque law was still based on unwritten custom.

The Basques simply wanted to be left alone, but suddenly, with civil war destroying Visigoth rule, a new and even more aggressive non-Christian group arrived. Muslims from North Africa landed in Spain in 711, invited to cross over from Morocco by a Visigoth ruler to help defeat his Visigoth rival. Once landed in Iberia, the 800-year struggle to expel the Muslims would leave a permanent imprint on Christianity and European culture.

In three years, they penetrated almost the entire peninsula, and by 714, Musa, leader of a North African Islamic alliance, was at the edge of Basqueland. Like other conquerors, he was not impressed by what he found there. An Arab history written six centuries later recalled, "Pamplona is in the middle of high mountains and deep valleys; little favored by nature." Of the people it says, "They mostly speak Basque which makes them incomprehensible."

The Muslims decided they would take the area anyway and use it as a base from which to move into the lands of the Franks north of the Pyrenees. But Musa, after so many successes on his way through Iberia, could not conquer Vasconia. Four years later, in 718, a second army took Pamplona. For centuries thereafter, the Basques and the Muslims lived side by side in a complicated relationship. The Muslims repeatedly took Pamplona but couldn't hold it. They could hold the southern flatlands by the Ebro, but when they ventured north into the mountains, the Basques would storm out of forests and down slopes and drive away the intruders.

In 732, the Muslim ruler of Spain, Abd-al-Rahman, led a force out of Pamplona northeast into the mountains of Navarra, climbing up into the narrow rocky pass above Roncesvalles, up the valley of the Nive, which meets the Adour at Bayonne, across the Adour to the swamps of Aquitaine and up the center of France to Poitiers, less than 200 miles from Paris, where he was finally stopped and turned back by the king of the Franks, Charles Martel. Poitiers was the farthest north the Muslims ever reached.

The legend of Charles Martel and the battle of Poitiers has grown. Every French schoolchild knows of it. Extreme right-wing racist groups still invoke the name of Charles Martel when speaking of purging Europe of non-Europeans.

It was during this long period of fighting with the Muslims that the Basques became Christians, part of the Christian struggle to drive out the infidel, what is called in Spain the Reconquista. The earliest estimates place the Christianization of the Basques in the seventh century, but some historians believe that the Basques were not a Christian people until the tenth or eleventh century. In any case, the Basques were not dependable Christians. They did not fight for Christianity; they fought for Basqueland, which the Franks threatened at least as much as the Muslims. Basques let Abd-al-Rahman pass through their mountains because he was on his way to fight the Franks. Some Basques even fought against Charles Martel in France a few years after Poitiers. But in Iberia they fought against the Muslim takeover.

And so this small people fought both Christians and Muslims and managed to survive and keep their lands.

In 1837, a forgotten manuscript from late-eleventh-century Normandy was published at Oxford. After centuries of obscurity, this epic poem titled *La Chanson de Roland* (The Song of Roland), became a classic of French literature. Revered for the extraordinary beauty of its Old French verse, it tells of Charlemagne's great victories in Iberia against the Muslims and how he had now decided to return to France. He marched his army through the Roncesvalles pass. Just as the last of his men were climbing out of the pine forest to the narrow rocky *port*, leaving Charlemagne's nephew, Roland, to hold the pass, the Muslims attacked. Roland fought valiantly with his great sword, but the Franks had been betrayed to the Muslims by Ganelon, a traitor from their own ranks, and faced with the overwhelming numbers of two huge Moorish armies, Roland died in the pass, saving Europe from that fate-worse-than-death, the Muslims.

The manuscript was written at the time of the First Crusade, when anti-Islamic bigotry had been elevated to the status of a religious belief and was being feverishly embraced. The poem has made the battle of Roncesvalles more famous than that of Poitiers. Even before the poem was rediscovered, the legend of Roland had the same stature in France as El Cid in Spain, an icon of national identity. In the sixteenth-century classic *Don Quixote*, Cervantes wrote of Roland and "that traitor, Ganelon."

But the truth is very different. The real battle had taken place three centuries earlier, in 778. From the opening lines— "King Charles, the Great, our Emperor, has stayed in Spain for seven years"—the poem is historically wrong.

Charlemagne had only spent a few months in Spain, and the ones betrayed were not the French but the Muslims. There was no Ganelon, but there was a Suleiman, a Muslim who was feuding with the emir in Cordoba over control of the Ebro Valley. In 777, Suleiman, wishing to take the Ebro away from the emir's control, had crossed the Pyrenees to offer Charlemagne a list of cities above the great river that he had arranged to have fall to the Franks without a fight. Seeing an opportunity, Charlemagne crossed into Spain in spring 778 from the Mediterranean side, the old Visigoth path of conquest. He was able to take Girona, Barcelona, and Huesca with almost no resistance. But in Zaragoza on the Ebro, the Muslim commander did not follow the plan, instead defending the city. Faced with a real fight for the first time in this expedition, Charlemagne decided to forgo Zaragoza and return to France. It was now August, and he had been in Spain only about four months. On his way back he chose to attack Pamplona, destroy its walls, and loot the town. In so doing he enraged not the Muslims but the Basques.

To return to France, Charlemagne chose the same pass as had Abd-al-Rahman in his ill-fated 732 conquest of Europe. Throughout history this was the pass chosen for conquest. Though narrow and rugged, it is wide enough for an army. It is easier to cross than the neighboring Ispegui pass, which leads up to sheer gray rock and narrow waterfalls, by means of a narrow ledge of a road along the mountainside. Smugglers used the

Early twentieth-century smuggler apprehended by the Spanish at the Ispegui Pass.

cloud-covered crests of the Ispegui pass, preferring its inaccessibility. But armies always chose Roncesvalles.

The Basques, being greatly outnumbered, waited in the pine woods in a place known in Basque as Orreaga, literally, the place where the pine trees grow, which has been translated into Spanish as Roncesvalles, valley of the pines, and into French as Roncevaux. The Basques allowed the huge Frankish army to pass, climbing up to the windswept heights today known as Ibañeta. From there, the Pyrenees can be seen all the way across to the rugged mountains of Basse Navarre. But after Ibañeta the army had to thin out to single file to drop down along a mountain trail to the rocky valley of waterfalls that parts the Pyrenees. Charlemagne made it through and up to the steep mountainside village of Valcarlos, where wild apples still grow in the steep woods. While waiting in Valcarlos, the rear guard, commanded by his nephew Roland according to the poem (though some records write of an official named Hruodlandus), was attacked.

The Basques ran out of the forest with rocks and spears, attacking the Franks, who were sluggish with their heavy arms. There, on the bald heights of Ibañeta where wild purple crocus push through the grass, according to one account written only about fifty years later, the Basques killed every trapped Frank. Possibly some escaped, but it is certain that they killed Roland or Hruodlandus, two others close to Charlemagne, and a significant part of the force. Then the Basque forces simply dispersed, going home to their mountain villages, so that there was no Basque army for Charlemagne to pursue in vengeance. Pamplona was left to revert to Muslim rule.

At the end of the poem, tears are rolling over the white beard of Charlemagne as he says, "Oh God, how hard my life is." But, in fact, Charlemagne never recorded the encounter. The Basque attack of August 15, 778, was to be the only defeat Charlemagne's army ever suffered in his long military career.

The first record of the battle was written in 829, after the death of Charlemagne, and states that the French army, although far larger, was defeated by Basques. The Basques built few monuments to their victories. In Pasajes San Juan, the great Guipúzcoan port, along the little street that follows the deep water harbor cutting into the mountains, stands a nearly forgotten stone shrine, built in 1580, that commemorates the Basque victory over Charlemagne.

The lesson of the battle of Roncesvalles should have been: Do not to alienate the Basques. Yet somehow, in the ensuing centuries, Roland became the battle's hero—in time, even to the Basques. The Basques went on to other battles against Franks and both with and against Muslims, against the Vikings and even the Normans. With their small population, ambush remained a favorite technique. But throughout northern Navarra, folk legends developed that are still heard today of a local character, a giant of Herculean strength named Errolan—Roland. Basque myth had become Christianized.

Constant warfare was changing Basque society. The people moved into fortified towns. A military chain of command gradually evolved in which once separate tribal chieftains became generals, the generals became a ruling class, and, in 818, Iñigo Iñiguez became king and ruled for thirty-three years. The Kingdom of Navarra, the only kingdom in all of Basque history, had begun. It would last until 1512, its dynasties becoming defenders of Christianity, a great regional power of the Middle Ages, and a critical force in the Reconquista. These Basques of Navarra helped create the country that Basques would one day see as their greatest problem—Spain.

# 3: The Basque Whale

*Many say that the first to take on this harrowing adventure
must have been fanatic–eccentrics and dare-devils. It would
not have begun, they say, with reasonable Nordics, but only
with the Basques, those giddy adventurers.*
*—Jules Michelet, on whaling,* LA MER, *1856*

IN 1969, a cave with drawings of fish dating back to the
Paleolithic Age was discovered in Vizcaya. The fish appear to be
sea bream. A sea bream drawing was also found in a cave in
Guipúzcoa, and drawings of a number of other fish species have
been discovered as well. These drawings are remarkable because
Paleolithic man, living in natural caves 12,000 years ago, usually chose to depict mammals, such as deer and horses, and not
fish. He had not yet gone to sea. But these same caves are also
significant because the remains of fish bones and shells reveal
an unusual prehistoric diet.

A reverence for sea bream, *bixigu,* has been conserved
through millennia on the coast of Vizcaya and Guipúzcoa. It is
a traditional Christmas dish, and in Guipúzcoa, a pastry shaped
in the form of a sea bream is served on Christmas Eve. On that
night, the people of San Sebastián gather by their perfectly
curved, elegantly lamp-lit bay, and climb Mount Igueldo, the
steep little mountain at the harbor entrance, carrying a large
effigy of a sea bream. This is because the fish is associated with
Olentzaro, a pre-Christian evil sort of Santa Claus who slides
down chimneys on Christmas Eve to harm people in their sleep.
Fireplaces are lit for the holiday to keep him away.

In the early twentieth century, when Basques who had
migrated to Madrid formed a gastronomic society, they named it
*Besuguin-a Lagunak,* Friends of the Sea Bream. In San Sebastián

such gastronomic societies make a near ritual of fishing sea bream on Saturday nights in January.

The following recipe from the gastronomic society Donosti Gain, which means "in San Sebastián," was collected by the well-known Guipúzcoan chef José Castillo.

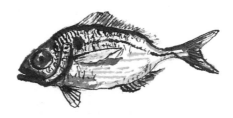

### SEA BREAM
### (for two)

*1 beautiful sea bream*
*6 tablespoons olive oil*
*4 tablespoons vinegar*
*2 slices guindilla pepper (a dried red, slightly hot, local*
  *pepper)*
*4 cloves garlic*

*Put the sea bream in a casserole.*
*Roast it well in an oven.*
*Put the vinegar in a skillet and turn up the heat. When the vinegar is reduced to half, add the juice from the fish that is left in the casserole and let it simmer a little.*
*In another skillet put the olive oil and the garlic cloves cut in slices. Heat the skillet with the oil and garlic. When the garlic begins to turn golden, add the guindilla and turn off the heat. Add the reduction of vinegar and fish juice.*
*Bring to a boil for 1 minute.*
*Uncover the sea bream and add the liquid.*

This leaves the question: What is meant by a "beautiful sea bream"? The answer was suggested in a 1933 book about fish written by the pseudonymous Ymanol Beleak, a native of Bilbao who lived many years in San Sebastián and whose real name was Manuel Carves-Mons. Beleak, an entrepreneur who, among other projects, manufactured chocolate boxes and created his own label of sparkling wine, wrote, "A sea bream of quality has a small head and thick back. It does not need to be large to be good."

ORIGINALLY, THE BASQUE idea of the sea, *itsaso*, was the Bay of Biscay, that part of the Atlantic between France and Spain that

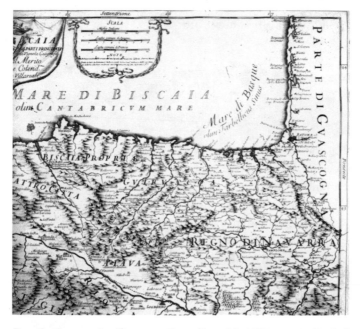

Detail of a map by Giacomo Cantelli entitled "Vizcaya is divided into four major parts," from *Mercurio Geográfico*, Rome, 1696. Note that the gulf is labeled *Mare di Basque*, the Basque Sea. (Photography archive of the Untzi Museoa-Maritime Museum, San Sebastián)

on some medieval maps is marked *El Mar de los Vascos,* the Basque Sea. This, by Atlantic standards, is a relatively unfertile corner of the ocean, because while fish tend to cluster in the relatively shallow water over continental shelves, the Iberian shelf is short, dropping off steeply close to shore.

With flair and imagination, the Basques have created great dishes out of even the least fleshy little creatures of their unfruitful Basque Sea: *txangurro,* the scrawny spider crab of winter; *txitxardin,* tiny baby Atlantic eel caught in the rivers, also in winter; *antxoa,* the spring anchovies; *txipiron,* small squid caught off the coast in the summer; and *sardina,* the fat summer sardines that were a specialty of the Bilbao area before the pollution that came with the industrial revolution.

Txipiron

Basque fishermen invented ways of cooking inexpensive local catch. *Ttoro* is a dish traditionally prepared by Labourdine fishermen based in towns at the mouth of the Nivelle: St.-Jean-de-Luz, Ciboure, and the village at the harbor entrance, Socoa. It is made from locally available fish, and the recipe varies from cook to cook. The following recipe is from Casinto De Gregorio, a Guipúzcoan who established a cozy little restaurant in St.-Jean-de-Luz in the 1920s. The restaurant, Chez Maya, is still in the family, and the cook, his grandson, Freddy, still uses his *ttoro* recipe.

### *TTORO*
### *(for six)*

| | |
|---|---|
| *6 hake steaks* | *2 large onions* |
| *6 very small monkfish* | *2 leeks* |

*3 rascasse (a local redfish
  in the same family as ocean
  perch, which is not a
  substitute)*
*2 large red gurnard
  (a bony European fish)*
*1 1/3 pound mussels*
*6 nice-sized langoustines*

*1 3/4 pound tomatoes*
*4 garlic cloves*
*1 pint white wine*
*1 bouquet garni
  (thyme, bay leaf
  and parsley)*
*pepper*

*Clean the fish. Cut the gurnard in slices. Fillet the rascasse.
Keep the bones.*

*Sauté the chopped onions, minced leek, and chopped garlic
in olive oil for 15 minutes; add the heads and bones of the fish
and cook slowly. Add the tomatoes, crushed, the wine, a quart
of water, the bouquet garni, and pepper. Cook 90 minutes.*

*Clean and open the mussels, adding the juice to the pot.
Strain the liquid.*

*Flour the fish and sauté for 1 minute in olive oil.*

*Combine everything and cook slowly for 10 minutes.*

*Serve in soup bowls with garlic croutons.*

Despite their inventive cooks, the Basques did not stay in
their little sea, content with its little creatures. What first drove
them out farther than the known world was the pursuit of a
deadly but profitable giant: the Basque whale.

PLINY, THE FIRST-CENTURY Roman naturalist, described whales
as creatures that lived off the north coast of Iberia. Until the
Basques overhunted them, giant whales, along with porpoises
and dolphins, made the Bay of Biscay their winter home.

Several varieties of whale, including the huge sperm whale,
could be seen off the rocky coastline. The most valued one has
the scientific name *Eubalaena glacialis*, referring to the fact that
it spent its summers amid the icebergs, cruising past pale blue

glacier faces off Norway, Iceland, Greenland, and Labrador. When these waters began to freeze for the winter, it would come down to the Bay of Biscay. Some scientists had proposed the Latin name *Balaena euskariensis* after its popular name, the Euskera or Basque whale.

An important feature of the Basque whale was that, like the sperm whale, but unlike many whale species, it floated when dead. The whale's back shone obsidian black in the water, though the belly was a brilliant white. Averaging about fifty to sixty feet in length, a quarter of which was the huge head, a single animal could weigh more than sixty tons. Such a whale would yield thirty tons of blubber, which could be cooked down to an oil valued for centuries as fuel. Most coastal Basque communities established facilities along their beaches for cooking down whale blubber. As with most things Basque, it is not certain when this oil trade began, but in 670, at the end of the age of the Visigoths, there was a documented sale in northern France by Basques from Labourd of forty pots of whale oil.

Whalebone was also valuable, especially the hundreds of teeth which were a particularly durable form of ivory. The tons of meat were a profitable food item. Whale meat had been eaten by the ancient Greeks and Phoenicians, who probably took beached whales since there is no record of commercial whaling. Romans also wrote of whale meat. Pliny wrote that eating whale meat was good for the teeth.

The first commercial whale hunters were the seventh- and eighth-century Basques, who found an eager market for this meat in Europe. Whale meat became a staple of the European diet partly because the Catholic Church forbade the eating of "red-blooded" meat on holy days—about half the days on the calendar including every Friday—arguing that it was "hot," associated with sex, which was also forbidden on holy days. But meat that came from animals—or parts of animals—that were submerged in water, including whale, fish, and the tail of the beaver, was

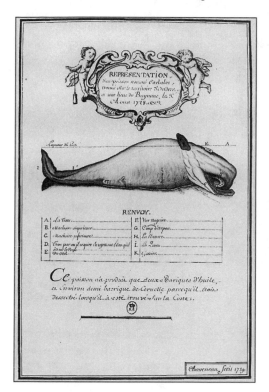

A beached whale brought to Bayonne in 1728. The caption says that the whale only produced two casks of oil because it had dried out from lying on the shore. (Collection of Charles-Paul Gaudin, St.-Jean-de-Luz)

deemed "cold" and therefore permitted. So with the exception of beaver tails and the occasional seal or porpoise, whale was the one allowable red meat. The Basques became the great providers of this holy red meat. They sold the leaner meat fresh or preserved in salt. Fattier parts were cured like bacon. In Paris, where these cuts were a lenten specialty, they were known as *craspois*. Tongues, fresh or salted, were regarded as a particular delicacy and served with peas. Being the choicest part, the only good part, according to some medieval writers, whale tongues were often demanded by local church or government officials as tribute. The port of Bayonne jealously guarded its monopoly on the tongue trade.

In the seventh century, the Basques, no longer content to

wait for ailing whales to beach themselves, built stone whale-spotting towers along the coast from Bilbao to Bayonne, manning them between October and March. One still remains on a mountaintop near San Sebastián and another in Guéthary in Labourd. The whale's undoing was the fact that it is a lunged mammal and must rise to the surface to breathe. When it does, a tall column of vapor is released. Spotting the spout of an approaching whale off the coastline, the lookout in the tower would let out a prolonged yell. His shouts were actually coded signals that told whalers the exact type of whale sighted, and whether it was a single whale or in a group. Five oarsmen, a captain, and a harpooner would then row out in a lightweight vessel.

The oarsmen would row as silently as possible, muffling the oars in their locks and even the oar blades in the water with oiled cloth. Then, having sneaked up on the unsuspecting giant foundering along the coast, they would strike suddenly with wooden-handled spears and harpoons. The oarsmen had to row close enough to the whale for the harpooner to plant the har-

Basque whalers. (Collection of Charles-Paul Gaudin, St.-Jean-de-Luz)

poon deeply into the body just below the head. Harpooning became the trade of the largest, strongest men. After harpooning the whale, the oarsmen had to row furiously in reverse, turning a fast circle, for an enraged whale could kill a dozen men with a flick of its huge tail. Or, instead of turning on its attackers, the whale might try to dive to the safety of great depths, dragging men and boats with it. The whale would dive with harpoon, line, and buoys until, out of breath, it had to furiously resurface, only to be harpooned again. The process was repeated numerous times until the whale spouted blood and died or the whalers capsized and drowned. Sometimes the boat and fishermen would just sink under the weight of the wet ropes.

By the late thirteenth century, whales marked the town seals of Bermeo and Fuenterrabía. Among the other towns that included whales in their town seals were Biarritz, Hendaye, Guetaria, Motrico, and Lequeitio. Not only did these towns keep the whale on their seals, but, from the use of whaling launches, they developed an early and enduring passion for rowing regattas.

Harpooning a whale. Shown on a Seal of Motrico, 1507, Municipal Archive of Motrico. (Untzi Museoa, San Sebastián)

The eighteenth-century British are generally credited with having invented this sport on the Thames, but it may be the Basques who originated it. Their first recorded contest, a legendary Mundaka-versus-Bermeo regatta, was in 1719, though they may have held many competitions before that with the fishermen of one town challenging the fishermen of a second town to a twenty-minute race. Even today, the Basque fishing towns compete every summer. The home team rows out to meet the visitors, in launches whose design has not changed in at least three centuries. After holding their oars vertically in a salute, they begin the race.

IN THE NINTH CENTURY, the Basques skirmished with yet another intruder, the Vikings who occupied the banks of the Adour River. The Basques always tried to learn from interlopers, and the Vikings, who had traveled farther by sea than anyone else at

BASQUE COASTLINE

Bay of Biscay

Bayonne
Biarritz
Bermeo
St. Jean-de-Luz FRANCE
Mundaka
Ciboure
Guéthary
Fuenterrabia
Ondarroa
Lequeito
San Sebastián
Hendaye
Nervión R.
Guernica
Motrico
Guetaria
Pasajes
LABOURD
Bilbao VISCAYA
Zarautz
Deba R.
Oria R.
Urumea R.
Bidasoa R.
GUIPÚZCOA
NAVARRA
ALAVA S P A I N
©1999 Jeffrey L. Ward

that time, became an important influence on Basque seamen. Instead of simply planking a frame, Basque shipbuilders began to use the Viking hull construction, overlapping the edge of planks horizontally and then fastening them with iron rivets.

Better-built ships meant the possibility of longer voyages, but despite the increased seaworthiness of vessels and even improved navigational skills, voyages were only able to last as long as the shelf life of the ship's provisions. Since most fish are found on continental shelves, a long voyage beyond the European shelf could not be provisioned by catching fresh fish alone. With no refrigeration, food spoilage was the undoing of many voyages beyond coastal zones. By the tenth century, Vikings were able to undertake longer voyages than other people of the time, able to travel between continents, because they provisioned their long journeys through the North Atlantic with cod that had been dried in arctic air. By the late tenth century, a century after leaving the Adour, they were crossing the North Atlantic to North America.

The Atlantic cod, a white-fleshed bottom feeder of the North Atlantic that was unknown in the waters off northern Iberia, has almost no fat, which enables it to preserve unusually well. The Basques refined the curing process by not only drying but first salting the cod, as they did with whale meat. Because cod were found in the northern summer whale grounds, the same rowboats that were launched from ships to chase whale were also used to fish cod. These Basque boats were the origin of the fishing dory that was later used in the North American cod fishery by most Atlantic fishing nations until the 1950s.

The Basques had extended their range in pursuit of the whale from the Bay of Biscay, across the northern coast to Galicia. But by pursuing northern cod, and provisioning their ships with salt cod, they then were able to start chasing the whale into its summer grounds, up to Iceland, Norway, the Hebrides, and the Faeroes.

By the year 1000, whales that had returned to safe northern waters, the snort of their spray echoing in silent fjords, were suddenly being pounced on by Basques, who had sailed more than 1,000 miles to hunt them down. The dangerous business became even more deadly with the move to subarctic waters where a fisherman, tossed into the icy water, would die in minutes. But long-distance whaling had the advantage that it avoided tributes demanded by local government and church, tributes which sometimes included the tongues, and often the entire first whale of the season or a strip from head to tail. Such tributes were inhibiting whaling. In 1334, to redress the declining fishing population of Lequeitio, Alfonso XI of Castile declared a five-year period during which whalers of that port were taxed a tribute of only one in eighteen whales, instead of the usual one in fifteen. In 1498, the whalers of Labourd rebelled and refused to pay the tongues demanded as tribute by the cathedral in Bayonne. But at times a more effective escape from tributes was to go far away to unknown corners of the globe, where their catch could not be easily monitored.

Salted and dried Basque cod lasted better than the Vikings' dried product and, through soaking, restored to something resembling a piece of fish. The dried Viking fish felt like a piece of balsa wood. To prepare it, the cook would break it into chips with a hammer. With salt cod, called *bacalao* in Spanish or *maikalao* in Euskera, the Basques further enhanced their whaling fortunes. While fresh fish was easily spoiled and expensive, the Basques had a cheap, long-lasting food for peasants—even inland peasants—that was Church-approved for holy days and that, unlike whale, seemed to be in inexhaustible supply. The Basques were so successful at marketing this product far from the fish's northern range that in Basqueland, Catalonia, Mediterranean France, Italy, Greece, North Africa—throughout the Mediterranean region—this northern import has remained a traditional food.

The Basques gradually became not only the world's purveyors of whale and cod products but the leading shipbuilders, pilots, and navigators. Capitalists before capitalism, Basques financed most of their shipbuilding through private venture capital. Typically, a single ship would have three or four investor-owners. Under the most common Basque contract, the crew worked for one-third of the profits. Basque ships, large and beamy and known for their exceptionally large hold capacity, were sought after by Europe's maritime peoples.

Shipyards emerged in the fifteenth and sixteenth centuries over the entire Basque coast from Bilbao, where the extensive waterfront of the Nervión River afforded many sites, to the fishing villages and riverfronts of Vizcaya, Guipúzcoa, and Labourd, all the way up to Bayonne. Villages with populations of a few hundred were producing what were considered the best ships in the world. Pasajes, a Guipúzcoan whaling port near San Sebastián with a village-sized population crowded onto a single street between the long waterfront and the steep mountains,

A nineteenth-century view of Pasajes.

developed some of the finest port facilities of the fifteenth century. Basqueland had not only the harbors but the iron fields and oak forests for this industry.

Basques built all kinds of ships: fishing, whaling, merchant, and warships. In 1505, a Basque General of the Fleet, Juan Lope de Lazcano, commissioned a ship with metal plating on the ribs; the precursor by centuries of ironclad warships. In 1543, a Basque engineer, Blasco de Garay, showed Carlos I a new idea: a ship powered by a giant wheel that was moved by vapor from boiling water. Though Carlos had a great interest in inventions, he was unimpressed with this one, and the idea was ignored for centuries, until the late-eighteenth-century dawn of the industrial revolution.

Maritime skill and engineering innovations were supported by legal prowess. In 1351, the Vizcayan fishing port of Bermeo signed a treaty with Edward III of England that was the first international accord to establish the principle of freedom of the high seas.

ONE OF THE GREAT Basque mysteries is: When did Basque whalers and codmen first reach North America? Although the pre-Columbian journeys of the Vikings are described in the Icelandic sagas, for centuries such anecdotal evidence was dismissed as legend, myth, or exaggeration. Then in 1961 the remains of eight Viking-built turf houses dating from A.D. 1000 were found in Newfoundland in a place called L'Anse aux Meadows. The Basques also left a trail of tales and myths but no physical evidence that they were in North America at an early date. Some have even speculated that the Basques were there before the tenth-century Vikings, a claim with very little basis. The more widely believed and more carefully reasoned theory is that the Basques arrived in North America, along the Newfoundland or Labrador coast, in the fourteenth or fifteenth century, that they visited, perhaps with some regularity, perhaps even had people working there, substantially before John Cabot's 1497 "discovery" of Newfoundland and Christopher Columbus's 1492 Caribbean find.

Throughout the century leading up to Columbus's and Cabot's celebrated voyages, widespread rumors persisted, especially among fishermen and maritime people, that Basque fishermen had found "a land across the sea," perhaps only an island. The Bretons even attempted to follow Basque fishermen.

In the early fifteenth century, many Europeans believed that two ships from Guipúzcoa, one captained by Juan de Echayde and the other by Matais de Echeveste, had reached land across the Atlantic at the end of the previous century.

But no physical evidence has been found of the Basques in North America before Cabot. Historians and archeologists who have searched for it and failed insist that the rumors are false. But the search for pre-Columbian Basques in America has yielded ample evidence of a surprisingly large-scale Basque presence in Newfoundland and Labrador soon after Cabot. The remains of extensive Basque whaling stations dating to 1530 have been found. It is now thought that by the 1560s the Basque population may have been as high as 2,000, and yet, until 1976, no physical proof of this had been found either.

Jacques Cartier saw Basques in abundance on his voyage of discovery thirty-seven years after Cabot. And Basque journals record seeing Cartier. Few of Cartier's place-names from the Gulf of St. Lawrence side of Newfoundland have survived because fishermen continued to use bastardized Basque names. Bonne Bay comes from the Basque name *Baya Adhere,* Beautiful Bay; Ingornachoix Bay comes from the Basque name *Aungura Charra,* Bad Anchorage; and Port-au-Choix from *Portuchoa,* Small Port. In 1594, Bristol merchant Sylvester Wyet observed that of sixty fishing ships in Newfoundland's Bay of Placentia, eight were Spanish and the rest were Basque.

The two leading arguments for placing the Basques in pre-

Columbian America are both based on deductive reasoning. The first is their catch. The Basques landed enormous quantities of cod and whale products throughout the Middle Ages. And yet their fourteenth-century competitors were convinced that the known fishing grounds alone could not explain the number of cod they brought to European markets. After Cabot, when Newfoundland and Labrador grounds became widely known, it could be seen that these were the principal Basque whale and cod grounds. Was that not the case before Cabot as well?

The second deductive argument is the improbability that the best sailors, with the best ships, the best navigators, and a tradition of sailing the longest distances could have missed North America during centuries of clearly being so close. There is evidence of the Basques in the Faeroe Islands as early as 875. This was a 1,500-mile journey, which, if they did not make landfall along the way, was a remarkably long distance to sail at that time. Is it possible that in all the following six centuries, working in the narrow area of the North Atlantic where the continents are not far apart, having known and learned from the Vikings, that the Basques never ventured the relatively shorter distance to North America? In 1412, an Icelandic account records that twenty Basque whalers passed by the western tip of Iceland off Grunderfjord, which is a 500-mile crossing to Greenland. From there another 1,200-mile voyage would have taken them to Newfoundland, or a much shorter crossing would have taken them to the northern Labrador coast. The total crossing from the Faeroes to Newfoundland is not much farther than from San Sebastián to Iceland. Most fishermen had little reason to cross the Atlantic, since the catches vanish with the end of the European continental shelf and do not pick up until the other side. But the Basques chased whales that traveled to subarctic waters and then dropped down along both the European and American coastlines.

Numerous reports claim that when Cabot and other early

explorers arrived in North America, they encountered native tribesmen who spoke Basque. In other accounts, the tribesmen and the Basques learned and intermingled each other's languages. In the sixteenth century, there was much speculation about the relationship between indigenous North American languages and Euskera. Esteban de Garibay used this as evidence that both North America and Basqueland were homes to survivors of the Flood. According to accounts from the late fifteenth and early sixteenth centuries, including those of Peter Martyr, cleric of the court in Barcelona, who reported on the early discoveries, the tribesmen encountered by Cabot were already using the word *baccallaos*. Even if this were true, however, they did not necessarily learn the word from the Basques. In this period the Basque word for cod had numerous variations in different dialects of Euskera, including *bacallau, bakaillo, makaillo,* and *makallao*. According to one theory, the word *bacalao* was originally Euskera and comes from the Euskera word *makila*, which means "stick." The cod were cured on sticks, and the Scandinavian word for dried cod, *stockfish*, has the same derivation, with *stock* meaning "pole." But other linguists point out that Euskera frequently converts *b* to *m* when adopting foreign words, and the word *makallao* was probably borrowed from Spanish, Catalan, or Portuguese. The tribesmen could have learned the word from any of these languages. The critical issue is: When did they learn it?

A St.-Jean-de-Luz merchant wrote in 1710, some 150 years after the fact, that when the French were first exploring the rivers of Nouvelle France, they found indigenous people already speaking a patois that was part indigenous and part Euskera. There were many accounts that the indigenous language "had come to be half Basque."

It has even been suggested that some indigenous words appear to be of Basque origin. The local name for deer is *orein*, which also is the Basque word. Pierre Lhande-Heguy, who became the first secretary of the Basque Academy of Language when this institute was established in 1918, observed a remarkable Basqueness in proper names of the Huron's language. Among the Huron names that suggested Basque origin to him were the men's names Anonatea, Arhetsi, Ochelaga, Ahatsistari, Andekerra, and Oatarra and the women's names Arenhatsi and Ondoaskoua. But the similarity could be a coincidence, and some historians who concede an Euskera influence on local languages argue that it could have happened after 1497 when Newfoundland became known and a large Basque presence there was well documented. If so, the difficult language was assimilated in only a few years.

On the other hand, if the Basques had been in America for decades, possibly centuries before Columbus, why would there be no record of it? Some say, as is always said about the Basques, that they keep secrets. But the real answer might lie not in the nature of Basques but in the nature of fishermen. When fishermen find an unknown ground that yields good catches, they go to great lengths to keep their secret. In most fishing communities, there are boats with notably better catches, and the crews are silent about the location of their grounds. The cod and whale grounds off the coast of North America was a secret worth keeping, the richest grounds ever recorded by European fishermen.

ANOTHER SIGN THAT Basque fishermen preceded explorers is the fact that when the fifteenth- and sixteenth-century Age of Exploration unfolded, the Spanish and Portuguese turned to Basque ships and mariners because the Basques were considered the people with experience. The Basques hunted voraciously and traveled restlessly. As the world became better known, Basque whalers were found everywhere. They were seen whaling off the coast of Brazil, far north in the Arctic, and down to the Antarctic. Many of the early European ships that explored Africa,

America, and Asia were built by Basques and often piloted by Basques as well.

The *Santa María*, one of the ships used for Columbus's first voyage, in 1492, was probably built by Basques. Among its crew were numerous Basques, including the boatswain Chanchu, who died on the voyage; the shipwright Lope de Erandio; and a carpenter from Lequeitio named Domingo. Among the Basques on the *Pinta* were two Guipúzcoans. Columbus's second voyage was organized in Vizcaya by two Basques, shipowner Juan de Arbolancha and naval commander Iñigo de Artieta. For that voyage, six Basque ships were built and ready to sail from Bermeo, in July 1493, with Basque pilots Lope de Olano and Martín Zamudio and many Basque crewmen. One of the ships, with eighty-five men, was outfitted by Juan Pérez de Loyola, the future Saint Ignatius's oldest brother. In 1494, Columbus's third voyage was also manned by Basques, and in 1502, the fourth included the *Vizcaina*, a ship out of Guetaria with a Basque pilot and many Basque crewmen.

Juan de La Cosa, a Basque explorer usually known as Juan Vizcaíno, which in the language of the time meant "Juan the Basque," was probably with Columbus on his first voyage and definitely on the 1493 second voyage. He continued to explore the Caribbean basin and in 1500 drew the first map of the world to include the Americas. In 1509, he was killed by tribesmen in what is now Colombia. Another Basque to be dubbed Vizcaíno, Sebastián Vizcaíno, was one of the early explorers of the California coast, exploring San Diego Bay, discovering Monterey, and sailing north of San Francisco Bay, giving California many of its present-day names.

Magellan, it is commonly taught, was the first man to circumnavigate the globe. But this is contradicted by the other well-known fact about Magellan: that he was killed on his voyage by tribesmen in the Philippines. The expedition with five ships and 200 men, of which at least 35 were Basque, left

Juan Sebastián de Elcano from an engraving by L. Fernández for "Portraits of illustrious Spaniards" commissioned by the Calcografía Nacional, 1791-1814. (Untzi Museoa, San Sebastián)

JUAN SEBASTIAN DE ELCANO, *Hábil Piloto y Argonauta inmortal por haber sido el primero que dió la vuelta al mundo. Nació en Guetaria, y murió en la mar del Sur en 1526.*

Seville in August 1519 under the command of Magellan, Fernão de Magalhães, a tough and burly Portuguese in the service of Spain. Only three ships made it to the Philippines. At Cebu, Magellan waded ashore with a few dozen men to attack a force of 1,500 tribesmen, enemies of a local sultan with whom he had made an alliance. He did not even bring his ship's cannons into firing range. When it became clear that the attack was a disaster, he stood with a handful of men to cover the retreat of his forces and was overwhelmed and slashed to death.

He had lost only eight of his men in the engagement. But by the time the expedition left the Philippines, fighting and starvation had reduced the crew to 110, and they scrapped one ship for lack of crew. Two continued, the *Trinidad* and the Guipúzcoan-built *Victoria,* under the command of Juan Sebastián de Elcano, a Basque from Guetaria, who learned his trade first on fishing boats and later, exploring the coast of Africa.

Elcano had already commanded larger ships than those of the Magellan expedition. But prior to Magellan's death, Elcano had not been a commander on this expedition. Early in the voyage, Magellan and Elcano had become bitter enemies, and Magellan had condemned Elcano to death for his part in a mutiny on the coast of South America. The only injury caused by the mutineers had been the stabbing of a fellow Basque loyal to Magellan, Juan de Elorriaga. Elcano had spent five months, a long gray winter, in chained hard labor in Patagonia while the crew waited for spring to find the straits to the Pacific.

Now in command, Elcano and the two ships engaged in the spice trade for some months, and then the *Victoria* continued around the world while the *Trinidad* was left behind for repairs. The latter was eventually stripped by the Portuguese and destroyed in a squall.

On September 8, 1522, almost nine months after leaving the *Trinidad,* three years and one month after setting sail from Seville, Elcano, the first man to circumnavigate the globe, sailed the *Victoria* up the Guadalquivir River and tied her up at a pier in Seville. On her decks was the surviving crew of eighteen men, including at least four Basques. In rags, carrying candles, the barefoot crewmen walked a mile to the cathedral, where they offered thanks at the shrine of Santa María de L'Antigua.

Elcano was given an annual pension and honored with a coat of arms featuring a globe with the words *Primus circumdedisti me,* Thou who first circumnavigated me. But many of the surviving eighteen received nothing. One, Juan de Acurio, stated two years later that all he had earned from the voyage was "glory, experience, and a bale of cloves."

The *Victoria* went on to the merchant service, making one

voyage to the Caribbean and going down with all hands on the second. To the enormous profit of the Basques, this was an age when an unprecedented number of ships were being lost at sea, and the demand for shipbuilding seemed limitless.

Basques returned to the Philippines. Andrés de Urdaneta, became the second man to circumnavigate the globe, completing a nine-year expedition in 1536. Then Miguel Lopez de Legazpi y Gorrocategui, who had gone to Mexico in 1528, where he amassed the fortune every adventurous Spaniard of the day was dreaming of, sailed to the Philippines, took Luzon, and established Manila as the capital of the new colony in 1571. Centuries later, when Spain lost its colonies and conflicting nationalisms divided the Spanish and the Basques, the angry Spanish military would no longer remember that it was the Basques who had secured much of Spain's global empire in the first place.

# 4: The Basque Saint

*Those who know the Jesuits know that Basque nationalism is completely Catholic.*
—*Sabino Arana,* EL CORREO VASCO, *July 29, 1899*

BASQUES MAY REMEMBER their own role in building the Spanish Empire, but almost no one wants to remember the Basque role in building Spain itself. By the beginning of the sixteenth century the Reconquista had been accomplished. The Moors—and while the victors were at it, the Jews and the Gypsies—had all been driven out of Spain. *Los reyes Católicos,* the Catholic monarchs, Ferdinand of Aragón and Isabella of Castile, had forcibly fused a huge country, taking control of every kingdom and fiefdom on the Iberian peninsula except Portugal and the Basque Kingdom of Navarra.

Basques, in search of wealth and nobility, had fought for los reyes Católicos against other Basques to take Guipúzcoa, Vizcaya, and Alava. In exchange, Ferdinand had promised the Basques that up to the Ebro, their ancient laws, the Fueros, were to be respected. Throughout their history, the Basques have been willing to compromise their independence as long as they could have self-rule by their traditional laws. Like the language, the laws are an essential part of Basque identity. For unknown numbers of centuries, these laws were based on custom and, unlike Roman law, had no formal code. In the twelfth century these traditions were, for the first time, written into a legal code. The Spanish language was used because Spanish was thought of as the language of legal codes, and they became known as the *Fueros,* a Spanish word meaning "codified local customs." Many other parts of Iberia, including Castile, had fueros, but nowhere were they as extensive or as revered as in Navarra and the Basque provinces.

The first article of the Fueros of Navarra states that the Fueros are "customs and practices, written and non-written," that guarantee "justice to the poor as to the rich." They comprised both commercial and criminal law, addressing a wide range of subjects, including the purity of cider, the exploitation of minerals, the laws of inheritance, the administration of farmland, crimes and punishments, and a notably more progressive view of human rights than was recognized in Castilian law.

A Basque assembly, the Juntas Generales, met under an oak tree at Guernica, to legislate and rule on Foral law. The meetings predate the written code. Meeting-oaks had been established in several Vizcayan towns but the Guernica sessions, which lasted two or three weeks, became dominant. Local assemblies sent elected representatives to Guernica and trumpets were sounded and bonfires lit on the nearby mountaintops. By tradition, a representative from Bermeo was the first to be heard. At the end of the session, a fourteen-man ruling body was chosen by lot to govern until the next meeting. Once Vizcaya was tied to Castile, a representative of the King of Castile came to each meeting to swear that the authority of the Fueros would be respected.

Ferdinand understood the importance Basques attached to their laws and customs because the other region that came closest to Basques in its reverence for its own Fueros was his native Aragón. Not all Aragónese shared his enthusiasm for merging with Castile to build a superpower, and he had calmed them by promises of limited self-rule. In time, Ferdinand reasoned correctly, the Aragónese movement, once pacified, would fade, and he probably made the mistake of thinking the same would happen with the Basques.

Among the privileges that came to the Basques with recognition of the Fueros were exemption from direct taxation by Castile, exemption from import duties, and exemption from military service outside their own province. When Castile wanted

Basque taxes, it had to negotiate the amount with the Basque government, which would then raise the agreed-upon sum from its own population. If the Castilians wished to have a Basque army or navy to use beyond the defense of Basqueland, the monarchs had to negotiate with Basques to raise an army or navy, usually in exchange for fees and privileges.

The Basques have little tradition of aristocracy—none outside of Navarra. In the *Fuero General*, the first written Basque code set down in 1155, there is only one reference to lords and vassals: "The Navarrese are to serve their King as good vassals." No other Basque titles exist. It was the Spanish who conferred titles of nobility and the right to a coat of arms to wealthy citizens. The Loyolas of Azpeitia, in central Guipúzcoa, were a notable example of a Basque family that had served the Castilians in exchange for wealth and titles. In 1331, Alfonso XII, king of Castile, presented the family with a coat of arms.

The Basques have a reputation of being warlike in the service of Basques. But the Loyola family exemplified another Basque tradition, known to both the Carthaginians and Romans, of being warriors for profit. Loyolas had been honored for battles they had fought against not only the Moors and the French but also fellow Basques. The family had played a critical role in making Guipúzcoa part of Castile. In September 1321, an army from Guipúzcoa joined forces with the Castilians to defeat the French and the Navarrese in the Battle of Beotibar. The exploits of seven Loyola brothers during this fight are still recounted in Euskera once a year in the little Guipúzcoan village of Iguerondo.

Beltran, a son of one of the brothers, fought the Moors for the king of Castile and was rewarded with land. In the Reconquista, as land was gained, a warlord would build a castle and encourage settlement under his protection. This was a Castilian concept, not a Basque one. Beltran not only built such a castle on his Castilian-granted land but also used his castle in Azpeitia

*67*

as a base from which to raid and pillage weaker warlords and even the Church. Eventually he was excommunicated by the bishop of Pamplona.

In 1491, Iñigo López de Oñaz y Loyola was born. A direct descendant of Beltran, he was destined to be the most famous Basque in history. Each generation of Loyolas had continued the family tradition. Iñigo's grandfather had attacked the two neighboring towns and lost. As punishment, the family castle was torn down and he was sentenced to fight the Moors in Andalusia. Allowed to return after four years, he rebuilt the family home out of brick in a Moorish style, and that house still stands. His son, Iñigo's father, Bertrand de Loyola, pledged himself to Ferdinand and Isabella, fighting the French for Castile in 1476 in Toro and Fuenterrabía.

A sixteenth-century Basque contemporary of Iñigo wrote, "The Loyolas were one of the most disastrous families our country had to endure, one of those Basque families with a coat of arms over the door, in order to justify the misdeeds that were the tissue and pattern of their lives."

By the time of Iñigo's birth, the family, though culturally still Basque, had amassed great wealth from royal favors. In the family tradition, his brothers were soldiers and adventurers. It was a new age of adventure, and the oldest shipped out on Columbus's second voyage and later died in a naval engagement against the French. Another died in battle in Naples. Another served Castile in the Lowlands. Another sailed to America in 1510 and died in a fight with angry tribesmen.

They were the knights of their age who, with no more Moors to defeat, looked to new lands in which to do combat. Only one brother, Pedro López, was different, turning to religion and becoming the rector of the local church.

Iñigo, too, was initially trained for the priesthood. His mother had died when he was very young, and, raised in a nearby cottage by a blacksmith's wife, he grew up praying in the local

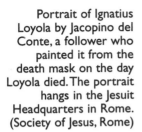

Portrait of Ignatius Loyola by Jacopino del Conte, a follower who painted it from the death mask on the day Loyola died. The portrait hangs in the Jesuit Headquarters in Rome. (Society of Jesus, Rome)

dialect of Euskera. But, realizing that, like his older brothers, he was more suited for action and worldly pleasures than a spiritual life, the family found him a position in the Castilian court as a page to Juan Velázquez de Cuéllar, treasurer general of Castile.

FERDINAND WAS CALLED "the Catholic," but a more accurate description was offered by Machiavelli. In *The Prince* he referred to Ferdinand as "the first king in Christendom." Ferdinand was a man who understood all of the tools for nation building. He could be a brilliant negotiator who wisely offered concessions, but he also knew when and how to use force. He took the bands of adventurers who had been crusading against the Moors and turned them into the best disciplined and most effective army in Europe.

Isabella was the real Catholic. Fanatically devoted to the Church, she personally completed the Reconquista. In 1492, dressed in white armor with the red cross of Castile, she led an army on Granada and drove the last of the Moors off the Iberian peninsula. Then she unleashed the Inquisition to purge Spain of heresy and impurity. Convert, die, or leave were the only choices she offered. She was Columbus's patron, and as new worlds were discovered, she charged the men of the Reconquista with spreading Catholicism.

In 1504, at the age of fifty-three, Isabella lay on her deathbed. She extracted two promises from Ferdinand: to bury her without ceremony in a homespun Franciscan robe and never to remarry. Ferdinand kept the first promise.

Germaine de Foix, Ferdinand's new bride, arrived from France with thirty shiploads of personal effects, including unimaginable quantities of cosmetics, perfume, and jewelry. A relative of the ruling family of Navarra, Germana, as the Spanish called her, was plump, alcoholic, approaching middle age, with, perhaps literally, a ton of makeup—the perfect embodiment of the Spanish stereotype of the frivolous and vain French.

Ferdinand, only a year younger than his late wife, was not in search of an autumn romance. Mortality was on his mind, and he wanted a son. His union with Isabella had given him, in addition to most of Spain, only a daughter, who was known as Juana La Loca—Juana the Mad. Now, sensing his time near its end, he had forged a magnificent birthright to pass on, and he wanted an heir who would know how to hold it together.

But Germana produced no heir, and Ferdinand was increasingly resigned to turning over his new European superpower to Juana's son, his grandson, Charles, whom the Spanish would call Carlos I. Charles was a teenager, born and raised in Flanders. He didn't even want to visit Spain to see his inheritance because to him, and many northern Europeans, Spain was a primitive and uncomfortable frontier.

Iñigo de Loyola's sponsor and protector, Juan Velázquez de Cuéllar, was married to the beautiful Doña María, lady-in-waiting to Germana. Iñigo, completely dazzled by María, entered the flighty world of Germana's court. María would entertain Iñigo by displaying her pearls and jewels, caressing certain glittery pieces and saying, "This one belonged to Queen Isabella."

Germana ran a court of shallow hedonistic amusements. Young Iñigo was taken by the jewels and the women. He had frequent infatuations and was especially smitten by the infanta Catalina. Catalina was the daughter of Philip the Fair and Juana the Mad. Unfortunately, the Mad triumphed over the Fair, and she spent much of her youth in the custody of her mother, who kept her in rags, locked up in the dark castle of Tordesillas. When she was eleven years old, her older brother, the future king of Spain, rescued her and brought her to court. During her brief stay, Iñigo was overcome with a teenage love for Catalina. But Juana refused to eat until her daughter was returned, and soon Catalina was taken away. She and Iñigo would remain lifelong friends.

Not all his romances were as pretty. Away from queens and princesses, his appetite for women seemed insatiable, and he was often violent and abusive to them, frequently brawling with other men over them. In his later life when he was given to confessions, he also admitted to criminal acts. He once allowed an innocent man to be convicted of a robbery he committed. He and his only religious brother stood trial for an incident involving a killing. They both escaped by pleading clerical immunity, which in Iñigo's case was a fabrication.

NAVARRA, THE ONE missing piece in Ferdinand's puzzle, remained independent. But in spite of its important role in the victorious Reconquista, the 700-year-old Kingdom of Navarra was weak. It had grown in the Middle Ages by shifting with and against the Moors, and in the eleventh century, Navarra had become the dominant kingdom of northern Spain. Under the rule of Sancho III, Sancho the Great, the Basques, for the only time in history, had expanded their rule far beyond their traditional territory.

Almost unique in Europe, Basques for most of history had no territorial ambitions. But Sancho doubled Basque territory. Under his reign not only had Navarra ruled Guipúzcoa and Vizcaya and taken Alava from Castile, but Sancho also had crossed the Ebro and taken Burgos and other parts of Castile.

Thirty years after his death, most of this land had been lost. In 1234, ninety-nine years after his death, the ruling Basque family had no more heirs, and the Navarrese turned to the French House of Champagne for a ruling family.

Ferdinand wanted this little Basque kingdom with the French rulers. By then, they had gone through two French families and were now being ruled weakly by the House of Foix, Ferdinand's new in-laws. In 1512, Ferdinand, who always insisted that the primary enemy was France, persuaded the Navarrese to let him enter their kingdom, claiming to be on his way to invade France. But he never engaged the French. Instead, he drove the ruling de Foix monarchs, Catherine and Jean d'Albret, across the Pyrenees, where they became king and queen of the little splinter kingdom of Basse Navarre.

Ferdinand, by repeatedly pledging to respect the Fueros, was able to take Pamplona without a fight. The rest of Navarra below the Pyrenees, seeing that Ferdinand would respect the rule of the Fueros, accepted him as king. Spain, with the exception of the Portuguese kingdom, was complete.

But the Navarrese were finding it difficult to be a mere province of this new Castilian-constructed peninsula-wide nation. They had been an independent country for seven centuries. Militant new movements pressed for a closer adherence to the ancient Foral laws. Others worked with an independence movement, based in Basse Navarre, whose goal was to reunite the two parts.

Ferdinand feared that after he died, his grandson, Charles, the boy from Flanders who did not even speak Spanish, would start losing the pieces he had so carefully put together. The first to go would be the Basques of Navarra. Navarra needed to be cemented to Spain. And so Ferdinand decided to make it a part of Castile. Attempting to win over the Navarrese to the idea, he made Charles swear to respect the Fueros and granted Navarra administrative autonomy within Castile.

In 1516 Ferdinand was in a deep depression. According to some accounts, Germana fed him "aphrodisiacs" to lift his spirits, though it is not clear what substance that might have been. On January 23, he died. Juan Velázquez de Cuéllar, who presided at the reading of Ferdinand's will, was soon to lose favor in court, and, in August 1517, he too suddenly died.

At the age of twenty-five, lacking a patron, Iñigo left his pretty court and went to serve his cousin, the viceroy of Navarra. He tried to continue his vain, self-indulgent court life, but this was a difficult time in the history of Navarra.

The deposed Catherine and Jean d'Albret, Ferdinand's in-laws in Basse Navarre, decided that Ferdinand's death was the moment to retake their kingdom. Jean d'Albret led an army from St.-Jean-Pied-de-Port up through the rocky pass to Ibañeta and there, in that historic and deceptively serene pine forest that descends to Roncesvalles, met spectacular defeat.

D'Albret, the last king of Navarra, died that year, like Ferdinand, in deep depression. Catherine, the queen-in-exile, died the following February. The only Basque kingdom in history ceased to exist.

IN 1517, with great reluctance, Charles came to Spain to ceremoniously tour his kingdom, region by region, as a monarch was expected to do. Before he ever reached Navarra, his other grandfather, Emperor Maximilian, died, and the new King Carlos I was off to Germany to become Emperor Charles V, the new Holy Roman Emperor. In his absence, rebellion broke out in towns throughout Iberia. The Basques of Navarra started to demand their independence.

The king of France, Francis I, was not a Basque sympathiz-er but a frustrated young man who also had wanted to be the Holy Roman Emperor. Now, to spite Charles, he took on the cause of Henri d'Albret, son of Catherine and Jean. On April 15, 1521, Hernán Perez, the mayor of Behobia, a Guipúzcoan bor-der town on the Bidasoa, reported, "King Jean's son is raising a mighty army with the help of the King of France to march on Navarra, and he is bringing seven thousand Germans and for-midable artillery."

Germans, Basques, as well as volunteers from neighboring Gascony and Béarn—in all an army of 12,000 men with twenty-six pieces of heavy artillery—overran St.-Jean-Pied-de-Port, the stone-walled mountain village on a fog-bound crook of the Nive. Once again, a French army climbed through the narrow pass to Roncesvalles and dropped down the piney slopes toward Pamplona.

This time they met no resistance. As they approached, Basque villagers overthrew their towns and joined the invading army. When they reached Pamplona, the townspeople opened the gates for them. Castilians fled the city, while the Navarrese sacked the ducal palace, tearing down the Spanish coat of arms. It was a great day for the Basques—or at least, for some of the Basques.

At this moment, pro-Castilian reinforcements arrived from Guipúzcoa under the command of Martín de Loyola, Iñigo's brother. Iñigo joined him. They were part of a larger Castilian force that tried to liberate Juana and her daughter, Iñigo's fan-tasy princess, Catalina, from their dank Tordesillas castle where local rebels were holding them hostage.

While most of the Navarrese saw the French-led army in Pamplona as liberators, these Guipúzcoans saw them as invaders. Martín was so disgusted with what to him was a betrayal by the townspeople that he refused to enter the city. Iñigo and some of his men entered the fortress, the unfinished castle Ferdinand had ordered before his death. As they went in, others were flee-

ing. He persuaded the commander to stay and fight. In his autobiography, which he wrote in the third person several decades
later, Iñigo noted, "While everyone else clearly saw that they
could not defend themselves and thought that they should surrender to save their lives, he offered so many reasons to the
fortress's commander that he talked them into defending it."
Though in the service of a mad cause, this was one of the first
indications that Iñigo had an extraordinary ability to lead.

Iñigo and the commander, holding nothing with which to
bargain but the castle they were ill-equipped to defend, emerged
to meet with the French commander. To Iñigo, all compromise
was cowardly, and, refusing to surrender, he walked back into the
fortress. As he awaited the bombardment, no priest being present, he said his confession, presumably a lengthy and colorful list
of transgressions, to a fellow defender. He was ready to die.

The castle held for several days until the heavy artillery
could be moved into place. Six hours of bombardment opened
a breach in a wall. Iñigo, sword drawn, was about to fight to the
death when a cannonball struck him in the legs.

The castle fell, and the French had Navarra. Then, repeating
Charlemagne's mistake, they needlessly antagonized the Basques
on their way into Castile by pillaging the Navarrese town of Los
Arcos for several days. The Castilians, desperately trying to
recruit an army to meet the French, were suddenly awash with
Basque volunteers. Navarra was quickly retaken, never again to
be regarded as a nation.

IÑIGO WAS TAKEN prisoner by the French, who performed surgery
on his legs, administered last rites, and sent him home to
Guipúzcoa by litter over mountain paths, covering the thirty
miles from Pamplona to Azpeitia in ten agonizing days. There
Spanish doctors operated on him again. In Iñigo's own words,
"Again he went through this butchery." His condition continued
to worsen, and he was again given last rites. Eventually, he

healed, but his leg had not been set right and was misshapen, with a bone sticking out in a grizzly manner. Despite being warned that it would cause excruciating pain, he insisted on having the protuberance cut off because, longing to resume his life as a handsome young courtier, he could not accept the idea of a disfiguring injury. After this horrid third operation, he was trussed up and told he could not move for months. Unable to sleep at night from pain, he stared at the ceiling and began reflecting on his life.

At first he read tales of knights, popular books of the period. But then he began reading about the lives of saints. He was especially moved by Saint Francis. He began having visions, one night seeing the Virgin Mary and the Christ child. The next morning, no longer the knight of Doña María or the infanta Catalina, he decided to be a knight of the Virgin.

His legs healed, though his right leg remained inches shorter than his left and he was to have a permanent limp. He became a restless religious pilgrim and, for a time, a hermit. He went to Rome and even was able to get an audience with Pope Adrian VI. But back in Spain he was arrested by the Inquisition. It was now the late 1520s, and the Spanish Inquisition was vigilant of heretical practices. Iñigo had shown far too much interest in various occult practices and worse, the Kabala and other magical teachings of Jews and Arabs. Released after three weeks of interrogation, he was barred from preaching.

Silenced in Spain, he decided to put aside preaching and went to Paris, where his Basque ways and hybrid beliefs would have little chance of a following, to study at the famous theological faculty. He so overloaded his donkey with books that he had to walk alongside on his damaged leg for two months to reach the capital. There, although a battle-scarred veteran of almost forty, he lived a student life, studying Latin, making his home in a shack on Rue St. Jacques, a main thoroughfare past the university area, the Latin Quarter. It was there that he received a degree in Latin as Ignatius and kept the Latin name.

The sixteenth-century Latin Quarter attracted other restless religious men from around Europe, and Ignatius gathered around him a small group of Spanish, French, and Basque students. Among them was Francisco de Jassu y Javier, a tall young Basque and champion high jumper who excelled at sports and was regularly seen playing by Notre Dame on the Ile de Cité. A seemingly lighthearted man, his craving for athletic excellence belied the trauma of a difficult childhood. He was a political exile from Navarra whose family had been loyal to the d'Albrets. His father had died fighting the Spanish, and his brothers had been imprisoned. Now he was rooming with Iñigo, a fellow Basque who had fought against their people.

When Iñigo, a natural leader who was consumed with his new religion, formed the small Latin Quarter group, Francisco laughed at him, found his sayings trite and his vows of poverty ridiculous. The once vain Iñigo, now lame and aging, showed a new tolerance for this tall young athlete whose family had been his enemies in war. Two decades later, Iñigo's secretary would write that Iñigo referred to Francisco as "the roughest clay he ever had to knead." According to legend, after two years of intellectual jousting, with Francisco mocking the less educated Iñigo's attempts to preach, and Iñigo flattering the younger man's vanity, Iñigo finally won him over.

On August 15, 1534, Iñigo and his group of seven founded their new order, the Society of Jesus, otherwise known as the Jesuits. The founding ceremony, typically Jesuit and, perhaps, typically Basque, took place by a crypt in Montmartre, a subterranean site beneath the hill north of Paris, said to be of pagan significance. The Jesuits, whose vows were simply chastity, poverty, and a pilgrimage to Jerusalem, would become known for a tendency toward the occult but also for their strict discipline.

They shunned the wearing of habits and renounced loyalty to local Church hierarchy. But they were fiercely loyal to the pope, leading the orthodox Counter-Reformation that tried to reclaim Protestant populations. True to the traditions of the Loyola family, the head of the order bears the title of general.

Ignatius was one of the Catholic Church's great mystics, given to visions and trances. His eyes would run with tears for hours as he tried to recite prayers. The Jesuits became the first worldwide order, accomplishing more than Queen Isabella's knights ever had to carry out her dream of spreading Catholicism to the new global Spanish Empire. In his battle against the Reformation, Ignatius made Jesuits in the tradition of medieval romance, knights who went forth in the world to conquer lands for the Church. Francisco, known as Francis Xavier, was his leading knight. Once the handsome and gregarious Francis, still only thirty-four, sailed from Lisbon for Asia in 1541, Ignatius would never see him again. Francis was a missionary in Japan, the Molucca Islands, and Malaysia, and died in 1552 en route to China. He is remembered as the patron saint of missionaries. After his death, other Jesuits went to Africa, to the Caribbean, and to the Americas.

In 1556 Ignatius fell ill, this time deteriorating so quickly that he died without receiving last rites. At the time there were 1,000 Jesuits.

The infanta Catalina, who had become the queen of Portugal, continued to support the Jesuits after Ignatius's death. In 1622, Loyola was canonized Saint Ignatius and his fellow Basque, Francis Xavier, was canonized alongside him.

Controversy has always accompanied the order. Known in Latin America as the preachers of revolution, they traveled up the unknown rivers of South America and tried to establish a model Christian society based on collectivism among the indigenous people they found there. In Europe they became, like Iñigo de Loyola, conservative-leaning and friendly to monarchs, although the Spanish Bourbon monarchs distrusted them. The French Bourbon monarchs, however, enlisted them as confessors to the royal house. Many progressive movements were vehemently anti-Jesuit, and their reputation in France was so reactionary that when Emile Zola wrote his famous 1898 defense of Alfred Dreyfus, "J'accuse," he called the military establishment that had persecuted Dreyfus "This band of Jesuits."

Today, with some 25,000 Jesuits in the world, they are the largest Catholic order. They are known throughout the world as builders of schools and promoters of education. Jesuit education has produced revolutionaries and archconservatives. It might have surprised Iñigo that the Jesuits also educated some of the most determined voices of Basque independence.

Cuba's Fidel Castro was once asked by a Dominican what he thought of his Jesuit education. "Everything was very dogmatic," he complained.

# 5: The Basque Billy Goat

*In ancient times and during the Middle Ages, Basques were
famous for their skills in the practice of fortune telling; today
it can be stated, at the risk of sounding prejudiced, that no
one in France is more superstitious than the Basques, except
maybe the Bretons.*
　　—*Francisque Michel,* LE PAYS BASQUE, *1857*

AS A SYMBOL OF their new order, the Jesuits chose not a cross
but a sun with its rays stretching toward a circular border. The
symbol is ubiquitous in Basqueland, although in modern times
the number of curved spokes filling the circle has been reduced
to four, giving the appearance of a cross—a concession Ignatius
de Loyola did not find necessary. This "Basque cross," as it is
frequently called, predates Christianity and is not a cross at all.

The Basque cross appears to be related to sun worship. The
original Basque religion was directly associated with nature—
sun gods, moon gods, rock gods, tree gods, mountain gods.
Such spirits were often animal-like but sometimes took human
form and often were a combination. Residents of different valleys worshiped different spirits. In many valleys, the sun, *eguz-
ki,* was the eye of God, *jainkoaren begi.*

Grave markers that pay homage to the sun have been found
in Basqueland dating from the first century B.C. well into
medieval times. These rough, thick stones tell the story of
Basque conversion, displaying every conceivable variation on
the sun from concentric circles to starlike bursts. In time, they
more and more resembled crosses, and some stones even have
a sun on one side and a cross on the other. Traditional rural
Basque houses are still built with the doorway facing east, the
direction of the rising sun. This is especially true in Labourd,

where the winds and rains are westerly, making the east the sheltered part of the house. Even in contemporary abstract art, the two leading Basque sculptors, Eduardo Chillida and Jorge de Oteiza, both use the circle as a central motif. Oteiza, who first

The image in the lower right-hand corner is a fresco of the Jesuit seal, circa 1600, from Ignatius Loyola's room in Rome. The remaining five images are ancient Basque gravestones, the dates of which range from 100 B.C. to A.D. 200 (top row) to after A.D. 833 (lower left-hand corner). The center images are opposite sides of the same stone. (Stones used by permission of Euskal Arkeologia, Etnografia eta Kondaira Museoa, Bilbao)

came to international prominence in 1958 by winning a sculpture prize in São Paulo for a steel ring with a strip curving through it, explains, "In the circle we have a tie to the sacred form, the solar circle and especially full moons, and such a primitive religious frame-of-mind, which is realized in these little circles, serves to regenerate our moral conscience."

But for centuries before contemporary abstract Basque art, these circular sun images, Basque crosses, were carved over the doorways of homes. Carvings of roosters were sometimes added to further greet the rising sun. "Sun, sacred and blessed, rejoin your mother" are the ancient words still repeated in modern times as a bedtime prayer.

Once the Basques turned to Christianity, they became, and have remained, the most devout Catholics in Europe. But because Basques keep their traditions, these devout Catholics have many strange practices, symbols, and beliefs. Basques have had a persistent belief in the existence of *jentillak*, gentiles, non-Christians who wander the woods and remote rural areas with terrifying pre-Christian magical powers. Some rural Basques still believe that an ax stored in the house with the blade up protects the house from lightning. Bread blessed on Saint Agatha Day is believed to protect against fire, and bread from Saint Blaise Day guards against floods. If this bread or blessed salt is fed to animals, these creatures will protect the house.

In the early years of Christianity, hermitism was a common phenomenon, not only in the Basque region but throughout northern Iberia. Devout men lived harsh, ascetic existences alone in mountain huts. In the year 800, one such hermit in the northwestern Galicia region of Iberia saw a shaft of brilliant light. Following this beam, he came upon a Roman cemetery. Under the shaft of light he found a small mausoleum concealed by overgrown vines, weeds, and shrubs. Since beams of celestial light don't lead to just anyone's grave, he concluded that this must

Silkscreen with relief by Eduardo Chillida for Amnesty International. Note the use of a circle with a line through it, a reference to the ancient Basque symbol.

have been the burial place of Saint James, Santiago, brother of John the Divine. The cemetery became known as Campus Stellae, the star field, and later Compostela.

According to legend, James, one of the first disciples chosen by Jesus, after the crucifixion went off to a distant land, sometimes specified as Iberia, to find converts. Having failed, he returned to Jerusalem, where he was beheaded by Herod, who refused to allow his burial. Christians gathered up his remains at night, placing them in a marble sepulchre, which they sent to sea aboard an unmanned boat. According to early Christian legend, the ship was guided by an angel to the kingdom of the Asturians, which is an area between Basqueland and Galicia.

The Church confirmed the hermit's finding in Galicia and had a church built over the spot. As the legend grew, an outbreak of miracles and visions was reported from Compostela. Sometimes Saint James was portrayed as a pilgrim and sometimes as a Moor-slaying knight. It was the age of Moor slaying, and many of the miracles and legends had to do with the triumph of Christianity over Islam. Much evidence even suggests that the French had fabricated the legends about Santiago, or his body, going off to Galicia, because they wanted to rally Christendom to defend northern Spain. One legend from the time claimed that Charlemagne himself, the great anti-Moorish warrior who died in 814, had found the body of Santiago in Galicia.

Just as it had become a fashion to demonstrate faith by making the journey to Jerusalem, thereby asserting that it was a Christian and not a Muslim place, it became a fashion to make a pilgrimage to Christian-held Galicia in Moorish Iberia and to pray at the tomb of Saint James. After the Muslims seized the Holy Sepulcher in Jerusalem in the late eleventh century and pilgrims stopped going to the Middle East, Santiago de Compostela became the leading Christian pilgrimage.

Pilgrims came from throughout Europe, especially from France. Some did not go by choice but were ordered as penance for some blasphemy or crime. Affluent criminals would hire impoverished people to make the pilgrimage on their behalf.

All of the European routes to Santiago passed through Basqueland. Some pilgrims crossed into Aragón and then traveled across Navarra, resting at the eighth-century monastery of Leyre, which means "eagerness to overcome" in Euskera. Today, seventh-century Gregorian chants are sung there seven times a day, before God alone or the occasional visitors, by exquisite voices selected from among the resident Benedictines. Other pilgrims took the coastal route from Labourd, crossing the mouth of the Bidasoa at Hendaye, to the cathedral town of Fuenterrabía across the bay and continuing along the coastlines of Guipúzcoa and Vizcaya. Still others crossed into Basse Navarre, resting at St.-Jean-Pied-de-Port before climbing through the narrow pass to Roncesvalles.

Because scallops are abundant in Santiago, the scallop shell became their symbol, which is why scallops are known in French as *coquilles Saint Jacques,* Saint James shells. Even today, pilgrims are seen in St.-Jean-Pied-de-Port with scallop shells on their backpacks, buying supplies before continuing into the mountains.

Basse Navarre is very different from the pretty farmland of neighboring Labourd. It has a wild look with reddish ferns on the slopes and, on the crests, rough rock outcroppings like huge, gray jagged teeth. The last refuge, where pilgrims arrived to prepare for the crossing, was the walled town of St.-Jean-Pied-de-Port. In early morning light the pilgrims would leave the red stone gate traveling toward the steep green pastures that looked soft as chenille against the Pyrenees. The mountains in the morning seemed to form a colossal wall with gauzelike fog draped over the peaks. But there is a path through the wall from the little village of Arnéguy, up to Valcarlos where Charlemagne had waited for Roland, down again past little waterfalls and

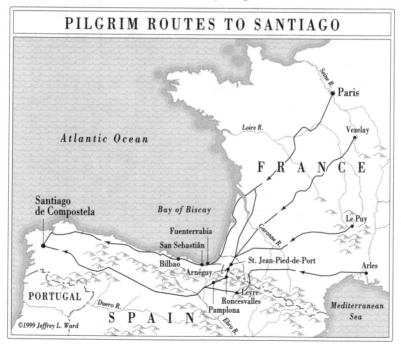

PILGRIM ROUTES TO SANTIAGO

©1999 Jeffrey L. Ward

streams and up again to the heights of Ibañeta and then down once more to the pines of Roncesvalles, where in 1127 a resting home for pilgrims was built, a home which still stands today.

Centuries of passing pilgrims brought Romanesque architecture to Basqueland with its huge scale and carvings and ornaments, depicting biblical lessons to instruct travelers. The pil-

Arnéguy in the early twentieth century. The small stone bridge is the border between France and Spain.

grimage also spread French ideas. Many French pilgrims settled in the region, and monasteries in the Spanish Basque provinces came to have more in common with those of France than those of the rest of Iberia. When the monastery of Leyre decided to build a new church, the design was taken from Limousin. Perhaps the ultimate expression of the growing French influence was in the thirteenth century, when the royal house of Navarra, devoid of heirs, turned to French families to continue the monarchy.

Yet in spite of this seemingly considerable openness to the French, Aimeric de Picaud warned pilgrims that they would be poorly received by the Basques. This twelfth-century French monk—the same man who concluded that Basques were of Scottish descent because they wore skirts—wrote a five-volume work, probably with the backing of the influential Cluny monastery in Burgundy, collecting all the stories, legends, and miracles connected with Saint James and including practical information for traveling pilgrims. This work, the *Liber Sancti Jacobi*, which is still kept at the cathedral of Compostela, became widely known in medieval Europe as the *Codex of Calixtus*. The latter title comes from a story circulated by Aimeric de Picaud, which is today dismissed as a complete fabrication, that Pope Calixtus II sent the text for editorial comment to the patriarch of Jerusalem and the archbishop of Santiago. Approval of the text, according to Aimeric de Picaud, arrived in the form of a vision.

Included in this divine text is a section on "the crimes of the bad innkeepers along the way of my apostle." According to Aimeric, the Basques, and especially the Navarrese, were crude, spoke primitively, and were given to crime. The *Codex* describes them as "enemies of our French people. A Basque or Navarrese would do in a French man for a copper coin." He recounted how pilgrims would find themselves surrounded by Basques demanding payment. If they refused, they would be stripped and robbed and sometimes, he claimed, killed.

Aimeric made numerous references to wanton sexuality.

"When the Navarrese get excited, the man shows the woman and the woman shows the man, that which they should keep concealed. The Navarrese fornicate shamelessly with animals. They say that a Navarrese keeps his mule and his mare chained up to keep others from enjoying them."

Aimeric de Picaud came from the Poitiers region and lived during the time of the Crusades, the *Chanson de Roland*, and considerable anti-Muslim frenzy. As pilgrims climbed through the pass to the heights of Ibañeta, now the famous site of Roland's death, and down to the hospice at Roncesvalles, taking time to contemplate in the pine woods where the Basque ambushers once hid, an understandable confusion about Basques and Muslims may have translated into anti-Basque sentiment.

In any event, no other record of the nature of Basque relationships with mules is to be found, and while a few stories of occasional unscrupulous innkeepers have been written, clearly the *Codex* exaggerated. Aimeric de Picaud himself may have had some bad experiences while traveling. Whatever the reason, no people have ever paid so dearly for negative coverage in a travel book. The *Codex* was widely circulated, and in 1179 the French Church called for the excommunication of "Basques and Navarrese, who practice such cruelties to Christians, laying waste like infidels, sparing neither elderly, orphans, widows, or children." In that epoch, a comparison to infidels was the harshest condemnation.

The Basques ever since have been chained to an enduring image as brutal, unfriendly, mercenary, and untrustworthy. The habit of distinguishing between "Christians" and Basques also endured.

WHEN A PEOPLE of strange practices and bad reputation collides with an age of intolerance, disaster seems inevitable. The time of the Protestant Reformation, in the sixteenth and seventeenth centuries, was such a period.

The Inquisition had been created in medieval Aragón to

guard the purity of the Church. Less than twenty years before the final defeat of the Muslims, it was reorganized and brought to Castile. After the victory of the Reconquista, Isabella extended its authority to the Spanish Empire from Sicily through Latin America. Other countries also had inquisitions, papal courts of inquiry. But the Spanish Inquisition was different because it was not controlled by Rome. The inquisitor general was appointed by the king of Spain, confirmed by the pope, and left to act however he saw fit. He had his own secret police, his own ministry, *La Suprema,* and his own prisons, ominously known as *las cárceles secretas,* secret prison cells.

All Inquisition officials and employees were sworn to secrecy, and all witnesses and accused were ordered to remain silent. The archives were closed. Not even the king could make inquiries about Inquisition proceedings except for financial matters, since the crown was owed a share of confiscated property. The accused, held incommunicado, vanished from sight for years with no explanation. Agents of the Inquisition were unpaid, but the coveted positions offered prestige, power, and privilege, including complete immunity from secular authority.

The Inquisition began hunting for hidden Jews following a 1391 order to convert to Christianity. In 1492, Jews were given four months to leave lands that had been family homes for almost a millennium in some cases. "We order them by the end of July to leave all the kingdoms and fiefdoms and never return," said the decree. After the mass expulsion, the primary preoccupation of the Inquisition was uncovering clandestine Jews and Muslims. The Muslims, hidden Moors, were called Convertis, Moriscos, or Moriscotes. The hidden Jews were called Tornidoros or Marranos—pigs.

Some 300,000 people were expelled from Castile and Aragón. If they lived in western Castile, they fled to Portugal; from the south they went to Morocco; and from Aragón to Basque country. Basques on both sides of the border, being by then exemplary Catholics, cooperated, often with enthusiasm, in the hunt for Moriscos and Marranos.

Unlike Spain, France allowed Jews, though their activities and living areas were severely restricted. But Convertis and Marranos, hidden Muslims and Jews from Spain, were illegal. Nevertheless, in the sixteenth and seventeenth centuries, a considerable population of Marranos from Portugal settled in French Basqueland, and the persistent accusation was that they engaged in contraband with Spain. In the late sixteenth century, French authorities were expressing great alarm over this discovery, even though smuggling had long been the stock-in-trade of the Basques without ever alarming anyone.

A Portuguese named Farcian Vaez was arrested in Labourd for Judaism, and it was reported that two bags of counterfeit money were found on him. According to his confession, probably forced, not only was he Jewish, but "all the Portuguese who pass through St.-Jean-de-Luz practice Judaism and buy merchandise to sell in Spain." He said the merchandise was purchased with counterfeit money made in Flanders.

In St.-Jean-de-Luz, the local clergy even suspected other priests, such as the Portuguese Father Antonio Leguel. Leguel was the only priest from whom his Portuguese community would receive the sacraments. He seemed an odd priest in that he never worked on Saturdays, and he was later exposed as a clandestine Jew. Local clergy knew to look for people who did not work on Saturdays or who made unleavened bread. Many Marranos made unleavened bread all year to avoid arousing suspicion at Passover time.

The Tribunal of Logroño, the regional tribunal of the Inquisition responsible for Spanish Basqueland, expressed the same frustration as have most institutions that have tried to control Spanish Basqueland: They could not control the French side. The Inquisition harbored a particular suspicion of Basques because they straddled the border. In 1567, an inquisitor reported from San Sebastián that the Basques were too close to the French and even spoke their language. In 1609, Léon de Araníbar, the abbot of Urdax, near the Dancharia pass that leads from the mountains of Navarra across the border to the woods of St. Pée, complained that mule caravans from Bayonne and St.-Jean-de-Luz could pass right under monastery walls and travel as far as Pamplona without anyone stopping them to search for heretical books.

The tribunal agreed that there was a problem with the area that was "under the jurisdiction of the Bishop of Bayonne." The tribunal explained, "The majority of the priests are French; and we cannot entrust the affairs of the Holy Office to them."

The Inquisition decided to plant its own spy in the St.-Jean-de-Luz Jewish community. Ironically, the French frequently and illogically complained that Marranos in their midst were spying for Spain. Now the Inquisition hired Marcos de Llumbre, a St.-Jean-de-Luz resident from San Sebastián, to pose as a Marrano and spy for Spain. But posing as a Jew posing as a Christian proved difficult, and the Jews of St.-Jean-de-Luz quickly saw through de Llumbre's attempts to infiltrate their community.

In 1602, yielding to popular pressure, the French king Henri IV ordered all Portuguese Jews out of Labourd in a month. A process of expulsion, town by town, began with Bayonne but was never effective since the Jews would just move to the next town. But Jews from Bayonne and St.-Jean-de-Luz began immigrating to Baltic cities with more open and accepting societies. Others resettled in other parts of France, including St. Esprit, a neighborhood of Bayonne designated as a Jewish ghetto because, being on the opposite bank of the Adour, it was out of Basqueland and in the region of Landes.

THE COUNTER-REFORMATION, so staunchly backed by the Jesuits, had ushered in the great age of persecution. The Council of Trent met in the Italian Alps between 1545 and 1563 and, recognizing that the Protestants were not going to come back to the Church without military force, defined the Catholic position. The council was supposed to usher in a reform of the Church, but only the most orthodox elements won the debates. Once the Church had redefined itself and irrevocably drawn the lines between Catholic and Protestant, the Christian world was found to be in an epidemic of heresy.

Now there were not only the Jews and the Muslims to flush out, but the Protestants, who in turn were having their own heresy hunts in the north. And there were the Bohemians (Gypsies) and Cagots.

Cagots were descendants of the Visigoths. The original Cagots may have been lepers, or perhaps just had a psoriasis-like skin disease. Outcasts in France, they were driven to the southwest, into Basqueland, and Cagot ghettos emerged in St.-Jean-Pied-de-Port, by the nearby deep green valley of the Aldudes, and in the port of Ciboure, which was on the wrong side of the river in St.-Jean-de-Luz. Water touched by Cagots was considered contaminated, and they were barred from all trades involving food, including agriculture. They became noted for their carpentry.

Until the early seventeenth century, despite their pariah status, Cagots were considered good Christians and were protected by the Church. But in 1609, Judge Pierre De Lancre, French Basqueland's most rabid witch hunter, said at his infamous St.-Jean-de-Luz witch trial that Cagots and Bohemians, both residing across the river in Ciboure, were consorting with the devil.

"Wandering Bohemians are part-devils," De Lancre said of Gypsies. "I say these nationless long-hairs are not Egyptian, nor from the Kingdom of Bohemia, and are born everywhere while passing through countries, in the fields and under a tree, and dance and juggle like at a witches' sabbath."

No one who could be identified as distinct and different was safe in this age. It is inevitable that in such an era, the Church would also grow concerned about Basque heresy. In past times of intolerance, Basques had been lumped with other undesirable groups. In fourteenth-century Huesca, an area east of Navarra, an ordinance forbade the speaking of "Alavan, Basque, or Hebrew" in the market place. The Basques had accepted the persecution of Jews, Muslims, Lutherans, Gypsies, and Cagots. They should have been able to see that they would be next.

BY THE SIXTEENTH CENTURY, witchcraft should have seemed a ridiculously old-fashioned accusation. In 787, Charlemagne had outlawed the execution of witches and made it a capital crime to burn a witch. A tenth-century Church law, Canon Episcopi, demanded that priests preach against belief in witchcraft as superstition. By the fourteenth century, stories of witchcraft were widely dismissed among educated circles as a primitive belief of peasants.

But by the late sixteenth century, the Canon Episcopi, which had been universal Church law, was being circumvented by the claim that society was faced with a new and more virulent form of witchcraft and therefore the old laws did not apply. Witches, poor rural women, were consorting with the devil just like the Protestants, Jews, Muslims, Gypsies, Lutherans, and Cagots.

Neither De Lancre's trials in St.-Jean-de-Luz nor the Tribunal of Logroño betray even a hint of cynicism. All evidence indicates that even some of the most fantastic tales told by witnesses and in confessions were believed at face value.

The Canon Episcopi had cautioned that women who claimed to be flying through the air on the backs of wild animals were in reality remaining on the ground and simply having hallucinations induced by the devil. Yet somehow, seven centuries later, men of the Church, of law, of learning, appeared to believe that women in the mountains of northern Navarra were rubbing an ointment on their bodies in order to fly through the sky to witches' sabbaths.

Doubts lingered. Interrogators earnestly tried to make a distinction between true events and the sort of delusions referred to in the Canon. Among the questions prepared by the tribunal was whether rubbing ointment and then flying was the only way to get to the sabbath.

In spite of the improbability of many of the accusations, it is striking how widely accepted they were. Even in modern times, this history is often treated as incidents of witchcraft, rather than incidents of mass hysteria. It seems likely that a frightened peasantry, attacked for being different, was coerced into absurd confessions. But rather than asking why this persecution took place, the question frequently asked is why the practice of witchcraft occurred. Pío Baroja, son of a distinguished journalist and himself a doctor and prominent twentieth-century novelist, rather than try to explain seventeenth-century witch hunting, attempted to explain why there were so many witches. He suggested that perhaps pre-Christian Basque beliefs had combined with a movement rebelling against the Church.

Baroja's nephew, Julio Caro Baroja, a leading ethnologist, set off a witch craze in Basqueland in the 1970s with the publication of scholarly studies. Despite Caro Baroja's reasoned books exploring the nature of the hysteria, it became fashionable once again to talk about Basque witchcraft not as a persecution by the authorities but as an exotic folk practice.

Pío Baroja had reversed the old bigotries, and rather than blame the Arabs and Jews, argued proudly that witchcraft was a uniquely Christian phenomenon. "In Semitic religions," he wrote, "the woman is always seen banished from the altars, always passive and inferior to men." In primitive European religions, on the other hand, according to Pío Baroja, "the great and victorious woman appears. Those first Christians—the Jewish race—did not have, could not have a cult of the Virgin Mary."

But if belief in witchcraft was about empowering women, as Pío Baroja asserted, the witch hunts themselves were clearly an attack on women. Although a few men were also accused of witchcraft, the essential belief was that a woman with power necessarily used it for evil. De Lancre made this clear in the 1600s in his embrace of an old Semitic myth about women. In explaining why the Basques were afflicted with so many witches, he said, "This is apple country: the women eat nothing but apples, they drink nothing but apple juice, and that is what leads them to so often offer a bite of the forbidden apple." And it is true, though not necessarily suspicious, that the people in Labourd, Guipúzcoa, and Navarra eat a great deal of apples and drink a lot of cider in the winter.

The antiwoman aspect of witch hunting becomes clearer when examining the nature of some of the allegations. The emphasis was on sexual perversion. Pío Baroja even offered lust as one of the possible motivations for practicing witchcraft. Women flew to secret rendezvous, where orgies were conducted with the devil. These clandestine orgies were known in Euskera as *akelarre*. The word comes from *akerr*, meaning a "male goat," and *larre*, meaning "meadow." The witches allegedly flew to a secret meadow and had group sex with a billy goat.

The accusation is reminiscent of Aimeric de Picaud's concern for mares and mules. What stronger denunciation of an agrarian society than the charge of bestiality? Even in modern times, when Basque peasants engage in the duel by insults known as *xikito*, the accusation of bestiality remains a classic attack. And though to most people, sex with a goat would seem sufficiently perverted, it was not even conceded that they had conventional goat sex. It was group sex, and the goat sometimes used an artificial phallus, with the intercourse sometimes vaginal and sometimes anal. According to some accounts, the goat would lift his tail so the women could kiss his posterior while he broke wind.

The goat was a typical convergence of Basque and Christian imagery. It is horned and therefore associated with the devil. Martin Luther was sometimes depicted as a goat. But a black billy goat was also an important spirit in the pantheon of pre-Christian Basques. In the modern-day carnival of Ituren, which, like witchcraft, is a complex blend of pagan and Christian, a goat appears. Carnival, the last fling before lent, celebrates permitting the impermissible. While the joaldunak, grim-faced men in sheepskin with high cone-shaped hats who ring copper bells strapped to their backs, come and go from the mountains, clanging their huge bells, people appear dressed as monsters spraying hoses or as farmers throwing mud. The most frightening character of all, the one that always scatters the children, is a man dressed head to toe as a huge billy goat.

THOSE ACCUSED OF WITCHCRAFT, being held in secret cells, their whereabouts unknown to the world, torture chambers awaiting, were urged to confess. Confession was rewarded with leniency. Many who confessed to the Inquisition were simply condemned to a few years' banishment from their native village. A convicted heretic was an outcast for life, forbidden to ride a horse, barred from owning weapons, silk, pearls, or precious metals. If a heretic was burned, the stigma was passed to her family.

The accused was not initially informed of the charges. She was simply told to confess what was in her heart. If the accused waited until being charged, it was too late to avoid torture. The Inquisition, contrary to popular belief, saw torture as a last resort and was suspicious of confessions coerced by violence, though all confessions were made at least under the threat of violence.

Accusations of witchcraft were usually initiated by Basque peasants settling a grudge or explaining a misfortune. In Pío Baroja's novella *La Dama de Urtubi,* a young man runs off to America to earn wealth and stature so he can court an aristocratic woman. But when he returns, he finds that she is interested in another man and concludes that the two have been bonded by a witch's spell.

This is typical. A crop fails, someone falls ill, the apple tree didn't bear fruit. Someone had clearly cast a spell. And there was often agreement on who the witch was—a woman who seemed to hold a grudge for some perceived wrong.

At the edge of St. Pée, a forest begins which crosses the border at Dancharia, near Urdax, and drops down into a deep val-

An illustration of the Basque billy goat by Jean Paul Tillac (1880-1969) for a book by Arthur Campión. Born in the French southwest, Tillac, whose drawings chronicled Basque life, had one Basque grandparent. (Collection of the Musée Basque, Bayonne)

ley where villages are built in the dark quiet mountain crevices and farmers work the rugged airy slopes. In 1608, a young woman named María de Ximildegui returned to her native village of Zugarramurdi in this self-contained little world. The village, whose name means "hill of elms," would never be the same.

Young María de Ximildegui had spent several years across the border in Ciboure. Her family had remained there, but she returned to her hometown, where she informed the local authorities that she had been a witch in Labourd, and during that time she had attended a sabbath in Zugarramurdi. She wanted to name names.

She said that while living in Ciboure, she had been an active witch for eighteen months before trying to break away, a struggle with the devil that resulted in weeks of illness. A priest in Hendaye had saved her through confession.

Ximildegui named twenty-two-year-old María de Jureteguía as one of the participants at the Zugarramurdi ceremony. Jureteguía, along with her husband, accused Ximildegui of lying. But in a public confrontation, Ximildegui was so convincing, offering meticulous details, that the townspeople began little by little to believe her and urged María de Jureteguía to confess. Too late, Jureteguía realized that she was now in the position of being a suspected witch. Overtaken with fear and the exasperation of what had turned into a losing shouting match, she fainted.

Later, the panic-stricken Jureteguía realized that since she was believed to be a witch, she could only save herself by the mercy that comes after confession. So she confessed to having been led astray by her fifty-two-year-old aunt, María Chipía Barrenechea. So began a string of denunciations that unraveled the village.

After her confession, Jureteguía said that she was being pursued by witches, whom she would try to fend off with the sign of the cross. She would see them in the yard disguised as cats, dogs, and pigs. The townspeople reacted to this news without a hint of skepticism and began searching houses for toads. They all knew that toads were necessary companions to witches. The toad search lead to Barrenechea's octogenarian sister Graciana, who would in time confess to being the queen witch of Zugarramurdi.

The first four witches in Zugarramurdi were accused of using an assortment of spells and powders to kill a total of eighteen children and eleven adults, and cause various harm to people, livestock, and crops. Eventually, ten witches confessed to a several-decade crime spree that included killing children and sucking their blood.

Incredibly, in a tribute to local Basque law, the village was able to resolve the entire affair bloodlessly, and the confessed witches were pardoned. The matter would have ended had not someone, the source remains anonymous, gone to the Inquisition.

In 1609, four accused witches and an Euskera translator were taken from the village by the Inquisition. More and more villagers were arrested, and the confessions were spectacular. Jureteguía admitted to a childhood of witchcraft. She had guarded a flock of toads and was punished if she did not treat them with the utmost respect. Her aunt would sometimes reduce her to a minuscule size, enabling her to pass through tiny chinks in walls. Many admitted to passing through small holes. They described elaborate initiations in which they were presented with a well-dressed toad. They had sexual intercourse in a variety of ways with the devil and with each other, both heterosexually and homosexually, including with members of their own family, all supervised by the elderly Graciana Barrenechea. They also confessed to infanticide and vampirism, cannibalism, defiling of tombs, eating of corpses. One admitted poisoning her own grandchild.

They confessed to breaking every taboo of their society. Were they furiously inventing stories based on the gravest cultural prohibitions they could imagine? The confession rate was not high. In the 1610 trial, only nine out of twenty-one witches had confessed. By then, another thirteen had died in prison and six had already been burned. Those who did not confess were certain to be burned alive. The Inquisition handed out sentences at an elaborate public ritual known as an Auto de fe, an Act of Faith. Although the 1610 Auto de fe of Logroño is famous for its witches, eleven of whom were sentenced to burning, an additional twenty-five heretics were also sentenced, including six people found guilty of Judaism, one of Islam, one of Lutheranism, twelve of heretical utterances, and two of impersonating agents of the Inquisition.

Auto de fe only unleashed more accusations throughout northern Navarra and Guipúzcoa. Rural Basqueland seemed in the throes of a spreading witchcraft epidemic. In some towns, panicking villagers lynched women. By March 1611, the Inquisition had discovered that in little Zugarramurdi, the hill of elms, 158 people out of a total population of 390 were witches and another 124 were under suspicion. One-fifth of the population of the twin villages of Ituren and Zubieta were found to be witches. In all, 1,590 witches were discovered in Navarra, with another 1,300 under suspicion. In Guipúzcoa, 340 witches were found.

AT THE SAME TIME, Pierre De Lancre, the witch hunter of French Basqueland, suspected that the entire population of Labourd might be witches. A reign of terror, based in St.-Jean-de-Luz, began when an official in St. Pée complained to Henri IV of an increase in witches in the area. De Lancre, a fifty-six-year-old lawyer from Bordeaux, was asked to investigate. He said that he found "so many demons and evil spirits and so many witches within Labourd, that this little corner of France is the nursery."

De Lancre had many theories on why the Basques were so afflicted. Part of their problem stemmed from Ignatius de Loyola and the traveling Jesuit missionaries. All that evangelizing in places like Japan and China had infected them with demons which they had carried back to Labourd.

Another source of difficulty unearthed by De Lancre was the side effects of tobacco. The Basques were the first Europeans to cultivate tobacco, and it seemed that this was rendering them a bit strange. "I feel, and it is certain, that it makes their breath and their bodies so foul smelling that the uninitiated cannot bear it and yet they use it three or four times a day," De Lancre pointed out. This use of tobacco, he supposed, was affecting their reason.

He also expressed disdain for Basque women and said they produced undersized and cursed children who died. This last accusation may have had some truth, due to the Rh blood factor.

Who was this Basque hater from Bordeaux who wanted to execute Basques by the hundreds? Before his father had earned a title, the family name had been Rostéguy, a Basque name, probably originally Errotegui, meaning "the place with the mill." His family had migrated to Bordeaux a century earlier and become aristocratic Frenchmen. De Lancre despised what he regarded as the backward superstitions of the Basques, their myths and folk remedies. But he seemed to truly believe in a physically manifest devil, who, he even claimed, visited his apartment one night.

Anyone found engaged in folk healing, divination, or other traditional practices, especially if it was a woman, was a candidate for burning. Like the Tribunal of Logroño, De Lancre believed that the devil marked the body of initiates. All he had to do was find the mark. A blood spot on the eye was the mark of the devil. But most marks were not this visible. Hundreds of men, women, and children were rounded up. The accused could confess and be spared the painful and humiliating inspection before being burned alive. Those who did not confess were completely shaved. The body was then pricked inch by inch until a spot was found that yielded no blood. To make sure, such a spot would be stuck deeper, but if no blood came forth, the mark had been found. Then, they too would be burned alive.

THE OFFICIALS OF the Spanish Inquisition came to understand that they were creating hysteria, that the more witches they burned, the more witches would be denounced. So they became more secretive and eventually even banned the burning of witches. The inquisitors went about their business, flushing out Lutherans, Jews, and Muslims, and even found a witch or two around Spain into the nineteenth century.

On the French side, as often happens with witch hunts, De Lancre's terror seemed unstoppable until someone had the courage to denounce it, and then it quickly disintegrated. Jesuits and tobacco merchants weren't the only Basques traveling the world. There were also the fleets that hunted whale and fished cod in Newfoundland.

When the St.-Jean-de-Luz cod fleet, one of the largest, heard rumors of their wives, mothers, and daughters stripped, stabbed, and many already executed, the 1609 cod campaign was ended two months early. The fishermen returned, clubs in hand, and liberated a convoy of witches being taken to the burning place.

This one popular resistance was all it took to stop the trials. Some French historians have estimated that 600 accused witches had been burned. A Spanish commission studying the De Lancre trials reported only 80 burned, which may be conservative, but the exact number will probably never be known.

De Lancre retreated to Bayonne, where he began condemning Basque priests. He was soon recalled by the French crown to Bordeaux, where he died of natural causes, his reputation intact, at the age of sixty-eight, in 1631. In 1672, a royal edict banned witch trials in France. But even into the twentieth century some rural Basques continued to believe that a blood spot on the eye is the mark of the devil and that prayer books left open in church will let witches into the community.

# 6: The Wealth of Non-Nations

*To be a true Basque, three things are required: to have a name
which bespeaks Basque origin, to speak the language of the
descendants of Aïtor, and to have an uncle in America.*
*—Pierre Lhande-Heguy, first secretary of the*
*Basque Academy of Language,* BASQUE IMMIGRATION, *1910*

EVEN IN THE SIXTEENTH CENTURY, the rural Basques, isolated in
mountain villages such as Zugarramurdi and Ituren, were not
the mainstream of the Basque population. While most Europeans were focused on their region, their country, their crown,
the successful Basque was a man of the world. He was interested in Africa and Asia and especially passionate about the lands
Basques called Amerika. Like the character in the Pío Baroja
witchcraft novella, an ambitious man could improve his station
in life by going to Amerika and returning with, if not wealth, at
least experience. *Amerikanuak,* Basques who returned from the
Americas, were people worthy of respect in the community.
This is a recurring theme in Basque literature, especially among
the early twentieth-century Basque writers, who tried to reassess
Spain after it lost its empire. In Miguel de Unamuno's short story,
"Every Inch a Man," a special masculinity is ascribed to the lead
character because he had made a fortune in America.

*Amerikanuak bezain,* good, like an American, is an Euskera
expression meaning "generous." *Ez gira Amerikanuak,* you're no
American, is a way of calling someone cheap. In both expres-
sions, the Americans referred to are *Amerikanuak.*

A people are shaped by their land, and the mountains of
Basqueland, the green slopes that no one else would fight as
hard for, could not support a population. Despite a lush appearance, the land is not fertile, and Basques always needed to look

beyond Basqueland for food. It had been this special need for imports that had induced Castilian kings to exclude the Basques from the Spanish customs zone. Goods that landed in Basque ports paid no Spanish customs. If the goods were bound for Spain, they were taken through Alava to Miranda de Ebro, a river town, to enter the Spanish zone and pay duties. But goods could also be landed in a Basque port and reshipped to Europe without entering the Spanish customs zone.

Both the need for food and the customs arrangement were incentives to trade. The Basques bought Castilian wool and sold it to the rest of Europe, where it was a highly prized commodity. By the fifteenth century, Basques were producing and supplying one-third of Europe's iron from Vizcaya's huge deposits. They also produced swords, musket barrels, and ship's anchors. Using the Euskera name for Bilbao, Shakespeare referred to "Bilbo swords."

Long accustomed to looking abroad, the Basques were among the first Europeans to realize that the unique products of the new American lands could become as valuable as the silk and spices of Asia. Not only did Basques trade new American products, but they were also open to using them. From rubber balls to tobacco, the Basques pioneered American products in Europe.

THE CHILI PEPPER was easy for Europeans to understand. In a sense, it was what Columbus had gone looking for, a spice. Exotic spices were already one of the most lucrative trades in the world. Columbus must have immediately recognized that hot peppers were valuable because he named them after the already high priced black pepper, *pimienta*. The new spice was called *pimiento*—masculine pepper, like black pepper but stronger. *"Mejor que pimienta nuestra,"* Better than our pepper, he reported.

The chili pepper was sold by Basques, Spaniards, and Portuguese to Africa, the Middle East, the Asian subcontinent, and the Far East. Its trading value soon declined because the plant was easily cultivated in these climates. Most Europeans ate only the mild sweet peppers. Basques were the only Europeans to have adopted a taste for hot peppers directly from America.

Guindilla peppers, grown in the Spanish Basque provinces, are pickled green or chopped into food when dried and red. Espelette, a whitewashed town next to St. Pée, is famous for its peppers. The small thin ones and the slightly hotter larger ones grow green but turn bright red in September, when they are harvested. The peppers are then strung through their stems and hung from the southern side of houses to dry, the lines of peppers echoing the traditional red trim of the white buildings. These peppers are used in the local sausage and many other dishes to give a subtle heat, nothing comparable to the fire of Caribbean or Mexican food, but the hottest burn of any cuisine in France. On the last Sunday in October, worshipers in Espelette are given a blessing and a string of dried peppers at Mass.

The following recipe is from Itxassou, the town next to Espelette that is famous for its cherries. The sauce is served by Jean Paul Bonnet at the Hotel du Fronton over skewers of grilled duck hearts.

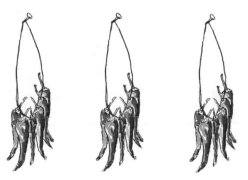

**ESPELETTE PEPPERS AND DUCK HEARTS**

*Brown shallots in duck fat, add 2 powdered Espelette peppers, and reduce to a sauce with créme fraîche for 8 minutes. I cannot*

*say how much pepper powder. In Espelette every bunch of pep-*
*pers is different depending on where it is grown and the weath-*
*er. You have to taste it and decide. If the peppers are too strong,*
*add a pinch of sugar.*

The European distaste for burning-hot pepper is in perfect balance with nature because hot American peppers when grown in Europe give off little heat. The burning taste comes from a substance called capsaicin, whose burn increases when the pepper is grown in strong sunlight. Capsaicin is a failed chemical defense for plants. Most animals won't eat plants that contain capsaicin, but many non-European humans are not deterred. The large red choricero, so called because it is used in chorizo sausage, has little heat when grown in Vizcaya on the wet fields near Guernica. When picked young and green, it is called a Guernica pepper. The same Guernica or choricero peppers, grown in the much sunnier Rioja, will begin to take on the sting of a chili. If Basqueland were sunnier, the Basques wouldn't like their peppers. The great mid-twentieth-century Guipúzcoan chef and food writer José María Busca Isusi wrote of hot peppers, "This sting, if it is strong is bad, but when mild is very digestible and even aids digestion."

In 1930 the Azcaray y Eguileor family published a book that promised to reveal the secrets of their Bilbao restaurant, El Amparo. It offered two suggestions for pimientos de Guernica, which have long been the popular ways of serving these peppers in Vizcaya.

## PIMIENTOS DE GUERNICA

*Rub the peppers with a cloth and fry them in sizzling oil, turning them so they cook on all sides.*

*or*

*Heat the peppers in an oven dish, peel them, and put them whole in a casserole with garlic and oil, simmer awhile, salt and serve them.*

BEANS ARE ANOTHER American product easily understood by Europeans because of their resemblance to European species, such as the broad bean, grown in Navarra and Alava, and peas, which, until the sixteenth century, were only used as a dried bean. American beans were quickly transplanted to most of Europe. In Vizcayan Euskera beans are called *indibabak*, Indian beans. Every Basque region prides itself on its own beans: red, pinto, black, white, or the unripened, soft, greenish white beans that Basques call *pochas*. Because pochas are picked exactly at the moment they ripen from green to white, Tirso Rodrigáñez, a Spanish government minister in the 1880s, called them "pubescent beans." In Tudela, in southern Navarra, pochas are served with eel for holidays. In the Alava section of Rioja, they are cooked with lamb tail. But because the optimum time for picking pochas coincides with the fall game bird season, these beans are most commonly associated with quail. An article in a 1967 Basque food journal pointed out that pochas are so highly regarded that the dish is always called "pochas with quails" and never "quail with pochas."

Before the Spanish Civil War, Nicolasa Pradera was the chef of a still celebrated restaurant, Casa Nicolasa, by the market in San Sebastián. This traditional recipe uses both beans and hot pepper.

## *POCHAS FOR QUAILS, GAME BIRDS, AND OTHER ROASTS*

*Put water in a stew pot with both lean and fat pork fatback or ham. [Cook the fatback or ham.] Let the water cool in the pan where the pork fat was cooked, and once cooled, add the pochas, chopped onions, raw peeled tomatoes, a hot pepper that is between red and green and is also peeled, a peeled, finely minced garlic clove, chopped parsley, a little white pepper, and a few drops of olive oil, and cook it slowly. Season with salt.*
—*Nicolasa Pradera,* La Cocina de Nicolasa, *1933*

The most celebrated Basque bean from America is the red bean of Tolosa, *alubias de Tolosa*. Borrowing even further from native American agriculture, the farmers in this mountainous part of Guipúzcoa plant beans in the shade between corn rows exactly as Central American farmers do. Busca Isusi wrote in 1972, "In the firmament of Guipúzcoan gastronomy there are many shining stars and *alubias de Tolosa* are generally considered one of premier magnitude."

These red beans actually are black, but when they are cooked they turn red and produce a thick, chocolate-colored sauce. Tolosans believe the beans must be cooked in earthen crocks. Basques have done elaborate studies involving gelatinization of starches and the breaking down of cellulose to explain why beans should not be cooked in metal. They also believe that Tolosa is an ideal bean town because the surrounding area has noncalcareous soil, soil without calcium or lime, which produces the best beans. But at the same time, the calcareous water of Tolosa is thought to be the optimal liquid in which to cook the beans. Though currently the forty-seven officially recognized producers of Tolosan red beans sell them to be used elsewhere, it is believed that the true dish can only be made with Tolosan water. Busca Isusi suggested that cooks elsewhere try using rainwater.

One weekend each year, Tolosa has an alubias contest. About twenty-five producers make the dish, each with the same recipe but with their own beans, and a panel of judges chooses the best one. The following day chefs using identical ingredients, including the winning bean, have their alubias judged. A famous place for alubias is the Fronton Beotibar, named after the 1321 battle in which Guipúzcoans defeated the Navarrese with the help of seven Loyola brothers. The Fronton Beotibar was built for bare-handed matches in 1890. In 1935, a club and restaurant of elegant Art Deco design was built in front of the court. The accompanying recipe for alubias comes from Roberto Ruiz Aginaga, chef of the Fronton Beotibar.

The dish is always served with cabbage. Old-time Tolosans, who recall an era when there was little but beans to eat, believe the heaviness of the bean dish can be moderated by the addition of vinegar, which seems to horrify the modern Basque gourmet, who will nevertheless add guindilla peppers pickled in vinegar.

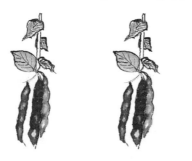

### ALUBIAS DE TOLOSA
#### (for eight)

*1 kilogram (2.2 pounds) alubias de Tolosa*
*4-5 liters (quarts) water*
*1/2 an onion*
*2 tablespoons olive oil*
*salt*

*For the frying:*
*4 cloves garlic*
*olive oil*
*1/2 onion*

*For garnishes:*
*1.5 kilograms (3.3 pounds) pork ribs*
*1 cabbage*
*3 blood sausage*
*guindillas de Ibarra (pickled green peppers)*

*Put the alubias de Tolosa in an earthen casserole with cold water.
Add oil and the onion and heat to boiling. Stop the boiling with
a little cold water, and cook slowly over low heat. Halfway
through, heat a skillet with oil, add the peeled garlic cloves, and
remove them when they are golden. Add chopped onion. After
they brown, add the beans from the crock. When the cooking is
finished, after about four or five hours, add salt and let the beans
rest a half hour.*

*Garnishes: Chop the cabbage fine, and put it in to cook with
the ribs over a lively fire for two hours. Salt and set aside. After
poking them with a fork, cook the blood sausages for 15 minutes.*

*Serving: Place the cabbage, well drained, in the center of a
platter. Cover with beans and place the ribs and blood sausage
around it. Serve the guindillas on a separate plate.*

AN INDICATION OF the Basque regard for corn is the fact that
rather than adopt a Castilian word, they gave the grain its own
name in Euskera, *arto.*

On his first voyage of 1492, Columbus encountered corn,
first in Haiti and then in Cuba. He did not seem to appreciate
that the plant he termed a "sort of grain" was a marvel of agricultural breeding. Thousands of years of experimentation by Meso-
American farmers had developed a high-yield hybrid more

evolved than any European grain. Corn is one of the few plants that has lost the ability to reproduce on its own. An ear of corn fallen to the ground remains sealed in sterility within its protective husk, but that husk makes it adaptable to almost any climate.

The men who traveled to America with Columbus, the Basques and Andalusians, brought corn to their farmers, who quickly realized what Columbus had not. Through trade and exploration, corn was spread around the world. Basques took corn to Asia, and by 1530, corn was growing in China.

The first mention of corn in France dates to 1523, when the governor of Bayonne complained about the husks. Apparently, Basques had been eating corn for some time by then because the city demanded that people stop throwing corn husks in the Adour, where they were accumulating by bridge pilings, posing a threat to navigation. Fishermen also learned to use corn husks to mask a hook, creating a squidlike lure. Labourdine tuna fishermen used corn husk lures until the 1930s, when a collaboration between a lighthouse keeper and a jeweler in Biarritz produced the spoon, a curved metal lure.

North of the Adour, the French eventually accepted the grain for livestock but would not eat it themselves until the second half of the twentieth century. Unlike almost all of the rest of Europe, Basques used corn not only to feed livestock but also as a staple of the peasant diet. Every town had its own corn mill. Peasants made, and still make, a flat bread similar to a Mexican tortilla but slightly thicker. Farmers wrap this Basque tortilla, known as *talo*, around the food they take with them to the field, much as a Central American farmer does. The talo was also eaten by miners and later by factory workers.

In 1502, on his fourth voyage, Columbus sailed to Pino, an island off present-day Nicaragua, where he was offered a drink that the natives called *xocoatl.* He was not impressed, even when it was explained that it was made from beans grown by gods in the Garden of Life. For the sake of thoroughness, he took some of these small, hard, brown, bitingly bitter beans back with him.

The Castilian court agreed that the beans were unusual but of no particular use. Then in 1519, the year he conquered Mexico, Hernán Cortés negotiated the release of a Spaniard, Gerónimo de Aguilar, shipwrecked in the Yucatán and held slave to a Mayan chief. Aguilar told Cortés of many curious foods including cocoa, and Cortés, apparently blessed with a greater gastronomic curiosity than Columbus, had the locals demonstrate how to use it. In 1528, when he returned to Spain, he had the foresight to take with him not just the beans but also three recipes: a drink, a "soup," and a paste. Understanding very well how to attract the interest of the crown he served, he pointed out that the local tribesmen so valued these beans that they sometimes used them as money.

The soup was a sauce known in Mexico as *mole,* and it had enough appeal so that the Basques still have a tradition of cooking game birds in chocolate, just as the Aztecs had made wild turkey in mole. Basques in Alava sometimes make hare instead of game birds with chocolate, which may explain why the Caltagirone region of central Sicily, once occupied by the Spanish, has a tradition of rabbit in chocolate.

In the 1980s, a noted Guipúzcoan chef, José Castillo, decided to document the recipes of elderly Basque women. Seventy-eight-year-old Emilia Sáenz de Vicuña from Alava gave him the following recipe.

### HARE WITH WALNUT AND CHOCOLATE

*Cut the hare in pieces and fry them. In the same oil, fry an onion cut in slices and a few garlic cloves. When the onion is tender, add a sliced apple, a little flour, a little chocolate, a glass of red wine, a glass of white wine, another of water.*

*Shell a dozen walnuts and crush them in a mortar, then throw the paste into the casserole with the hare. Simmer together very slowly, and when the hare is tender, remove it to an earthenware dish. Run the rest through a food mill and pour it around the hare. Let the whole thing simmer a little, then toss in a little chopped parsley and serve.*

The drink that Cortés brought back also quickly became popular in Spain, and when both Louis XIII and Louis XIV married Spanish princesses, their brides brought the drink to the French court. Louis XIV's bride, María Theresa, the same bride who was served macaroons at her St.-Jean-de-Luz wedding, did little to dispel the belief that chocolate was a toxic and evil addiction. She could not stop drinking chocolate every day, and this was thought to be the reason that she lost all of her teeth.

Chocolate's bad reputation may have come in part from reports from Mexico, where chocolate seemed a potent drug because the Aztecs mixed it with hallucinogenic mushrooms to drink in religious ceremonies. In any event, for chocolate's first European century, its unsavory reputation grew along with its popularity. In 1628, the Spanish poet Francisco de Quevedo wrote, "There came the devil of tobacco and the devil of chocolate, which . . . avenged the Indies against Spain, for they had done more harm by introducing among us those powders and smoke and chocolate cups and chocolate beaters than the King had ever done through Columbus or Cortés and Almagreo and Pizarro. For it was better and cleaner and more honorable to be killed by a musket ball or a lance than by snuffing and sneezing and belching and dizziness and fever."

Time has shown him right about the tobacco, though more than a little unfair to chocolate. But in the sixteenth and early seventeenth centuries, both were regarded as vile habits the Basques had picked up in America. A seventeenth-century Englishman in San Sebastián wrote that the locals "wake up and have a chocolate, and wouldn't leave without it even if their house were on fire."

What happened to Cortés's third recipe, the paste? When he returned with beans and recipes, the court entrusted them to a monastery. The monks of Guajaca softened the beans and mixed them with cane sugar, which was itself a new food at the time. The Spanish crown immediately realized the commercial value of this new confection and attempted to keep the formula secret. For almost a century the Spanish were able to keep chocolate making exclusively Iberian.

Their secret chocolate was a peculiar brick-red block. Since chocolate was American, the Spanish seasoned it with other new American foods including hot peppers and vanilla. The reddish color came from annatto, the dye that Caribbeans rubbed on their bodies, giving birth to the term *redskins*. And since chocolate was an exotic food, they added other exotic foods to it such as cinnamon, anise, and nuts.

It was the Inquisition that ruined the Spanish monopoly on chocolate confection. During the sixteenth century the Portuguese had quietly discovered chocolate making in Brazil, but they were not sharing their discovery with the rest of Europe either. However, Jews, driven to Portugal by the Inquisition, learned the craft while there. From Portugal, the Jews migrated to Bayonne—St. Esprit, the ghetto across the river and out of Basqueland.

The fame of the Jewish chocolate makers of St. Esprit spread throughout both sides of Basqueland and into the rest of France. At first the town fathers thought chocolate making was a low and immoral trade and barred it from Bayonne proper. But the chocolate makers were already barred from the city because they were Jews. Those who wanted the evil chocolate went to St. Esprit. After the French Revolution guaranteed Jews the full rights of citizenship, Jews moved into town, and the city of Bayonne has been boasting of its "Bayonne chocolates" ever since.

In the 1970s, Robert Linxe, a native of Bayonne, became one of the leading chocolate makers of Paris, founding the Maison du Chocolate. He offered this recipe from his native city:

*Take 1 liter of heavy cream and bring it to a boil. Pour it slowly over 3 pounds 12 ounces of semibitter chocolate until the chocolate melts. Whisk it like mayonnaise until thickened. Add 3 1/2 ounces of softened, high-quality butter.*

*Remove pits from Itxassou cherries and put the cherries through a food mill until a fine pulp is produced. Heat the pulp, add a little alcohol (brandy or local fruit alcohol), and reduce the liquid. Incorporate in the chocolate mixture. Chill it. Then cut it in pieces and dip in melted* couverture *(covering chocolate). That's a bit difficult. But you can always shape it into balls and roll them in cocoa powder as truffles.*

*[Linxe sometimes mixes this filling with citrus juices from Spain and forms it into little flat rectangles that he hand-dips in dark satiny chocolate. He calls his creation an* Arnéguy.*]*

THE BASQUES GROUND the cocoa beans with a stone roller against a stone block, the metate. The tool, a copy of the ones used by the Aztecs, remained the Basque way of grinding chocolate until into the twentieth century. Perhaps it remained in use because

Metate

it was so much like a Basque tool: chunky, made of rough-hewn stone, either unadorned or with very simple ornamentation. From prehistoric ruins, to early grave markers, to ancient and enduring tools, to the huge cornerstones on houses, to the modern sculpture of Eduardo Chillida and Jorge de Oteiza, massive, rough-hewn stone has always been the Basque look. *"Bai./Harri eta herri,"* Yes./The stone and the people, wrote the Basque poet Gabriel Aresti. Kneeling and leaning over a rough stone metate, grinding husked beans, just as the Aztecs had done for pre-Columbian millennia, became a part of Basque life.

A FEW AMERICAN products were rejected. "Not very good" was the judgment of Antonio Pigafetta, who sampled cassava on Magellan's voyage. The Basques, like other Europeans, were cautious about eating roots and tubers. The Arawak taught Columbus to make bread from grated cassava root, but Spaniards and Basques yearned for wheat. Perhaps they were put off by the fact that a poison had to be extracted from cassava before it was edible, and that the Caribs who attacked them poisoned their arrow tips by dipping them in cassava juice.

The potato did not get any better reception. Peruvians who introduced potatoes to Pizarro lessened their appeal by leaving them to dehydrate on brown bald mountaintops above the timberline, which produces bland and blackish things called *chuños.* Today, Peruvians still mystify outsiders by savoring such potatoes. But even fresh, these dull-colored, irregular lumps did not look promising. Europeans believed that the physical appearance of food indicated hidden properties. Red food cured anemia but caused lust, which led to the Friday ban on red meat. Walnuts enhanced intelligence because they resembled the brain. The potato, it was reasoned, caused leprosy.

Neighboring Galicians were the only ones in Iberia to be excited when the new discovery was brought back to Spain by Pizarro's men in 1539. They popularized it in Italy but nowhere in Spain. Even after most Europeans had given in and were eating potatoes, though still feeding corn only to pigs, the Basques were doing just the reverse. Basques do not seem to like any tubers. They feed turnips to pigs and seldom eat beets. In 1783, a Bayonne chemist wrote to Antoine-Augustin Parmentier, the French nutritionist who finally persuaded his country to eat potatoes, informing him that the Basques eat corn, not potatoes, and "no province produces healthier, more vigorous people." The Basques of Alava were broad bean eaters before American beans had arrived, and it was taken as a sign of their Castilianization, along with the decline in the Euskera speaking there, that they tended to replace broad beans with potatoes rather than American beans. Nevertheless, the Basque pejorative for an Alavan, *babazorro*, broad bean eater, has endured. Alava aside, it was only in the 1940s, during a time of famine following the Civil War, that the potato became a common food in the rest of Basqueland.

ACCORDING TO A popular story, potatoes were introduced to Ireland when some washed ashore from ships of the Spanish armada, blown off course and wrecked on shoals. The story is probably not true because the men of the armada, being predominantly Basque, would not have provisioned with potatoes.

By the late sixteenth century, armadas, fleets of warships, were usually crewed by Basques. Many of the ships of the 1588 Spanish armada that headed for England were Basque whaling vessels requisitioned by Felipe II. One of the commanders, Miguel de Oquendo y Dominguez de Segura, was a Basque from San Sebastián who had begun as a shepherd and then worked his way up at sea as a shipwright. A second commander, Martines de Recalde y Larrinaga, was a Basque shipbuilder.

Martines de Recalde managed to make his way back from the debacle but died of exhaustion soon after. Oquendo, after a long struggle, arrived back in Pasajes with a few surviving ships,

*117*

including his own *Santa Ana,* said to be one of the finest ships of the epoch. He also died of exhaustion a few days later.

The Spanish defeat by British gunners in the English Channel was not as decisive a blow as is often thought today. The battle gave the British confidence and weakened that of the Spanish, but it did not alter the naval balance of power, which had already favored the British because they had better gunners. The engagement simply destroyed the myth of Spanish naval power. The Spanish quickly rebuilt their fleet, but so many Basque fishing vessels had been lost that Guipúzcoan long-distance fishing was diminished for a decade.

As wars and treaties reduced fishing and whaling opportunities, the cultivation of corn provided work and drew many maritime Basques into the landed rural life. By the seventeenth century, growing corn, a crop that easily adapted to the mediocre farming conditions of Basqueland, became so profitable that it was thought to be creating a manpower shortage in the fisheries.

It was a hard life onboard Basque ships. Cod fishermen worked months off the Newfoundland and Labrador coast, while whalers went to the Davis Straits between Greenland and Baffin Island. They navigated around uncharted shoals and icebergs, rode out gales, chopped ice off the windward rigging to keep from capsizing. As with all professions of hardship and danger, a distinctive machismo developed. It was considered cowardly to "waste" deck space by stocking lifeboats. Basques in home port would wear a ring-and-chain gold earring to indicate that they had fished a spring-to-fall cod campaign in Newfoundland.

Adding to the danger was the Basques' peculiar status as an unrecognized nation. Basques pursued their far-flung fishery during centuries in which the French and Spanish were repeatedly at war with each other and with the Dutch and British. While French and Spanish warships were squaring off on the high seas, Basque fishermen, some from French ports such as Biarritz, St.-Jean-de-Luz, Ciboure, and Hendaye, and others from

Spanish ports such as Fuenterrabía, Pasajes, and Bermeo, were shipping out together, speaking their common language, in pursuit of whales and cod and the enormous profits they brought. They had little interest in the affairs of France and Spain.

But no one else saw it that way.

The Dutch and British navies attacked and sank Basque fishing boats on their way to and from the North. In 1625, the Compañia de Ballenas de San Sebastián was formed. This San Sebastián Whaling Company built an armed fleet of forty-one ships with 248 rowing skiffs and 1,475 fishermen. But the British continued to seize Basque fishing boats in Canadian waters and force the fishermen into what amounted to slave labor. When the Danish navy could find Basque ships off Iceland and Norway, it would expel them from those waters. As the North Atlantic opened up and became more competitive, North American fishing was increasingly difficult for the nationless Basques. Their 1351 treaty that established the principle of freedom of the high seas had been long forgotten. St.-Jean-de-Luz fishermen turned to the French government, which based four heavily armed warships in their port to protect Basque fishermen going to and returning from North America. In the mid-sixteenth century the Spanish, hoping to destroy French competition for Newfoundland cod, began attacking French Basque ships. Heavily armed ships out of St.-Jean-de-Luz began defending their fishermen. Eventually these ships, Corsaires, became privateers, operating independently but harassing Spanish ships in the service of France. Basque mariners were increasingly being separated into French and Spanish camps.

Spain regarded Basque maritime skills as a valuable strategic commodity to be controlled by the crown. In 1501 the Spanish crown had prohibited Basques from building ships for other nations. The same measure was tried again in 1551. The crown also declared it a capital crime for a fisherman to serve on a foreign ship.

But in 1612, England's King James I petitioned the Spanish crown to allow Basques to go to England and teach whaling. The first British whaling fleet was established with six Basque officers under contract. The Dutch also recruited Basques, who defied threats by Madrid of both the death penalty and confiscation of all property.

The Basques would have done well to have obeyed the Spanish crown. Instead, by the seventeenth century, the Basques had lost their monopoly on whaling. Once numerous countries had fleets, the European powers gained control of the whaling grounds.

Then, in 1713, the Treaty of Utrecht dealt a blow to the Basque long-distance fishing fleets, from which they never recovered. This treaty, ending the war known in Europe as the War of Spanish Succession and in the Americas as Queen Anne's War, attempted to give something to each power. The Bourbons got to keep Spain. The Hapsburgs were given smaller nations to make up for the Bourbon victory. The British gained control of Newfoundland and Nova Scotia at the expense of the French, who were only compensated with limited fishing rights.

The result was that the Basques lost access to Canadian waters. They argued for historic fishing rights as the discoverers of the continent and the first to fish it. But power politics, not right of discovery, mattered in the Utrecht negotiations. The Basques who lived in France could use the limited French fishing grounds, but if they were from Spanish ports, as most Basque fishermen were, they had nothing. The king of Spain, having won Spain, did not have to be offered fishing concessions.

But in the long view of Basque history, a more important outcome of the war was that the Basques saved their homeland. The Bourbons, more than previous monarchs, wanted central power over their Iberian realm. They stripped Catalonia, Valencia, and Aragón of their regional privilege. But unlike these provinces, the Basque provinces and Navarra had supported the Bourbons

Fishermen off the coast of Guipúzcoa, 1910. (Kutxa Fototeka, San Sebastián)

in the War of Spanish Succession and, at this critical era in the formation of Spain, the Basques were allowed to keep their Fueros.

The old commerce, salt cod and whale, was over. The Basques were driven back to whaling in the Bay of Biscay. In the sixteenth century, Basques had landed several hundred whales a year in Newfoundland and Labrador. Between 1637 and 1801, Zarautz, a major whaling town in Guipúzcoa, landed only fifty-five whales from the Bay of Biscay. By 1785, when the Spanish government decided to form a whaling company and sent an emissary to find a Basque harpoonist, he could not find one.

By then, the Basques had found new opportunities in America. New products would be made into Basque fortunes, and the whale would be forgotten. Whales themselves were vanishing from "the Basque Sea."

THE HOT PEPPER or the bean may be the American product that best shows the Basques' genius for cooking, but the cocoa pod is the one that reveals their commercial skills. By the end of the seventeenth century, affluent Europeans craved chocolate, were addicted to it, some said. The leading producer of cocoa was the Spanish colony of Venezuela, and the principal purveyors were the Dutch, who, enjoying a near-total monopoly, were able to demand extremely high prices.

In 1728, in yet another example of the confidence and ambition of the Basques, a group of wealthy Guipúzcoans, led by Francisco de Munibe, the count of Peñaflorida, formed a Basque company, the Real Compañia Guipúzcoana de Caracas, the Royal Guipúzcoan Company of Caracas, to compete in the Venezuelan cocoa trade. The seventeenth-century Dutch West India Company had built a trade empire along the Atlantic coasts of Africa and the Americas. The British had established trading companies to dominate North America. If the British and the Dutch could have trading companies dominating sectors of American commerce, why not the Basques?

The company attracted private investors as well as the city of San Sebastián, the province of Guipúzcoa, and even the Spanish crown, which was enthusiastic about the idea of breaking the Dutch cocoa monopoly in a Spanish colony. But it was essentially a Guipúzcoan company. The five directors were required to have San Sebastián residence, and most investors were from the province, as were the majority of sailors.

At first the Real Compañia Guipúzcoana de Caracas struggled to find suppliers and the necessary contacts in Venezuela. The first ships were not sent for two years, until 1730. But once the company secured enough cocoa, it was able to get an ever-increasing share of the world market, and as its business strengthened, so did its standing in Venezuela, until it became the company with which producers sought contracts. Because Basque ports were not in the Spanish customs zone, they could operate like a free zone for trade in the rest of Europe.

This had a huge impact on the Basque economy, especially at the ports of San Sebastián and Pasajes. Stores, warehouses, commercial houses prospered. Shipbuilding boomed, especially in the company's own shipyard in Pasajes. The Royal Company alone operated forty-eight ships. In the first decade, it paid the investors dividends from 20 to 25 percent.

From cocoa, the Real Compañia Guipúzcoana de Caracas expanded to leather, coffee, and tobacco. It was the company's shipments of Venezuelan red beans that made them a staple in Tolosa. It also shipped turkeys, which became a mainstay of the Guipúzcoan diet. In 1751, it even tried to bring back whaling, resurrecting the seventeenth-century Compañia de Ballenas de San Sebastián and sending two armed whalers to the South Atlantic and the Pacific. One returned empty, and the other was forced to turn back for repairs.

But the company was not only concerned with bringing goods to San Sebastián and Pasajes. It also sold Basque goods in the colonies. A fundamental concept was that the ships should be full in both directions. It was still a dangerous fifty- to sixty-day crossing. Basque iron products, weapons, chemical products, sardines, and construction wood were shipped to Caracas. Other Basque provinces, and especially Navarra, began to see the opportunity the company offered. Navarrese wine was shipped to Latin America. Other regions of Spain began to do business with the Royal Company. Valencia shipped silk and ceramics; Aragón shipped cotton; Catalonia shipped textiles and manufactured goods. And ports all over Spain received cocoa and other goods from the Royal Company.

In 1751 the company seat was moved to Madrid. But it did not operate as a Spanish monopoly. Its owners were the first pan-Europeans, caring little about the arbitrary borders that split up the continent. At the dawn of capitalism, the Royal Guipúzcoan Company of Caracas became a multinational. Deeply involved in inter-European trade, it had relations with the French, Dutch, and Germans and even operated some ships out of French ports. And French ships brought hams, flour, and other agricultural products to Pasajes to sell to the Royal Company. The company shipped a great quantity of French flour to the Latin American market.

Wanting a share of all profitable commerce of the epoch, the company even attempted to enter the slave trade but, finding the monopolies by European powers in their own Caribbean colonies to be unbreakable, it had to give up this plan.

In 1766, Xabier María de Munibe, the son of one of the founders of the Royal Guipúzcoan Company, founded the Real Sociedad Bascongada de los Amigos del País, the Royal Basque Society of Friends of the Country, an eighteenth century think tank that, in addition to studying everything Basque from science and engineering to gastronomy, discussed and promoted the precepts of modern capitalism.

In this new age of capitalism, the Basques were demonstrating what their British contemporary, Adam Smith, would write about decades later. It was Smith's contention in his 1776 bible of capitalism, *The Wealth of Nations,* that the wealth of a country was not the gold that it held but the goods and services it provided. When Smith was articulating this theory, he took the example of Spain. The nation was in precipitous decline after centuries of trying to enrich itself by extracting wealth, often literally gold, from its Latin American holdings. What Smith, however, did not go on to say—but which illustrates his point exactly—is that while Spain was wasting its energies amassing American gold, the Basques generated affluence throughout the Iberian peninsula by providing goods and services to and from Latin America.

Another lesson in capitalism practiced by the Basques and later espoused by Smith: Having broken the Dutch cocoa monopoly, the Basques caused the price of chocolate to plunge. Far from causing a crisis, the almost halved price made chocolate more accessible and greatly expanded the market, making the trade far more profitable than it had been under Dutch price fixing.

The company produced spin-offs such as the Real Compañía de Habana for trade with Cuba and another for trading with the Philippines. Lasting fifty-six years, the Royal Guipúzcoan Company of Caracas had an enormous impact not only on Basqueland but on Latin America. It greatly facilitated the Basque dream of making a fortune in America, but the prosperity that it brought to Caracas, as well as the unbridled exploitation, also had much to do with the Spanish loss of colonies and the creation of an independent Venezuela. In 1749, a violent uprising against the Royal Guipúzcoan Company erupted in Caracas. To avoid further uprisings, producers were paid better, causing dividends to drop to only 5 to 10 percent.

Ironically, the aspirations of these South American rebels were realized a generation later by the father of Latin American independence, Simon Bolivar, El Libertador, who was born in Caracas in 1783 to a Vizcayan family that had grown wealthy in South America.

But it was in Basqueland itself that unrestrained capitalism and the emergence of a new wealthy class were creating a rift that would lead to more than a century of civil war.

*Part Two*

# THE DAWN OF EUSKADI

*The Basques are said, with good reason, to be agile and deft and have earned their reputation of being good shots.*
—ILLUSTRATED GUIDE FOR THE TRAVELER TO SAN SEBASTIÁN, *1909*

*The Basques . . . are a religious, deep drinking, non-swearing race who live on the mountainous south-eastern shores of the Bay of Biscay. They are profoundly nautical; they swing and fish in the Bay without ever feeling sea-sick.*
—*George Steer,* THE TREE OF GERNIKA, *1938*

# The Basque Onomatopoeia

*Food is always, more or less, in demand.*
*—Adam Smith,* THE WEALTH OF NATIONS, 1776

FOR THE REST of the world, the little-remembered Carlist Wars were to have only two lasting consequences: the invention of the political term liberal and the popularizing of the beret. These two brutal and complicated nineteenth-century civil wars were to shape the destiny of at least six generations of both Basques and Spaniards. Their enduring impact is most easily seen in features of daily life such as food and clothing. Carlism resulted not only in the famous Basque hat but in the creation of their most mysterious, and therefore some might argue, most Basque sauce.

According to popular and unverified legend, in 1836 a Bilbao salt cod merchant named Gurtubay placed an order by telegram saying, "Send me by the first ship that lands in Bilbao, 100 or 120 top quality salt cods," which in Spanish was written *"100 o 120 bacaladas."* The telegraph code was misinterpreted as *"1,000,120 bacaladas."*

In any event, Gurtubay got a lot more salt cod than he had expected, and had no possibility of returning it, because by then the First Carlist War had begun and Bilbao was under siege. The mistake might have been ruinous had not the city started running out of supplies. As the food shortage became more severe, Bilbaínos became an eager market for Gurtubay's million dried fish, and Gurtubay became a rich man, which is the way Basques like their stories to end.

It is often said that this is why the people of Bilbao eat so much salt cod, which is probably not true. The Basques, including Bilbaínos, had been eating salt cod since they developed the

The First Carlist War, drawn by M. Miranda, *Panarama Español*, Madrid, 1842.

product many centuries earlier. But a typical salt cod dish of the day was a stew with many ingredients. During the siege, no fresh food could get in to the city, which in time left its inhabitants with little more than three nonperishable staples: olive oil, garlic, and dried pepper.

Salt cod cooked in olive oil with slices of dried guindilla pepper and garlic became a popular dish called *pil pil*, though the origin of this name is not clear. The tendency is to assume that this odd-looking term means something in Euskera. Disappointingly, it has no more meaning in that ancient language than it does in Spanish or English. As with the origins of the Basques themselves, explanations abound, ranging from a reference to pelota to the sound of sizzling olive oil. As with many Basque words, the orthography became almost a question of personal preference. *Pil-pil* with a hyphen was often used, and a 1912 book called it *pirpir,* one in 1919 said *pin pin,* and one in 1930 wrote of *pirpil.* The 1892 *General Dictionary of Cuisine* published in Madrid defined "pil pill" as "the name of a new red sauce the Bilbaíno gastronomes have invented now to eat with their famous *chipirones,* or squid." The only explanation for this definition is that it was neither the first nor the last time a Madrid publication got its Basque facts wrong.

All of these variations on the name lend credence to the theory that the word is an onomatopoeia attempting to capture the sound of sizzling olive oil. An 1896 book, *Lexicón Bilbaíno* by Emiliano Arriaga, stated that the dish while cooking made the sound "bil-bil" but that, since there is a tendency to transpose *p*s and *b*s, which he also stated is the origin of the name Bilbao, the sauce became known as "pil-pil." The only problem then is that pil pil doesn't go "pil pil" anymore.

At some point later in the century, it was discovered that if the cooked salt cod was placed in an earthen casserole with warm but not at all sizzling oil and garlic, and the casserole was moved in a circular motion over a very low heat, the oil would thicken into a creamy, opaque, ivory-colored sauce.

The people of Bilbao like to say that the chefs of San Sebastián are French influenced, and though this may sound appealing to the outside world, especially the French, it is not intended to be a compliment. But the unpleasant truth is that in the late nineteenth century, Bilbao chefs were developing a number of sauces for their salt cod, because sauces were the fashion in French cuisine.

Nevertheless, this particular sauce was brilliant. Called *ligado,* meaning "bound" or "thickened" in Spanish, it had more craft and more originality—and more mystery—than the older, sizzling, clear-oil pil pil. Today almost no one makes the original pil pil, whereas ligado is considered the litmus test of a Basque chef. But apparently everyone still liked to say "pil pil," and it has become the name for the thickened, ligado sauce.

There is a sense of alchemy to the emulsification of a good pil pil. It happens slowly as the casserole is being moved, the low temperature perfectly maintained, a little—not too much—of the water the fish was cooked in added to make more liquid. This is not a mayonnaise; there is no solid suspended in the oil. It is a sauce made purely of liquids, some of which somehow become solidified and suspended in the remaining liquid. There is not even a change in temperature. In fact, most cooks agree that all parts of the pil pil should be maintained at the same constant tepid state.

That is one of the few things agreed on. As with all Basque salt cod dishes, almost no one agrees as to how and for how long to soak the dried fish. Then, some insist it must be made in an earthen casserole or the emulsification will not take place. Many claim the secret is "in the wrist," that is, in the correct circular motion of the cook's arms while holding the casserole. Most recipes make a point of insisting on only the best-quality virgin, cold-pressed olive oil, but some cooks whisper that a few drops of corn oil helps the emulsion. But no Basque chefs would ever go on the record with corn oil in their pil pil.

The gelatin in the cod skin may be what creates the emulsion. In any event, pil pil would not be made without skin because to a Basque, a skinless salt cod is a deep offense. It has been discovered, some accounts say it was at the Restaurant Bermeo in Bilbao, that a sauce made with leftover skin and bones and then poured over the fish has a stronger bind.

The sauce is often described as a "triumph" of Basque gastronomy, but it is a triumph that was born of defeat. Bilbao put up a determined resistance and the siege was a disaster from which the Carlist cause never recovered. Bitter sentiments endured for more than a century, but both sides recognized that the siege of Bilbao gave the Basques a great sauce.

JENARO PILDAIN of the Restaurant Guria in Bilbao is considered one of the masters of pil pil. His technique is unusual in that he cooks the fish directly in the oil and not in water beforehand. Pildain learned pil pil from his mother, who had a country inn in the 1930s, and her technique may date back to the original pil pil sauce, since the recipe begins that way and then develops into the ligado sauce.

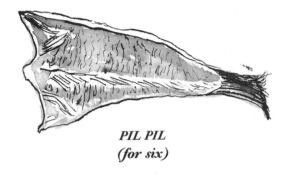

*PIL PIL*
*(for six)*

*12 pieces of top-quality salt cod*
*4 cloves garlic*
*2 red guindilla peppers*

*Soak the salt cod for between 36 and 44 hours. During this time, change the water every 8 hours. Taste to see if this period of time has been long enough for the fish to be perfectly desalinated. Remove the desalinated salt cod from the water and let it drain. Scale it well and remove the bones. Then place it skin side up in an earthenware casserole with abundant olive oil and garlic over a low flame, removing the garlic when it has been browned. If the salt cod is top quality, 5 minutes cooking will be sufficient. When done, remove the olive oil and begin to move the salt cod against the casserole in a circular rolling movement and add, little by little, the oil that was removed until the sauce is thick, ready to be served.*

*Decorate with garlic that has been fried in oil and with sliced rounds of guindilla.*

# 7: The Basque Beret

*Federalism and superstition are expressed in low-Breton, emigration and hatred of the Republic speak German, counter-revolution speaks Italian, and fanaticism is expressed in Basque. Destroy these harmful and misguided instruments.*
*—Bertrand Barère to the French National Assembly, 1794*

IT WAS THE FRENCH REVOLUTION that set off the chain of violent struggles—Basques against Spaniards but also Basques against Basques—that lasted well into the twentieth century. The Revolution quickly divided Europe between those for whom events in France held the promise of progressive reform and those for whom it was a menacing assault on traditional values.

Under the French monarchy, like the Spanish one, Basques had carved out a complicated relationship in which their Foral rights of self-determination were respected. But the Revolution sought change. Even calendars and maps were to be redrawn. To carry out a detailed agenda of radical change, a true revolution, the revolutionaries in Paris wanted complete control. In 1789, the revolutionary National Assembly, which was to establish liberties, eliminated the three Basque provinces—Labourd, Basse Navarre, and Soule—and fused them with Béarn into a single Département. The entire Département system was created to break up the many ethnic identities within France and make all regions "equally French."

Having lost their provinces, French Basques would now be required to pay taxes to the French government rather than to their own Foral administration and to serve in the French military wherever they were sent, instead of being responsible exclusively for the defense of their own region. Paris even attempted to obliterate Euskera place-names. Ustaritz became Marat-sur-

Nive, Baïgorry became Thermopyles, Itxassou became Union. Even already Frenchified names were changed. St.-Jean-de-Luz, long ago translated from its Basque name of Donibane Lohitzune, was now changed to Chauvin-Dragon. None of these revolutionary names would endure, but the centralism would.

With the abolition in French Basqueland of the Fueros, or Fors, as they were called in French, Basques were suddenly required to abandon their traditional laws, codified more than 250 years earlier, and accept an entirely different system of law, eventually to be established in the Napoleonic Code of 1804. The ancient custom of collectively owned land would be abolished. The law of inheritance would be changed. Ancient Basque law distinguished between acquired goods, which could be willed, and inherited goods—the house, the etxea, and what belonged to the house—which had to be passed down, without distinction of sex, to the firstborn. Under the new legal code, each child had an equal claim to all property, which would result in ever smaller holdings. In time it would cause many etxea to disappear.

Revolutions are always easier to admire from across the border. The affluent commercial class of San Sebastián and Bilbao was not concerned about the dismantling of the French Basque provinces. Instead, with great excitement, they were following news of the establishment of parliamentary rule in an elected republic. Guipúzcoans greeted the dramatic events in Paris with such enthusiasm that the Spanish began censoring press coverage of the Revolution. This could not stop pamphlets and political tracts from flowing into Guipúzcoa, nor could it stop Basque businessmen who had regular contact with France from bringing back news.

The Basques got news of France faster than it arrived in Madrid. But in 1793, when the elected Convention, charged with creating a new democratic French state, declared a French republic and had Louis XVI executed, it took only thirteen days for the startling news to reach Madrid by mail. Spain, ruled by a related Bourbon monarch, marched 20,000 troops toward the Basque border.

As the French moved their troops toward the Pyrenees, the inevitable conflict was certain to endanger Spanish Basque independence. Ever since the Basque provinces were first tied to Castile, the policy in Madrid had always been to let the Basques be Basque, let them have their Fueros—their own laws, taxes, and import duties. Then Madrid could count on these warlike people to be on Spain's troubled border, ready to defend it, because they would be defending their own liberty. Basques were not even required to serve in the Spanish military, just as long as they were ready to defend their own provinces, which happened to be the border.

It had been centuries since this defense clause had been invoked. Some towns and villages had at one time been divided into religious societies, and each society had been responsible for the defense of a specified section of the town wall. Once a year, this home guard would be reviewed. The day of the review had by now become the town festival, but its significance had been lost. Basques no longer trained in defense, nor did they have a draft capable of raising an army. When they finally did raise one, they had to deal with their own Foral issues. When Vizcaya sent an additional 500 men to the defense of Guipúzcoa, only 200 actually went, because the Fueros specified that Basques could only be required to fight in their own province.

The French crossed the passes of Basse Navarre and encountered little resistance as they marched through the deep Bidasoa Valley toward Guipúzcoa. Fuenterrabía, the fishing village with a hilltop cathedral, fell without a fight. In San Sebastián, the mayor turned over the city. The Junta General de Guipúzcoa even sent delegates to the French Convention and, apparently not noticing the fate of its sister provinces in France, proposed to the French that "the province [Guipúzcoa] be independent as it was until the year 1200." Ten days later the Convention decided that, instead, Guipúzcoa would be governed by French military occupation without recognition of any special Basque rights.

Nor did the troops of the Convention treat occupied Basque towns kindly. They burned churches and houses and destroyed religious relics as they swept through Guipúzcoa, Vizcaya, and into Alava. They even took Victoria, the Alavan capital in the south. Only in the Roncesvalles area did the locals do what they always had done, what the Spanish counted on Basques to do: resist and drive the invader back over the border.

At this point, Basqueland was almost entirely in French hands and the closest it had ever been to a united seven provinces. But the Spanish won back at the peace table what they had lost on the battlefield. All they had to give up for the return of their Basque provinces were their claims to the western third of the island of Hispaniola, present-day Haiti, an area where a slave revolt would explode in a few years and destroy two elite French armies in a decade of brutal conflict.

Many factors had contributed to the humiliating failure of the Spanish troops. The French had three times as many soldiers, and they were better trained and better equipped. But the Spanish military blamed the failure on the Basques. The fierce Basques on the border failed to be fierce, had not crushed the invader, had not even tried. A strong element in Madrid became hostile to traditional Basque rights and increasingly questioned the sanctity of the Fueros.

CHRONIC WARS, or perhaps they were the same recurring war, erupted for the next century and a half between the two sides that had been defined by the Convention War. From the beginning, the divisions were complex. This was a dispute not only between pro-French and anti-French, the reformers and the conservatives, but also between urban and rural.

While the people in San Sebastián were sending delegates to the French Convention, rural Guipúzcoa had been organizing to fight the French. The *baserritarrak,* people of the *baserri,* the farm, felt their world was besieged and being undermined by modernism, while the *kaletarrak,* people of the *kalea,* the street, were eager to embrace a new kind of society.

The most volatile conflict of the nineteenth century involved the discord between declining rural agricultural societies and the growing urban industrial societies. This social fissure was at the root of many nineteenth-century conflicts, including the American Civil War. In Spain, much of this wrenching conflict was to be focused in Basqueland, where the industrial revolution had been introduced to Iberia.

Basqueland, unlike southern Spain, did not have the problem of huge wasteful landholdings, the so-called *latifundia* that led to centuries of social conflict in Andalusia, from where it was exported to Latin America. In those regions a small aristocracy controlled the latifundia, tracts of land that were too vast to be completely utilized, while the peasantry suffered from a shortage of arable land. Basques like to say that they avoided the latifundia problem because they had a more democratic tradition. But the reverse may well be true. Perhaps it is the land that shapes the laws. Fueros are a less feudal and more democratic code than other European medieval law because the land did not lend itself to the feudal system. The Basques lacked large tracts of fertile farmland. Nature broke up Basqueland into smaller plots.

Small-scale farming has made the countryside picturesque, its produce of excellent quality, and its farmers poor and frustrated. But that is not to say that there were not rural Basques who tried to concentrate the wealth.

One of the few Euskera words to have become part of popular American English is *jauntxo,* which in English has kept the same pronunciation and become the word *honcho.* A *jauntxo* was a wealthy, powerful, rural landowner. Derived from the word *jaun,* which means "sir," "a lord," or sometimes even "a god," *jaun-*

*txo* has an ironic negative undertone. There is the implication of exploitation.

The Basques had jauntxos. Between the voyages of Columbus and the eighteenth century, jauntxos amassed great wealth from grain speculation and agricultural expansion spurred by Latin American products and trade. But in the eighteenth century the prices of agricultural products plunged, and the jauntxos maintained their profits at the expense of the poor farmer.

Neither the wealth nor industry that was changing urban life reached the agricultural sector. Into the twentieth century, soil was still being turned by Basque women using the two-pronged *laia*, the basque hoe.

The most striking feature of modern industrial Bilbao is at

Farm women with *laias*, photographed by Eulalia Abaitua Allende Salazar. Born in Bilbao in 1853, she began documenting Basque life during the Second Carlist War. She died at the age of ninety in 1943. (Euskal Arkeologia, Etnografia eta Kondaira Museoa, Bilbao)

the end of most any downtown street: The green, steep slopes of the Basque countryside can be seen with shepherds tending grazing flocks. Bilbao is an urban population surrounded by a rural one. Farming families look down from their low-pitched, red-tile-roofed country houses into the busy streets of the largest, most industrial Basque city. The *baserritarrak* look down at the scrambling *kaletarrak*.

In 1801, Simón Bernardo de Zamácola, a jauntxo, approached the regional Basque government, the Juntas Generales, meeting in Guernica. Zamácola wanted to break the trade monopoly of the Bilbao commercial class, which had exclusive rights to the port of Bilbao. He proposed that the Juntas open and manage a new port in Abando, which is today part of Bilbao.

The Juntas sent Zamácola to the next step, the required Royal approval from Madrid for a new port. Madrid named its terms: The Basques could have their port, but in exchange they would have to agree to perform Spanish military service. The explosion that this counteroffer produced in Bilbao in 1804 has become known as the Zamacolada.

The Zamacolada of 1804 was a miniwar in Bilbao. Spanish troops occupied state buildings, closed down the Juntas, suspended self-rule, and held the city under a state of siege for three years until yet another war broke out—this time against Napoleon.

NOWHERE IN SPAIN was there more loyalty to the Spanish monarchy, and more hostility to the antimonarchist, anticleric reforms of French republicanism, than in Navarra. Oddly, the Spanish kings did not share the ferocity of their supporters. In February 1808, when a Napoleonic army climbed through the pass over the ghosts of Roncesvalles and down to Pamplona, it met little resistance because the Spanish monarchy had declared the French to be allies. In March, Charles IV abdicated and fled to France. His son, Ferdinand VII, sought only to be a servile puppet to

Napoleon. But, reasoning that a relative was more dependable than a collaborator, Napoleon forced Ferdinand to step down and made his own brother, Joseph Bonaparte, ruler instead.

On May 2, 1808, a date remembered in Spanish history as Dos de Mayo, the Madrid citizenry rose up against the French. A French ruler was one step too far, which is why the six-year Iberian war—the Spanish, Portuguese, and British against Napoleon—is called the Spanish War of Independence. Most combatants were fighting to keep Napoleon from incorporating Spain into his growing empire. But the Navarrese fought for the monarchy itself. Ferdinand, the pathetic prince who had capitulated, was referred to by the Navarrese as *El Deseado*, the longed-for.

Though Pamplona remained in French hands for most of the war, Napoleonic troops had to contend with relentless Basque guerrilla attacks from the mountains. The first of the guerrilla movements was organized at the mouth of the Roncesvalles pass in Valcarlos.

Napoleon had originally shown contempt for local Basques. His troops had harassed them when they attempted to hold meetings of local Foral administration. Now, realizing his error, he proposed a constitution with special Basque provisions.

Neither Spain nor the Basques had ever had a constitution. Napoleon not only imposed his own absolute rule but, by drawing up a constitution for his Spanish holdings, also imposed a new form of government. The issue of constitutions has been an enduring controversy in Spain. This first taste was bitter for most of Spain since the new constitution abolished almost all institutions of regional self-government. But in Navarra and the Basque provinces, Napoleon allowed the Fueros to remain in force. Kings of Castile had controlled Basques with this same concession. However, being by nature obsessed with centralized authority, Napoleon could not resist adding that the Fueros would be subject to review at a later date.

In France, Napoleon had been determined to end regionalism. Préfets, government officials charged with carrying out the will of Paris, were sent to each region. A uniform school curriculum in France banned Basque and other regional languages, an act that was not repealed until the election of François Mitterrand in 1981.

But in Spain, Napoleon promised, it was all to be different. He even let it be known that he was thinking of creating a Basque state. Called Nueva Fenicia, it was to have had two parts: The three French provinces would become Nueva Tiro, and the four Spanish ones, Nueva Sidon. It is not clear how the Basques felt about becoming "new Phoenicians," nor even how serious Napoleon was about this plan. The broader plan, one that he was ready to act on, was moving the French-Spanish border to the Ebro. North of the Ebro would be France, and south of it would be a puppet Spain ruled by his brother.

The Navarrese guerrilla resistance, apparently not impressed by any of these plans, continued. A small group called the División de Navarra was particularly effective at defeating far greater French forces, heroics for which the French regularly retaliated with the execution of citizens in Pamplona, gruesomely displaying the corpses after each Navarrese victory.

By 1813, the Spanish-Portuguese-British alliance had swept through Iberia and driven the Napoleonic army back everywhere. But the French stubbornly held Pamplona through a four-month siege, finally surrendering after losing 2,300 men.

Spain was rid of Napoleon and once more free to choose its own destiny. But the French had set off a controversy which to this day has not been resolved: the idea of Spain. Not only did the French Revolution proclaim "liberty, equality, and fraternity," but it also established a new kind of nationhood. Instead of an inherited kingdom whose borders were defined by the wins and losses of a ruling family, France had established a strong, centralized state that incorporated many peoples and cultures, backed by a constitution, which, of course, could always be rewritten.

In the beginning of the nineteenth century, Spain was still more of a geographic demarcation, like Iberia, than a state. In the fifteenth century, Ferdinand of Aragón, through his diplomatic skills, had created an amalgamation of distinct kingdoms. And that is what Spain remained. As such, it was willing to negotiate a special relationship with the Basques. There was no monarch with the title king of Spain. Rather he was king of Castile and León, king of Navarra, of Aragón—the list of titles was long. So that he could rule Basque provinces that had never been kingdoms, titles were invented such as "count of Guipúzcoa." It took a long paragraph to give the monarch's full title. Many would die before the title would be condensed to "king of Spain" in the late nineteenth century.

AFTER THE DEFEAT of Napoleon, as so often happened at these critical moments, the Spanish had one idea of how to proceed and the Basques another. The Basques, as always, wanted regional autonomy and rule by the Fueros. But to the Liberals in Madrid, the problem had been an inept monarchy, and the solution was the French concept of strong central constitutional government.

A group of radicals who had escaped the war in Cádiz, calling themselves "the Liberals," now wanted to create a homegrown version of constitutional government. The term *liberal* is an Old French word meaning "a completely free man," which was to say, a nobleman. The Spanish Liberals in Cádiz were the first to use the word to refer to those who believed in greater liberty.

But to the Liberals, greater liberty did not mean autonomy for the Basques. The preamble to their 1812 constitution paid tribute to the Fueros, but the body of the document dismantled them. Francisco Espoz y Mina, the former commander of the

División de Navarra, one of the great heroes of the war, took a copy of the constitution, placed it on a chair, and ordered it shot.

The stage was set for civil war—conservative against liberal, Church against secular, populist against bourgeoisie, rural against urban. But in Basqueland, a crucial factor was regionalist against centralist—the Liberals wished to abolish the Fueros. To many Basques, and to the Catalans also seeking to preserve their self-determination, it was a struggle for survival.

The first civil war to occur, the Royalist War of 1820-23, was the smallest. While the Liberals had opponents throughout Spain, armed resistance occurred only in Navarra and Catalonia.

When Ferdinand VII died in 1833, a decade later, the rift deepened. The two sides backed different candidates for the throne. Ferdinand had named his daughter Isabella, three years old at the time of his death, as his heir, with her mother, María Cristina, as regent. But many wanted to see Carlos, Ferdinand's younger brother, as king instead and invoked the so-called Salic Law, which had barred women from inheriting the throne in France.

In Spain, it was not clear what the laws of succession were since there was no real king of Spain but only a collection of titles with varying rules. The real debate was not over who had the right to succeed but over what kind of monarchy to have. The rule of Isabella and María Cristina would be Liberal: a weakened monarch and a strongly anti-Church constitutional government that wanted to move Spain closer to the new French model of a secular republican society.

Carlos stood for absolute monarchy. His supporters, Carlists, were mostly Basque, Aragonese, Catalan, and Valencian. These passionate monarchists were also the people of Iberia who enjoyed special measures of home rule. They wanted strong monarchy, but from a distance. Among the Basques, Carlists were clergy, peasants, and aristocrats. The urban middle class, the

commercial class, and the high-ranking military officers supported Isabella and María Cristina. It was the same enduring split
that began with the French Revolution.

The Carlists often seemed fanatically right-wing. They opposed an elected representative parliament as a foreign concept.
They opposed universal male suffrage because it dismantled the
privilege of rural landowners. Freedom of religion was objec-
tionable because it diminished the power of the Catholic Church,
and they were infuriated by the long overdue abolition of the
Inquisition even though it had persecuted Basque peasants.

Freemasonry, a nonsectarian religious movement, was singled out by Carlists as a particularly odious enemy that, according to the bishop of Urgel, chaplain of the Carlist army, "has been
robbing Europe and the new world of its beliefs and Christian
morality." Mystifyingly, Freemasons, by virtue of their lack of
Church affiliation, have always been a target of denunciation,
but especially in the nineteenth century. In the United States,
the Anti-Masonic Party of 1827 was the first third party.

Though today Carlism seems extremist, in the volatile nineteenth century, Carlists were often seen as romantic figures.
They were the underdogs, the brave and hardworking people of
the countryside, fighting the powerful. Curiously, the great anticleric voice of the nineteenth-century industrial masses, Karl
Marx, praised the Carlists and not the anti-Church Liberals:
"The traditional Carlist has the genuinely mass national base of
peasants, lower aristocracy and clergy, while the so-called Liberals
derived their base from the military, the capitalists, latifundist
aristocracy, and secular interests."

The term *liberal* has become synonymous with reformist,
progressive politics. And that is how some of the Spanish Liberals
saw themselves. Yet Marx and subsequent Marxists have always
viewed the original Liberals in Spain as the epitome of bourgeois hypocrisy. This is in part because, as always happens, many

of the Liberals were not liberals. Isabella, the Liberal choice for monarch, grew up to be no liberal, nor was her mother, the regent María Cristina.

Nor was Carlos himself wholly Carlist. Unlike his brother Ferdinand, he was deeply religious and sincere in his sense of royal responsibility. He did not compromise and deal away royal authority. But he had no interest in restoring the Inquisition, which, to him and most of the world, seemed an obsolete institution.

Nothing so illustrates the romance of the Carlist cause as their hat, the Carlist trademark, a large red beret. The Carlists brought the beret into fashion in Europe, and it has never since gone out of style. Although the first known use of the word *beret* dates to a 1461 text in Landes, and though Gascognes and others in the region had worn this hat of unknown origin, there has been a long-standing association between Basques and berets. Jesuit novices wore a *birette*, and a bas-relief in Tolosa dated 1600 shows berets. The Carlists wore it in red, the color traditionally worn on Basque holidays, and made it their own. *La Boina*, "the beret," was the name of a Carlist newspaper, and it was during the First Carlist War that the French began referring to the hat, as they still do, as *le beret Basque*. Since the First Carlist War, the hat not only has become a central symbol of Basqueness but has also gained international popularity and is generally associated with the political left. Argentine leftist revolutionary Ernesto Che Guevara saw no contradiction in using the image of the beret, because it is the hat of the underdog fighting the establishment.

"WHEN YOU SAY BASQUE, you say Catholic" is an old proverb. To the Basques, a principal attraction to Carlism was its defense of the Church. The rural priests, almost always local because they had to hear confession in Euskera, were among the most dedicated Carlists. Miguel de Unamuno, in his first novel, *Paz en la*

Making berets in the nineteenth century at the Elosogui Beret factory in Tolosa, still a leading beret maker. (Museo San Telmo, Donastia Kultura, San Sebastián)

*Guerra,* wrote, "All the villagers thought the same, hearing it directly from the mouth of the priest." These local priests were instrumental in rallying Basque peasants to the Carlist cause by making it sound like a religious crusade. To an anti-Carlist Liberal such as Unamuno, this alone was a reason to curtail the power of priests. But to a Carlist, this was the reason to leave the power of the Church unhampered. The difference had no resolution.

Under Joseph Bonaparte and the French occupation, religious orders had been suppressed. In 1808, Bonaparte was the first to abolish the Inquisition. Once back in power, Ferdinand reestablished it, also restoring the religious orders, including, of special significance to Basques, the Jesuits.

But the legislature, the Cortes, continued to pass anticlerical laws, and after Ferdinand's death anticlericism became an avowed policy. Though, in 1833, the Liberals installed Isabella as Queen Isabella II, the Vatican refused to recognize her rule. On July

15, 1834, the Spanish Inquisition was finally abolished. Economic and political privileges of the Church were dismantled. The Carlists were furious and prepared to go to war for the Church.

Many Basques rallied for Carlos. Most of Vizcaya, all of Alava, much of Guipúzcoa, though not San Sebastián, and most of Navarra but not Pamplona; declared their support for Carlos. Although his intellect was not held in high regard and he was not a skilled military commander, he inspired intense loyalty. Counting on that, he made no attempt to secure the crown when his brother was alive but assumed that his loyal minions would bloodlessly hoist him to power after Ferdinand's death. He waited at the Portuguese border, yet no such movement materialized.

THE FIRST CARLIST WAR, from 1833 to 1839, was fought on three separate fronts: Basqueland, Aragón, and Catalonia. But the most concentrated fighting was in Basqueland, the Carlist stronghold. While Carlists went into battle singing songs of Ignatius Loyola, the Liberals burned churches and monasteries. Most of Europe took sides: England and France, for once on the same side, backed the Liberals, and Russia, Prussia, and Austria supported the Carlists. To Europe, it was a war for or against absolute monarchy.

The British and French both sent troops to fight for the Liberal side. The British troops were amazed by the Basque way of fighting, comparing it to the "Indian" tactics of the American colonists in the Revolution, resenting their "un-European" tactic of only firing from under cover.

No longer waiting for the masses to triumphantly carry him in, Carlos slipped into Spain through Basqueland to Elizondo, a valley town in northern Navarra. He found a war under way and an able general with several victories behind him in command.

The general, from Guipúzcoa, was Tomás Zumalacárregui, whose family name of imposing length means "willows on the mountain slope." Zumalacárregui's image—the daring young general with the fine long Basque nose, thick mustache, and side-burns framing a strong Basque chin, wearing a large red beret with a tassel draped from the middle—caught the international imagination.

This poster revolutionary, whose portrait helped make berets fashionable, was made a romantic figure by those who wrote of the war. In 1835, Augustin Chaho, one of the great Basque propagandists, wrote a popular account, *Journey to Navarra during the Basque Insurrection,* in which he quotes Zumalacárregui as saying, "Isn't this the land of our fathers? What are the Christians to us Basques except thieves who come in the night to attack the innocent man at home with his family?" Despite their attachment to the Church, speaking of the enemy as the Christians, as though the Basques were still animists fighting off the Visigoths, became a fashion of Basque nationalists.

Zumalacárregui was a brilliant tactician who had built a fine defensive military, schooled in hit-and-run guerrilla tactics but capable of major assaults. His army was fiercely committed, loyal, and disciplined. They took town after town: Vergara, Guernica, Tolosa. But they still had no port. In 1835, Carlos ordered them to take Bilbao. Zumalacárregui thought this was a mistake, but he obeyed orders from Carlos. This was the siege that is remembered for pil pil. The attack failed, and, wounded in the fight, Zumalacárregui died eleven days later.

A warring people with more wars to come, the Basques had in Tomás Zumalacárregui their last great military commander. Carlism never recovered from this loss.

THE PROBLEM WITH the army Zumalacárregui had built was that, typically Basque, it was based on the defense of Basqueland against invaders. Except for a brief period under the Kingdom of Navarra, Basques never fought to take new land. But now they were in a war for more than the defense of their own borders. To bring Carlos to power, they needed to seize the offen-

Tomás Zumalacárregui, from *Don Carlos et ses Défenseurs,* by Isidore Maquès, Paris, 1837.

sive. In a surprise attack they almost made it to Madrid and were within striking distance of kidnaping María Cristina. But instead, they retreated back to Basqueland.

Again they tried and failed to take Bilbao. Another foray into Spain failed. After they crossed the Ebro, progress was slowed by the insistence on saying Mass in every liberated church. They finally got as far as Valencia, took it, started to march toward Madrid, but confronted with a superior force, they reverted to guerrilla tactics, retreating back to Navarra.

Needing to strengthen his base, Carlos did what monarchs always did when they wanted Basque support. From this point on, when raising money or recruiting volunteers among rural Basques, the Carlists declared that Carlism stood for the Fueros against María Cristina and the Liberals who wanted to abolish all of the traditional rights. Suddenly the motto of Carlism, *Dios, Patria, Rey,* God, Country, King, became *Dios y Fueros.*

But in 1837, a Carlist writer-turned-general, José Antonio Muñagorri, began questioning the value of Basques killing Basques in the name of Carlos. He suggested that the Basques on both sides give up fighting, that the cause of Don Carlos be abandoned in exchange for an agreement from Madrid that the rule of the Fueros would be respected in Basqueland. "Our first objective is the total restoration of the Fueros," he said. Few listened.

Both armies were brutal. Prisoners were frequently massacred. Espoz y Mina, the constitution-slaying hero of the División de Navarra, in a fury over a defeat, burned down the Navarrese village of Lecároz and executed one in every five of its men. The Carlists, always poorly provisioned because they did not control major ports, captured town officials and tortured them to locate caches of money and supplies. As often happens in war, women were singled out for their collaboration. When Carlists took a town, they would tar-and-feather women who were said to be Liberal sympathizers. Because Carlist general Ramón Cabrera was infamously brutal, Liberal forces in Aragón captured and murdered his mother.

On August 29, 1839, an end to hostilities was signed in Vergara. To prove that hostilities had ended, the two opposing generals embraced, which came to be known as the *Abrazo de Vergara*, a phrase which in Basqueland became synonymous with sellout. The troops from Alava and Navarra did not even appear for the signing. After their defeat, thousands of Basque peasants immigrated to the Americas. A curious footnote is that Muñagorri, the reluctant general, was assassinated in 1841, not by a Carlist angered by his willingness to give up fighting for Carlos, but by a Liberal.

IT WILL NEVER BE known if a victorious Carlos would have defended Basque independence. But his claim that their enemies were out to destroy it was proven true. The process that began with the century of chipping away at Foral rights continued. Already under Ferdinand, the Navarrese had lost their right to review royal decrees. In 1833, the Ministry of Interior in Madrid had ordered Spain to be divided into forty-nine provinces, meaning that even Navarra, which had still been recognized as a nominal kingdom, was reduced to being just another province. In 1836 the traditional Navarrese ruling body was replaced by a provincial legislature. The following year the same was ordered in the three other Basque provinces.

The Liberals had for a number of years been forcing anti-clerical and antiregional measures on a reluctant María Cristina. In 1837 they forced her to reinstate the 1812 constitution. Three years later a more liberal faction came to power, and, unable to accept further demands, María Cristina resigned, leaving Spain and her daughter, now ten-year-old Queen Isabella II. With the victorious Liberal general Baldomero Espartero acting as regent, there was no longer any hope of saving the Fueros. The Navarrese, through compromise, were able to negotiate better terms than the other Basque provinces, but in the law of August 16, 1841, Basque autonomy was largely ended. Customs controls now began at the Pyrenees border and not at the Ebro. Provincial governments retained control only over internal affairs.

As the assassinated and forgotten Carlist general Muñagorri had warned, the war for Carlos had been disastrous for the Basques. But even worse disasters were to come.

The First Carlist War had resolved nothing, merely intensifying society's divisions. The Liberals, in control, did not try to assuage the Carlists, and with each new Liberal measure restricting regional autonomy or eroding the position of the Church, the Carlists grew angrier. Throughout northern Spain, the veterans of the First Carlist War were restless and occasionally violent. In 1844, the Spanish government responded by creating a national police force, the Guardia Civil, which became and has remained the greatest single irritant in Basque-Spanish relations.

# 8: The Basque Ear

*I am tempted to say about metaphysicians what Scalinger would say about the Basques: they are said to understand one another, but I don't believe it at all.*
—Nicolas Chamfort, French writer, 1741–94

SOON AFTER THE CARLIST defeat, disillusioned peasants in farmhouses on the green slopes above Bilbao looked down and saw an eerie red glow tinting the night sky along the Nervión River. That strange man-made volcano told them the world was changing—all the more reason to fight for the old ways.

A revolution was taking place in the cities and even some towns of Guipúzcoa and Vizcaya. Aside from these urban Basque regions and parts of Catalonia, the great changes of England, Germany, eastern France, and the northern United States—the industrial revolution—were not reaching Iberia.

The defeat of the Carlists and dismantling of the Fueros had presented Basque industrialists with an opportunity. When the Basque economy was focused on trading between Latin America and Europe, being outside the Spanish customs zone had been a great advantage. But while Basqueland was mired in the First Carlist War, Britain had revolutionized metal making by fusing coke and iron to produce steel, which destroyed the iron industry of Vizcaya that had once been a world leader. As the British eroded the Basque competitive edge for industrial products in Europe, and Latin American colonies became increasingly rebellious, the Basques were beginning to find the internal Spanish market attractive, especially since the population of Spain almost doubled during the nineteenth century. Once Vizcaya was inside the Spanish customs zone, the Basques were in a position to dominate the Spanish market against foreign competition.

In 1841, the same year that Basque autonomy was dismantled, the first blast furnace was built in Basqueland at a steel plant called Santa Ana de Bolueta. This one plant produced as much steel as 100 of the small mills that had been operating in Vizcaya. In 1846, Ibarra Hermanos, a leading Basque iron mining company, built the first completely modern Basque steel mill, Fábrica de Nuestra Señora de la Merced, down the Nervión River from Bilbao. In 1855, the Fábrica de Nuestra Señora del Carmen was built on the left bank of the Nervión.

In 1856, Henry Bessemer, working in Britain on an improved artillery shell, found that by blowing air through molten iron, he could speed up the process of converting iron to steel. No longer requiring tremendous time and energy, the new Bessemer converter process made steel cheap enough to be a practical metal for common use.

Ninteenth-century steelworkers in Vizcaya. The fact that they are wearing canvas espadrilles on their feet while working with molten metal is an indication of the safety standards for workers at the time. (Kutxa Fototeka, San Sebastián)

Bessemer had by chance used for ore a low phosphorus iron called hematite, and it was later discovered that this was a requirement for the Bessemer process to function well. There was only one place in Europe that had known deposits of this type of ore in easily exploitable fields near a coastline for efficient transport: Vizcaya.

A rail line was built from the mines to the coast, and the port of Bilbao was modernized. Confident that iron exports could generate enough capital to build Basque industry, the new infrastructure was financed with public money. The smaller mills merged into Altos Hornos de Vizcaya, Vizcaya Blast Furnaces, which by the end of the nineteenth century was the largest steelmaker in Spain and one of the largest in the world. By exporting iron to England, Basque mills were able to get advantageous arrangements for British coal, which was the return freight. From 1885 until the early twentieth century, Vizcaya produced 77 percent of Spain's cast iron and 87 percent of its steel. With the ability to manufacture the cheapest steel in Europe, the banks of the Nervión from Bilbao to the sea, once a world capital of shipbuilding, became one of the world's great steel centers, creating enormous wealth and thousands of jobs. Basques also invested in chemical factories, and in 1878 one of the first oil refineries in Spain was built on the Nervión.

There have always been two kinds of Basques. While some were fighting for the Basque way, the Basque tradition, other Basques, naming their steel mills after saints, just as they used to name the ships in their commercial fleets, fought for a place in the forefront of modern industry and became very wealthy.

These industrial Basques did not want serene isolation in their mountain lairs. They wanted rail connections to move raw materials, manufactured products, and people. These Basques wanted to be physically connected to Spain, which to them was nothing more or less than a market. In 1845, a rail link was completed between Irún, Guipúzcoa, on the French border, and Madrid. In 1863, a line from Bilbao to Tudela connected Vizcaya, Guipúzcoa, and Navarra. Both the railroads and the industries were financed by investments attracted from England, France, and Belgium. Basqueland was no longer to be a rugged enclave of isolated valleys.

The Basques were not only the leading industrialists but also the first modern bankers in Spain, providing the capital for growing industry. First came insurance companies in Bilbao, which underwrote shipping. In the 1850s, new laws allowed joint stock companies to finance banking and railroads. In 1857, the Banco de Bilbao was founded by the leading industrial and commercial families of the city to finance industry and infrastructure. Though hailed as a great success when it opened in 1863, the Bilbao-Tudela train line was bankrupt three years later, and the intervention by the newly formed Banco de Bilbao averted a severe economic crisis. In 1868, the Banco de San Sebastián was created. The Banco de Vizcaya invested in hydroelectric companies that controlled rights to the Ebro and not only provided for Bilbao's energy but that of Barcelona, Santander, and Valencia.

The reason Marx admired Carlists and not Liberals is that Carlists were profoundly anticapitalist, the sworn enemies of the new banking and industry. Rural Basques could see the new capitalist class profiting on the loss of Basque privileges. The moving of the customs zone to the French border had greatly profited Basque banking and spurred the creation of Basque industry. Carlists were appalled by bank and industry efforts to attract foreign investment. They saw foreign banks such as Crédit Lyonnais opening branches in San Sebastián and British engineers taking over mines. Vizcaya's huge iron deposits were noted as long ago as Roman times, when Pliny wrote of a mountain "composed entirely of iron." But this source of wealth was not inexhaustible, and only 10 percent of Vizcayan ore was going to Basque steel mills. The rest was being shipped abroad, 65 or 75 percent to British steel mills, which was contrary to Foral tradition. For centuries the Fueros had regulated iron mining as Basqueland's most valuable resource, forbidding the exploitation of Vizcayan iron by non-Basques.

The Carlists were vehement anti-Communists, but they were among the first to speak out against the mistreatment of industrial workers. V. Manterola wrote in his Carlist newspaper, *La Reconquista*, "The factory worker is a virtual slave, turned into a machine by Liberalism, good only to produce, but without regard for his morale."

In 1869, THE Spanish government instituted secular marriage. In giving the state, rather than the Church, the right to create families, the government was shifting the fundamental control over Basque society. The family was the primary Basque institution, not only socially but economically, since most farms, stores, and businesses were family run. Even today, a high percentage of Basque businesses are family operations.

That same year, freedom of religion became law. No longer would Catholicism be the only legal religion in Spain. During debate in the legislature, the Cortes, it was pointed out that "the Jews descending from Spanish families, in London, Lisbon, Amsterdam, Bordeaux, and other parts of Europe, will want to return to Spain where their ancestors are buried, in the expectation that the elected Cortes has given them the freedom to practice their religion." The Carlists warned that there could soon be mosques, synagogues, Buddhist shrines, and protestant churches in Spain and that the Jews and Muslims would take control of business and Spain would lose "not only its religion but its money."

In 1872, a Basque Carlist rebellion financed by provincial Foral governing bodies grew into the Second Carlist War. The Banco de Bilbao funded Liberal forces to fight the Carlists. It was to be yet another war of Basque against Basque.

The two sides battered each other from 1872 to 1876, each

side losing 2,000 men over Bilbao alone. The Liberal troops fighting for a secular state burned churches and monasteries, while Carlist forces torched town halls and civil records.

The Carlists established their own state in territory they held, crowning Carlos "king of the Basques" and establishing schools and other institutions, even issuing their own money and postage stamps. But in the end, once more, the Carlists lost. Their grandchildren would be the next Basques to have a taste of self-government.

The law of July 21, 1876, ended the remaining Foral rights. Now the Basques would not even have the right to manage their financial affairs. They would pay taxes to the Spanish government and be required to serve in the Spanish military.

To THE BASQUES, culture has always been a political act, the primary demonstration of national identity. One of the keys to Basque survival is that political repression produces cultural revival. The loss of independence in two Carlist wars produced a conscious effort at a cultural rebirth known as the Basque Renaissance. Arturo Campión (1854-1937), a Navarrese writer on the myths and culture of Navarra, in 1884 produced a landmark work on Euskera, *Grammar of the Four Dialects.* Campión wrote that Euskera "is the living witness which guarantees that our national independence will never be enslaved."

In 1891, Resurrección María Azkue, son of a noted poet, wrote a major book on Euskera, *Basque Grammar,* and went on to write an Euskera-French-Spanish dictionary and numerous other pivotal works on the Basque language. He also gathered folk songs and myths, village by village, to use as subjects for huge choral works. He was returning to a tradition started in the fifteenth century by a Guipúzcoan choral master, Johanes Antxieta, who arranged ancient Basque songs for choral works. The Basques are noted for their love of singing. *On chant comme un Basque,* You sing like a Basque, is a French expression for someone who

Choral group in St.-Jean-de-Luz. (Collection of Charles-Paul Gaudin, St.-Jean-de-Luz)

sings loudly, well, and often. By the turn of the century the Basques were again singing like Basques, asserting their Basqueness in choruses that were larger than ever before, performing booming choral works in Euskera for soaring sopranos and chocolaty basses. Choral groups were established in Pamplona, Vitoria, Bilbao, and San Sebastián. The Orfeon Donastiarra, the San Sebastián Lay Choir, founded in 1897, and the Bilbao Choral Society, started the following year, are still performing.

To the Carlists, and to many other Basques, preserving Basqueness was the first step toward regaining the Fueros. It was this concern about the Basque past that led to exploring prehistoric caves—such as Santimamiña cave, found in Vizcaya in 1917—for drawings and artifacts from the Paleolithic Age. Prehistoric discoveries led to assertions about the ancient Basque people in numerous tracts and books written by both French and Spanish Basques. In French Basqueland, that underdeveloped corner of France, ignored by the industrial revolution, where sons whom the farms could not support immigrated to America in large numbers, this cultural reawakening, especially a fascination with the ancient Basque past, was embraced. The invention of Aïtor, the father of the Basques, by Augustin Chaho, who was born in Soule in 1810, was typical of the kind of creative mythologizing of the period.

But of even greater interest on the Spanish side was the recent past. The Fueros became the great martyr of Basque Carlism, and their restoration, a sacred cause. The hymn of a new Basque militancy, "*Gernikako Arbola*," The Tree of Guernica, became to the Basques what the "International" was to Communism, or the "Marseillaise" to the French Revolution. From the Middle Ages until 1876, Basque leaders had met in front of the oak tree at the edge of Guernica. Once the Basques agreed to live under the monarchs of Castile, each king had been obliged to come to Guernica to stand under the tree and pledge continuing support for the Fueros.

Until the nineteenth century when the Fueros were threatened, the meeting spot was a simple place consisting of the tree

The oak of Guernica. (Sabino Arana Foundation, Bilbao)

and an old church. In 1826, a new pillared, neoclassical *Batzar-retxea*, or meeting house, was built. In 1860, the then-300-year-old oak tree died and was immediately replaced with an off-spring that still stands there. José María Iparraguirre, a Carlist volunteer in the first war at the age of thirteen, wrote "Gernikako Arbola" in 1853. He would sing it in unrestrained Euskera with his guitar in cafés. It begins:

| | |
|---|---|
| *Gernikako arbola* | O tree of our Guernica |
| *de bedeincatuba,* | O symbol blessed by God |
| *euskaldunen artean* | Held dear by all euskaldunak |
| *guztiz maitatuba.* | By them revered and loved. |
| *Eman ta zabalzazu* | Ancient and holy symbol |
| *munduban frutuba,* | Let fall thy fruit worldwide |
| *adoratzen zaitugu* | While we in adoration gaze |
| *arbola santuba.* | on thee our blessed tree. |

Spanish authorities responded to the growing popularity of the song by arresting Iparraguirre in Tolosa and expelling him from Spanish Basqueland.

IN 1872, DURING the Second Carlist War, modern Basque nationalism may have accidentally begun when Santiago Arana, a passionate Carlist from Vizcaya, hid a wounded Carlist general, Francisco de Ullíbarri, in his shipyard. Arana was a wealthy industrialist who had purchased arms for the Carlists. When the Liberals learned of the general and the arms, Arana was forced into hiding, abandoning his wife and eight children. Then, fearing capture and interrogation, the family also went into hiding, eventually fleeing to French Basqueland. Sabino, the youngest child, was only seven years old.

Though the family was reunited at the end of the war, life was never the same for the Aranas. Sabino grew up with the weight of the Carlist defeat, a disintegration of family life that had only begun with separation and exile. Santiago's bitterness over the defeat and the abolition of the Fueros made him seem physically and spiritually diminished. Even the family business, shipbuilding, was declining. Basque shipbuilding had reached new heights after the First Carlist War. With the new steel mills along the Nervión, the industry adapted to steel. Huge new shipyards such as La Naval were established along the riverfront. But the Arana family was still building wooden ships.

The two youngest children, Sabino and Luis, were sent off for a Jesuit education. Sabino would later write, "When I was ten years old I felt intense patriotic feelings, only I didn't know what my country was." He questioned why his father had so spent himself on Carlos, a would-be king of Spain. In 1882, according to Sabino, the two brothers were passing the morning talking in the garden, and they slid into a debate. Sabino championed the Carlist point of view, but Luis, echoing the forgotten argument of the slain Carlist Jose Antonio Muñagorri, thought the cause of Don Carlos had nothing to offer Basques. "Vizcaya is not Spain," Luis argued to his brother. This was a deep revelation to Sabino.

The following year, their father as well as an older brother died, and Sabino drifted into a deep depression from which he emerged with an intense interest in the study of Euskera. He wanted to write a book on Euskera grammar, *Elemental Grammar for Vizcayan Euskera*, which could be used to teach the language. He also became convinced that Basques needed to study "the glory of their past in order to understand their current degradation."

But, to please his mother, he studied law in Barcelona. As soon as she died, in 1888, he left law school and returned to the family estate in Vizcaya. That year a professorship of Euskera was created at the Instituto Vizcaíno, and Sabino applied. The winning candidate was Resurrección María Azkue. In second place, was Miguel de Unamuno. Sabino Arana had not attracted a single vote.

FOR TWO MEN who are almost perfect opposites, Sabino Arana y Goiri and Miguel de Unamuno y Jugo had a great deal in common. Both were deeply religious, and both saw the loss of the Fueros, the cataclysm that darkened their childhood, as the great tragedy of their times. Like Arana, Unamuno was devoted to issues of the Basque language and identity. His first book, his university thesis, was *Critique on the Issue of the Origin and Prehistory of the Basque Race*. His early dream, never realized, was to write a twenty-volume history of the Basque people. Both men were born in Vizcaya, Unamuno in Bilbao in 1864 and Arana the following year in a nearby town. The town and the city, Carlism and Liberalism. But in the beginning they did not seem so different. Perhaps their clash was heightened by the fact that neither man was much given to humility.

When older, Unamuno said that in his youth he had been a "staunch nationalist." He used the Euskera word, *bizkaitarra*, that Arana had given to his journal, the first Basque nationalist publication. But it was clear even in his university thesis at age twenty that Unamuno was not a *bizkaitarra*. He was too honest an intellectual to be a true crusader. He was a *contrapelo*, someone who liked to comb his hair against the natural flow. In his *Critique*, he attempted to expose the romantic half-truths, the preposterous myths about Basque origin. Later he would write an essay titled *Ideocracia* about the tyranny of ideas. He declared himself an "ideophobe" who never wanted to see his thoughts turned into a movement.

Sabino Arana did not suffer from this fear of ideas. The tyranny of ideas was to be his kingdom. He did not want to expose myths; he wanted to create them. While Miguel de Unamuno is remembered as one of the greatest intellectuals Spain has

Sabino Arana. (Sabino Arana Foundation, Bilbao)

ever produced, Sabino Arana was a fanatic, perhaps a lunatic, certainly a racist, and a man who spent his life in a hotheaded fury, dying young and absurdly. During a half century Unamuno produced a large body of work, including novels, poetry, and essays; Arana's few writings are seldom read, and he is rarely spoken of with fondness even by his supporters. Yet it is Arana, not Unamuno, who has had the great impact on history. That is partly because Arana, unlike Unamuno, did want to start a movement.

The more Unamuno reflected, the more he turned against Basque nationalism, which he called, in his first novel, *Paz en La Guerra,* "exclusivist regionalism, blind to all broader visions." Typical of middle-class Bilbao, he became a Liberal, and remained one even after that movement had become, by his own admission, irrelevant. He was always proud of his Basqueness, but he concluded that Basques were simply an interesting and valuable element in the greater quilt that was Spain. He regarded Euskera as an inferior language to Spanish, an oral language of peasants, unsuitable for literature, and claimed that agglutinating languages were not capable of articulating sophisticated ideas.

Contemporary writers have proven Unamuno wrong about Euskera. He failed to see how the Basque Renaissance could change the language. Until then, Euskera had not been used as a literary language. But in 1898, a priest named Domingo de Aguirre wrote the first novel in Euskera, *Aunamendiko Lorea* (The Flower of the Pyrenees), a romantic historical story set in the seventh century.

Arana was that dogmatic nationalist, "blind to all broader visions," that Unamuno had described. He had a single idea: that the Basques were a nation and should have a country. In fact, so narrow was his focus that originally he spoke only of his native Vizcaya. But Arana instinctively understood nation building. He reflected on why his nation was not a country and resolved to give it the missing elements. He gave it a name, inventing the word *Euzkadi* from *Euskal,* meaning "Euskera speaking," and the suffix *di,* meaning "together." Before this, Euskera had only the phrase *Euskal Herria* "the land of Euskera speakers." Euskal Herria was the name of a place, but Euzkadi was intended to be the name of a country. Arana invented other important words in Euskera: *aberri,* meaning "fatherland," from *aba,* meaning "father," and *erri,* meaning "country"; *abertzale,* meaning "patriot"; and *azkatasuna,* meaning "liberty." He not only invented new words but changed the spelling of existing ones, to make them look more Basque. The Castilian *c* was replaced with the Basque *k* and the *s* with *z.* He gave Euzkadi a mythology of national origin in works such as *Bizkaya por su Independencia* (For Vizcayan Independence), which mythologizes the medieval struggle for independence of the Basques.

*Bizkaya por su Independencia,* originally published in 1890 as *Cuatro Glorias Patrias* (Four Glorious Acts of Patriotism), is considered the founding act of modern Basque nationalism. Critics argue that it was founded on a lie; supporters would call it simply an embellishment.

Compared with other Basque writing of the nineteenth century, such as Chaho's invention of Aïtor, these four stories of great battles in Vizcaya between the Basques and León and Castile were not outrageous. Arana was not as interested in historical facts as he was in turning these events—the battles of Arrigorriaga in 888, Gordexola in 1355, Otxandiano in 1355, and Munguia in 1470—into epic struggles for the founding of the Basque nation. Complications such as those other Basques, including the Loyolas, who were ready to fight to the death for Castilian privileges, were not to be part of the founding myth. Arana was a propagandist, not a historian, and he understood the importance of simplicity. This was a Basque declaration of independence.

The book ends by asserting that "Yesterday," each of the four places:

> *fought against Spain, which tried to conquer it, and remained free.*
> *Today—Vizcaya is a province of Spain*
> *Tomorrow— . . . . . . . . . . . . . . . . . . . . . . . ?*
> *Heed these words, Vizcayans of the nineteenth century, the future depends on what you do.*

ON JUNE 3, 1893, Arana organized the first public demonstration openly declaring Basque nationalism. His early supporters were mostly young men under twenty-five years old, but his following grew at a rate that sometimes alarmed his adversaries. On July 31, 1895, Ignatius Loyola's Saint's Day, Arana officially founded the Basque Nationalist Party, his underground independence movement.

Arana wrote the Basque national anthem, *"Gora ta Gora,"* though it was set to music only after his death. He worked with his brother Luis on designing the flag, the *ikurriña*, originally for Vizcaya and later as the flag of Euzkadi. The flag established the Basque national colors: red, green, and white. Typical of

Arana, the reasoning behind the flag's design was arcane and alienating, but the reality of it is appealing. According to Arana, the red background symbolized the people, the green *x* stood for the ancient laws, and the white cross, superimposed over it, symbolized the purity of Christ. But what makes the ikurriña work is that it echoes the colors of Basqueland, recalling a red-trimmed, whitewashed Basque house set against a lush green mountain.

ACCORDING TO ARANA, ninth-century Basqueland was "a confederation of republics . . . free and independent, harmoniously and fraternally united." But, like many sons and daughters of old Carlist families, Arana exaggerated the democratic quality of the Fueros.

In some ways, the Fueros were remarkably progressive for medieval law. The revision written in 1526 under Guernica's oak tree was one of the first legal codes to outlaw the use of torture. It was also one of the first European codes to ban debtors' prison. It protected citizens from arbitrary arrest and unwarranted house searches. But contrary to what is often asserted, traditional Basque government was not a representative democracy. It favored rural people and did not give proportional representation to urban dwellers. The code did not give full rights to women but gave women more consideration than most medieval law. For example, inheritance law emphasized keeping an estate intact and favored surviving widows. An older sister had priority over a younger brother. The Fueros were sympathetic to family-owned business and small holdings. When Socialist-led democracy came to power in Spain in 1982, wanting to rewrite property laws to break up large holdings, it looked to the Basque Fueros for a model of property law.

In any event, Arana, who touted the Fueros as the perfection of democracy, did not have a notably high standard of democracy. His ideal was closer to a Catholic theocracy, a notion which traces back at least to 1881, when he was fifteen and had fallen so ill that he was given last rites. Miraculously, he recovered, and ever after he credited the Virgin Mary with this unexpected reversal. His slogan for the Basque Nationalist Party, a motto which is still used, was *Jaungoikua eta Lagizarra,* God and the Old Laws, today frequently abbreviated on official Basque Nationalist Party messages as *JeL.*

Arana wrote that if the Basques were ever to abandon the Church, he would abandon the Basques. He called for Euzkadi to be "an essentially Catholic state" and added, "It will not admit in its midst any individuals affiliated with a false religion, sect, schism, masonic or liberal." In 1888, when he was twenty-three, he learned that a London-based Bible society had obtained permission to sell Protestant books in Bilbao. He applied for permission to distribute Catholic literature next to them, giving his away without charge, until he drove the Protestants out of Bilbao. As for Jews, on the occasion of the death of French writer Emile Zola, Arana wrote a profile describing the hero of the infamous Dreyfus case as *"el nuevo Judas* who got filthy-rich by using his pen to help Jews fight Christ."

ARANA WAS ONE of the first Basques to address a question destined to plague Basque nationalists forever: Who is a Basque? This was an especially contested issue in his epoch because, for the first time in history, a large percentage of the population of Basque country did not come from Basque families. Vizcaya had a labor shortage soon filled by the poor of Spain.

This new and different kind of invasion was one that history had not prepared Basques to face. From 1857 to 1900, the population of Alava grew by only 2.5 percent, which was about the same growth as Navarra. But during the same period, Guipúzcoa's population grew by 25 percent and Vizcaya's by almost 94 percent. For the first time in history, more people were moving to Vizcaya than leaving it.

This immigration to industrial areas tended to further exacerbate the differences between rural and urban life. The countryside was remaining Basque, while the cities were becoming cosmopolitan. In 1850, the population of Bilbao was 20,000. By the end of the century, the population had grown to almost 100,000, more than half of the residents born outside Vizcaya. Some of these outsiders—British, Germans, and other northern Europeans—were entrepreneurs, managers, and supervisors who came with foreign capital. They had a huge impact on the cultural life of Bilbao, especially the British. The Athletic Club of Bilbao, Vizcaya's now-much-loved soccer team, was founded and trained by the British in 1898. Even Arana's ikurriña was modeled on the British Union Jack.

But the great majority of the new residents were workers from Andalusia and other poor regions of Spain. The new wealthy Basque industries were creating jobs that drew desperately poor people. They lived near the mills in dark, crowded housing, often provided by the companies, worked long hours, earned little money, and spent it at company stores. They had no better choice, coming from places that had no work and nothing to eat. Working twelve hour days, breathing black smog, they died young of lung disease or alcoholism.

An underclass was being created in Basqueland, and Basques sneered at it the way societies usually do at poor immigrants. Basques emphasized the foreignness of these workers by referring to them as Chinese, Manchurians, or Koreans. Another popular expression was *maqueto,* later translated into Euskera as *maketo.* This was one of Sabino Arana's favorite words, and, having a Basque explanation for most everything and a creative approach to linguistics, he theorized that it came from *makutuak,* which he said was an Euskera word meaning "those with bundles on their back." However, *magüeto* is a pre-Roman word from northern Spain meaning "outsider," and the Greeks used the word *meteco* to mean "outsider." In 1904, Unamuno wrote, "With mines and industry facilitating the accumulation of great wealth, now is when a change in spirit can be noted. Enterprising and active, yes, but it has made the Bilbaíno unbearable, with his wealth convincing him that he is of a special superior race. He gazes with a certain petulance at other Spaniards, those who are not Basque, if they are poor, calling them contemptuously, *maquetos.*"

If racism is not clear by the use of this word, another Basque term for foreign workers, *belarri motx,* stumpy ear, leaves little doubt. One of the peculiar characteristic of Basques is their long earlobes. But *stumpy ear* was not a term of endearment. In the 1870s there had even been a soldier's song among the Basque Carlists that included the line:

*eta tiro, eta tiro/belarrimotxari*
*And shoot, and shoot/at the stumpy-eared ones*

Arana had several objections to the Stumpy Ears. Until they came, the great majority of the population had spoken Euskera; now, these Spanish workers and their families were turning it into a minority language. This was only the most obvious example of how the Basque culture was being diluted. The Stumpy Ears were also less religious than the Basques, and they were increasingly involved in that anathema antireligious movement—socialism.

Arana's attempts to define who is a Basque make apparent the racist nature of his vision. He declared that for people to be considered Basque, their four grandparents must all have been born in Euskadi and have Euskera names. If married, true Basques must have spouses of similar purity.

This view was not entirely removed from Basque tradition. Normally, to be eligible for a Spanish title of nobility, a family was required to obtain a certificate of "blood purity," which proved that the family had no Jewish or Moorish blood. But since Vizcaya had never been controlled by the Moors, the Spanish waived the requirement for Vizcayans. To preserve this status, the Basques had established rules to bar outsiders from settling in Vizcaya. Of course, as with many Basque laws, there was also a commercial angle: It kept outside competitors from setting up shop in the province.

Arana and his Basque nationalism, like Carlism, idealized peasants, though the ideologues themselves were rarely of peasant background. Basque culture is, in many ways, rural. The etxea, facing the sunrise with the Basque solar cross over the doorway, is a rural concept. And so traditional Basques, even if they live in a city, make reference to a rural origin when they introduce themselves by the name of their ancestral house.

In 1900, Arana married a peasant, Nicole Atxika Iturri, who had little education and little chance of understanding her husband. But Sabino pointed out that his bride fulfilled his definition of Basque with her two Euskera family names. To him, this marriage was a perfect symbolic act, and Sabino cared far more about symbolism than reality. Instead of applauding his uncompromising beliefs, some in the movement feared the cause of Basque nationalism would be harmed by this mismatch. But while everyone else saw an uneducated impoverished girl from a farm, Sabino saw that great institution, the Basque peasant. He protested to a friend, "She is an original Vizcayan—all of the original Vizcayans descend from nobility, all Basques descend from villagers, farmhouses."

Marriage to Sabino, however, was not to be a peasant's fantasy of marrying into the upper class. He ordered his original Vizcayan to cloister herself in religious contemplation to prepare for the marriage. For a honeymoon, he took her to Lourdes, the Catholic shrine near French Basqueland where thousands of infirm peasants flocked for faith healing.

Soon came an event in the life of Spain and the Basques, of

Unamuno and Arana, of singular importance. Americans call it the Spanish-American War, but in Spain it has always been known as El Desastre, the Disaster.

THE SPANISH-AMERICAN WAR, the Disaster, the Cuban War of Independence—it was a different war for different people. But only the United States won. Though the war's boosters in America had promoted it as the war to rescue poor Cuba in its noble struggle against Spanish tyranny, once the new territories of Cuba, Puerto Rico, and the Philippines were taken by military force, the United States had little interest in setting any of them free. In fact, the United States granted Puerto Rico and Cuba less self-government than the Spanish had offered. The new territories were, to the Americans, delicious war booty. Books with titles such as *Our New Possessions* excitedly introduced these prizes to the American public. Meanwhile, the Spanish public had to adapt to suddenly being without these places, the last of the empire that they had known for four centuries. Spain had lost the lands won by Columbus, Magellan, Elcano, and all the other great men reproduced in stone and bronze. The places with which they traded, the places to which a Spaniard went to seek a fortune or adventure, the places to go when things went wrong in Spain, the places that were Spain's claim to being a world power, were gone.

This disaster produced the greatest flow of literature Spain had seen since the period from the mid-fifteenth century to the late sixteenth century known in Spanish literature as the golden age. The new turn-of-the-century writers and artists were called "the generation of '98," a group who responded to El Desastre by seeking to analyze and redefine the newly diminished Spain. Through paintings, novels, poems, and essays, they searched for the essence of Spain in Castilian landscape, in the history of the golden age, in critical examinations of classic lit-

Miguel de Unamuno by Ignacio Zuloaga (1870–1945). Born in Eibar, Zuloaga, with his dark vision of Spain, was one of the leading painters in the generation of '98. (The Hispanic Society of America, New York)

erature such as Cervantes's *Don Quixote de la Mancha.* The pivotal question was: How can Spain undergo a regeneration?

Curiously, this search for the soul of Spain was led by Basques. Experiencing the Spanish simultaneously as both "us" and "them" is essential to discovering the soul of Spain. Castilians, for whom Spain is only "us," are the exception. Unamuno was a central figure in the generation of '98, as was San Sebastián-born Pío Baroja, the doctor-turned-novelist. Lesser-known members of the group, such as Ramiro de Maeztu, were also Basque. A number of the central figures were non-Basque, notably philosopher José Ortega y Gasset and poet Antonio Machado. But even most of these non-Basque writers were not from the Castilian heart of Iberia. Yet Spain, even Castile, was their focus.

It was not the focus of Sabino Arana, who referred to Spain as *Maketania* and said, "It doesn't matter to us if Spain is big or small, strong or weak, rich or poor. They have enslaved our country and this is enough for us to hate them with all our soul, whether we find them at the height of greatness or the edge of ruin." Arana's followers sometimes shouted, even on the streets of Madrid, "Down with the army! Die Spain!"

In truth, the defeat of Spain, perhaps the sight of it shedding territory, inflamed both Basque and Catalan nationalism. It was at this moment in history that both the Basque and Catalan yearnings for nationhood, which had been romantic dreams, developed into serious political movements.

To those other nationalists, the Spanish nationalists, this was an affront never to be forgiven. Spain, the great nation, had gone down in humiliating defeat, and in this dark hour, the Basques and Catalans were attacking, hoping to further amputate the already truncated nation.

The defeated military developed a festering resentment of Catalans and Basques. At their urging, in 1900, the penal code was revised to categorize claims of separatism as acts of rebellion against the state. In 1906, such statements became "a crime against the army" and military justice was given jurisdiction over these cases.

Sabino Arana came to an end, absurdly testing this new and furious rift. In May 1902, he attempted to send a telegraph to Washington:

*Roosevelt. President of the United States. Washington.*

*In the name of the Basque Nationalist Party, I congratulate Cuba, which you have liberated from slavery, most noble federation, on its independence. You have shown in your great nation, exemplary gen-*

*erosity, learned justice and liberty, hitherto unknown in history and inimitable by European powers, especially the Latin ones. If Europe were to imitate this, then the Basque nation, the oldest people, who, for the most centuries, enjoyed the kind of liberty under constitutional law for which the United States merits praise, would be free.*

*Arana y Goiri*

The telegraph office, rather than send it, delivered the telegram to the appropriate authorities, who arrested Arana. Never a healthy man, he had often been arrested and survived short prison terms. But now, at thirty-eight, his health seemed to be finally failing. Arana's supporters circulated a petition asking for his release and got 900 signatures. The response of a government official, Segismundo Moret, was "It would be more gallant to leave him die in prison. The peace of Spain outweighs the life of one man." After almost a half year, his frail health ruined, he was released. Fearing further legal action, he fled through the Roncesvalles pass to St.-Jean-de-Luz. Finishing the writing of a play titled *Libe,* he went to Vichy in the hope that the waters would restore his health.

Arana believed that theater was second only to the press as the best vehicle for propaganda. *Libe* is the story of a woman who chooses to die, rather than be married to a Spaniard.

Only weeks after his release, Arana returned to his home in Vizcaya to die, which he did on November 25, 1903, at the age of thirty-eight. According to legend, his last word was *"Jaungoikua,"* God. On a rainy day he was buried in Sukarrieta, leaving no descendants. His wife remarried a Spanish policeman.

WHILE BASQUE NATIONALISM has grown, its detractors always find Sabino Arana the easiest of targets. Even most nationalists have few illusions about their founding father. Ramón Labayen, like his father and many other family members, a lifelong activist of the Basque Nationalist Party, said, "Sabino Arana was an unpleasant man with no sense of humor. A wealthy man who never worked a day for money."

But Sabino gave the Basques their colors, a flag, a vocabulary, the name of their country, and the political party that would produce many of their future leaders. Though he himself remained a seemingly preposterous figure, he gave credibility to his movement by attracting significant numbers of followers. Ramiro de Maeztu, one of the Basque generation of '98, said of Arana's success, "Unfortunately we can no longer say—and here I am on the side of the Madrid press—that separatism is just four nuts."

It can be argued that it was the times, that between the end of the Fueros and 1898, Basque nationalism would have arrived even without this unpleasant zealot. What is certain, though, is that when Sabino was born, the Basques had a culture and an identity. Thirty-eight years later, when he died, they had the beginnings of a nation. A country was the great unfinished work.

# 9: Gernika

| GERNIKA! | GUERNICA! |
|----------|-----------|
| *Xoratzen iluntzen daut* | This name inflames |
| *hitz horrek bihotza.* | and saddens my heart |
| *Mendek jakinen dute* | Centuries will know its misfortune . . . |
| *haren zorigaitza . . .* | We can no longer say |
| *Numanze ta Kartagoz* | the names Numancia and Carthage |
| *ez gaitezke mintza.* | Without saying in a loud voice |
| *Goraki erran gabe* | In Euskadi, |
| *Euskadin, han, datza:* | lying in its ruins: |
| *GERNIKA!* | GUERNICA! |

*—Jean Diharce, a.k.a. Iratzeder, 1938*

EVEN THOUGH IT BEGAN in 1931 as, at last, Spain's first democracy, only the most optimistic of dreamers could have believed the new Spanish republic would end up well. It was called the Second Republic because there had been a first, but that had only lasted a wink of an eye between dictatorship and monarchy in the nineteenth century.

Today the cause of the Second Republic and that of the Basques are so closely linked that to say someone was a Basque Republican seems redundant. But in 1931, at its birth, the Second Republic had few Basque supporters. Steeped in a traditional leftist ideology, the Republic was too socialist and too anti-Church for most Basques. Across Navarra, including Pamplona, the majority voted against the Republic. The only strong support for the Republic in Basqueland was among the urban population of San Sebastián, Bilbao, and Vitoria.

Carlists were never likely to be Republicans. Their doctrines had far more in common with those of that other twentieth-century Spanish movement, the Falange, or Fascists. Many Carlists

La Pasionaria, Dolores
Ibarruri during the
Spanish Civil War by
David Seymour.
(Magnum Photos, Inc.)

were close to another far-right group, the monarchists. However, Basque Carlists had one fundamental disagreement with both Fascists and monarchists: They wanted Basque self-determination.

On the eternal other side were the Liberals. But they were linked to the industrialists, whose main concern, in addition to resisting the leftist labor movement, was protectionist tariffs for their industries. By the time of the Second Republic, Basque iron fields were already showing signs of decline, but Vizcaya was still producing half of the iron and three-fourths of the steel in Spain. Basque banks controlled one-third of all investment in Spain. Basque industrialists worked closely with Catalan industrialists, not because they shared the issue of local autonomy, but because Catalonia was the only other important industrial center in Spain and the Catalans too wanted to stop the wage-and-working-condition demands of organized labor.

The ruthless capitalism of Vizcayan and Guipúzcoan industrialists produced strong labor movements and Communist and

Socialist parties in those two provinces. Such leftist figures as Vizcaya-born Dolores Ibarruri made up a third group of Basques who passionately supported the Republic. Ibarruri, always dressed in black, with her sculpted Basque face—the strong nose, deep-set eyes—had been a young *sardinera*, a woman who sold sardines from town to town in Vizcaya from a tray carried on her head. Until the twentieth century these women, covering as much as twenty miles in a day, selling on foot, were the primary distrib-

A sardinera in Bermeo, Vizcaya, by David Seymour. (Magnum Photos, Inc.)

utors of fish in Basqueland. Ibarruri had married an Asturian miner and was elected to the Republican legislature as a Communist representing Asturias. During the Spanish Civil War she would become a symbol of the entire Republican cause. Known as La Pasionaria for a speaking style that brought tears to the eyes of thousands of listeners, she turned the World War I battle cry of Verdun, "They shall not pass," into the motto of the Spanish republic. But she and other Basque leftists, for all their Basqueness, had little connection to Basque nationalism, its leaders from elite industrialist families, or its conservative Catholic ideology.

The heirs to Sabino Arana, the Basque Nationalist Party, were avowed enemies of socialism. The party leader, José Antonio Aguirre, once theorized that Basques became socialists when they lost religious faith. In 1931, the Basque Nationalist Party was still racist and anti-Spanish, working toward the day when the Castilian language would no longer be spoken in Euskadi, disapproving of Basques who married Spaniards. Basque nationalism was strongly backed by the Basque Church, which rejected the anticlericism of the Republic and rejected the Spanish language as "the language of Liberalism." The Basque deputies had protested the prevailing anticlericism of the legislative debates on a new constitution for the Second Republic by walking out.

Later that year, after the Republic had been established, General Luis Orgaz, a perennial conspirator for the monarchist cause, having witnessed a Basque nationalist demonstration in Bilbao, tried to persuade José Antonio Aguirre to participate in a coup d'état against the Republic. "If you put at my disposal the 5,000 young Basque nationalists who marched at Deva the other day, I would quickly make myself master of Spain."

The monarchists understood, as did so many of their predecessors, how to obtain Basque cooperation, and a few days later, the exiled King Alfonso sent an envoy to Aguirre with the old proposition: Support us, and we will back the Fueros. "The means of restoring the Fueros are being studied," Aguirre was informed.

But this Basque leader, Aguirre, did not snap at the Fueros being dangled before his eyes. Once rejected, the monarchists reacted with what would prove to be an enduring animosity toward Basque nationalism.

AGUIRRE WAS BORN in Bilbao in 1904, shortly after the death of Sabino Arana. During Aguirre's childhood, Basque culture—language, literature, choral music, and painting—prospered. Like Basque youth of today, Aguirre's generation could express their Basqueness with a natural fluency of both language and culture that thrilled and astounded older, more oppressed and assimilated Basques.

The first *ikastola*, a primary school that taught in Euskera, was opened in San Sebastián in 1914 by Basque nationalists as an alternative to the Spanish-only educational system. Many communities in Guipúzcoa and Vizcaya soon followed. Aguirre's Euskera-speaking parents sent him to Bilbao's first ikastola. Later, like Sabino Arana, Aguirre was educated by Jesuits. Also like Arana, he had come from a traditional Basque industrialist family and he studied law. When his father died, he took over the family business, a chocolate factory called Chocolates Bilbaínos. Aguirre was a handsome man and, though small, a great athlete, a star soccer player for the Athletic Club of Bilbao at a time when soccer was the exciting new sport in the city. Because Aguirre is a very common Basque name—it means "an open field cleared of weeds"—shouting fans distinguished him by the nickname "Aguirre, chocolate maker."

Though his athletic success contributed to his popularity, so did his looks and an undefinable charisma. He is still remembered for such traits as "the liveliness of his eyes" and the quality of his smile. A natural leader, as a teenager he headed the Catholic youth movement. At age seventeen, he joined the still-underground Basque Nationalist Party and became its youth director. Though it may be true, as Pío Baroja once observed, that Basques produce great poets and singers but no great orators, with the exception of Ibarruri who seldom spoke on Basque issues, Aguirre was as close to one as there is in Basque history. In private he had a calm, soft voice that gave little hint of the booming tones of which he was capable. But it was difficult to identify anything in his oratory style that explained his ability to hold the attention of Basque crowds. George Steer, the British correspondent who often covered Aguirre during the Civil War, observed that Aguirre's leading gesture was shoving his hands in his pockets.

But Aguirre could project himself to the world as "the Basque"—not only a Basque speaker, with a Basque face, who could appear in a beret with a *makila*, the Basque walking stick, but someone who contradicted the outside world's Basque stereotypes by being moderate and nonbelligerent.

He was a devout Catholic but believed in a gentle Christianity, disavowing self-proclaimed defenders of the Church such as the Carlists and the Falange. "I dream with all the nostalgia of a Christian," he wrote years later in exile after having endured the assaults of Franco and Hitler, "in the evangelical precepts of the Sermon on the Mount, a return to primitive Christianity which would have nothing in common with the opportunistic and spectacular affiliations with which we Christians rush to disfigure the most august of doctrines."

He also preached a gentler Basque nationalism: "Our nationalism should be universal: if we don't want to become selfish and petty, it should not be turned into a source of discord between peoples." Unlike Arana and many other Basque nationalists, Aguirre never spoke badly of Spain or the Spanish.

In 1931, Aguirre understood that the Republic, for all its leftist anticlericism, might still be friendly to Basque nationalists. The new Republican government had been elected with the nationwide expectation that it would bring Spain into the twentieth century, into Europe. To accomplish this, it needed the Basques and the Catalans, the only Iberians who enjoyed a European standard of living. Catalan nationalists were closer, politically and culturally to the leaders of the new leftist government than were the Basques, and the Catalans had already negotiated their own statute of autonomy at the start of the Republic.

While polarized Spain was splitting even farther apart into a leftist and a rightist camp, Aguirre had the political courage to lead his conservative Basque Nationalist Party toward the leftists in Madrid. Neither the leftists nor the rightists of divided Spain could understand the seeming contradiction of this party—a conservative, pro-business, Catholic movement that in calling for Basque independence was embracing what to other right-wing movements was the worst of all heresies. To this day, the position of the Basque Nationalist Party, known in Spanish as the PNV, is little understood, but it was never more clearly articulated than in 1931, when Aguirre addressed the Cortes in Madrid:

*I am affiliated with the Basque Nationalist Party, founded by Sabino Arana Goiri. The PNV has for a motto:* Jaungoikua eta lagizarra, *God and the ancient laws. In naming God in the first word, we understand that the party wishes to be religious, and in the phraseology of the left and the right, ridiculous phraseology, we have a well defined position: We are Catholics, virile and upright, in a human Catholicism, not a bigoted sentimentality. For us, in this phraseology to which I have alluded, if you are on the right, you are opposed to the legitimate progress of democracy, since it opposes absolute power. If that is what being on the right means, then we are leftists. If being on the right means defending any kind of regime, as long as it is identified with religion, and against the absolute separation of powers of church and state, than we are leftists. And if by being rightist, it is understood that in social matters we oppose progress for the working class, if that is what is meant by being on the right, then we are leftists. But, on the other hand, if to be a leftist means we are going to be against family, against the holy principles of the Catholic Church, whose rules we observe, then in this phraseology which I find ridiculous, we are right-wingers.*

THE NEGOTIATIONS FOR a Basque autonomy statute were difficult. The composition of the Republican government was constantly shifting, and becoming more authoritarian, less friendly to regional autonomy. In 1934, Madrid reduced the Basque tax-levying rights and, realizing the angry reaction this would probably provoke, canceled Basque municipal elections.

But then, on July 18, 1936, something happened that turned negotiations in the Basques' favor—a coup d'état attempt.

The conspirators were not simply Fascists. Francisco Franco, who because of both political and military skills gradually came to be the leader of the uprising, was not a member of the Fascist movement. Because Franco was so nimble with ideologies, because he managed to direct a diverse coalition, not only of Fascists but of Carlists, monarchists, rightists, and clergy, historians have labeled his side in the Civil War after their founding act—the Rebels. His adversaries, those who refused to go along with his attempted putsch, have been labeled the Loyalists.

The uprising was largely a failure. Most senior officers remained loyal to the Republic, as did the great majority of the Spanish population. But the Assault Guard and the Guardia Civil were solidly behind the uprising, and in areas where these two armed factions were strong—a few pockets of the south and in Galicia and León in the north—the rebels prevailed. In Catalonia the Guardia Civil remained loyal, and the rebellion failed. Vizcaya and Guipúzcoa were safe because Aguirre, having foreseen the questionable loyalty of the Assault Guard and Guardia Civil, had managed to have them both disbanded in his region before the rebellion had occurred.

But the rebels did succeed in splitting the two Basques. Alava and Navarra supported the coup. Through the strange contortions of Spanish history, the Guardia Civil, which had been established to repress Carlist veterans was now allied with the Carlists, for whom the Republic was an unbearable assault on the Catholic Church. The Carlist stronghold, Navarra, may have been the zone where the rebels enjoyed the most solid backing.

The day after the coup, the two generals who had best established themselves were Francisco Franco, who ruled by terror with Moroccan tribal troops who looted towns, killed any men they captured, raped any women, and left behind sexually mutilated corpses, and General Emilio Mola, who took Navarra by popular acclaim. Mola was cheered in Pamplona, with Carlists lining the streets shouting "Long live Christ the King." It was the kind of Catholicism from which Aguirre had tried to disassociate himself.

Securely behind rebel lines was Miguel de Unamuno, now seventy-two, master of sixteen languages—according to legend, he learned Danish because he wanted to read Kierkegaard—the venerated leading intellectual of Spain. He was professor of classical languages and rector of the university in rebel-held Salamanca. Franco's headquarters was in the nearby bishop's palace. Columbus Day, or "the day of the race," as the newly empowered Spanish ultranationalists liked to call it, was observed in October 1936 at the University of Salamanca. A war hero was on the dais: General José Millán Astray of the Foreign Legion, veteran of too many Moroccan colonial campaigns, some fingers missing from his one remaining arm and wearing an eye patch. Also present was Salamanca bishop Enrique Plá y Deniel, who had taken to calling the Fascist rebellion "a crusade"; Doña Carmen, the wife of Franco; and assorted other Fascists and monarchists.

*185*

And with them, officially taking the place of General Franco, who was unable to attend, sat the slender, gray-bearded, bespectacled Rector Unamuno.

He didn't want to be there, but he had gotten himself into this unlikely position. Many of the generation of '98, including Pío Baroja, initially supported the Republic. But Unamuno, who had opposed the previous dictatorship, refused to support the new republic that had allowed him back into Spain from political exile. He had reached the height of his international fame by opposing the dictatorship. The daring rescue of Unamuno from prison in the Canary Islands by means of a boat sent by a Paris newspaper, *Le Quotidien,* had been covered by much of the international press including the *New York Times.* But once back in Spain, Unamuno, the international literary hero, had openly admired leaders of the Falange and even contributed money to the Fascist cause. Several months after the rebellion, the ideophobic intellectual began to realize that he had made a mistake. He called the uprising "an epidemic of madness." The previous week he had visited General Franco to plead, without success, for the release of several of his friends whom Franco's forces had taken prisoner.

After numerous rousing speeches on Spain's lost imperialist glory, Professor Francisco Maldonado, perhaps forgetting in whose company he was speaking, told of Spain's epic struggle to preserve traditional values against the scourges of contemporary Spain: the reds, the Catalans, and the Basques. The Catalans and the Basques, argued Maldonado, were "cancers in the body of the nation." Fascism was the surgeon that would cut into the body and exterminate these cancers. From the back of the university hall came a seemingly spontaneous cry, the slogan of the Foreign Legion, *"Viva la muerte!"* Long live death. What remained of Millán Astray, the battered Legion commander, then shouted *"España!"* to which he received the formulaic reply *"Una!"* The general shouted again, "Spain!" and got the reply "Great!" and to the third round the audience shouted back "Free!"

Several young, dark-shirted Fascists, stirred beyond self-control, rose, and facing photographs of Franco above the dais, gave the stiff-armed Fascist salute.

The room fell silent. It was time for the rector to close the meeting. But what would he say to all of this?

His exact words are unknown, because the press, which reported all of the other speeches the following day, made no mention of Unamuno's words. But a number of accounts were later pieced together by historians of the Spanish Civil War.

Among other remarks, he said, "Let us waive the personal affront implied in the sudden outburst of vituperation against the Basques and the Catalans. I was myself, of course, born in Bilbao. The bishop, whether he likes it or not, is a Catalan from Barcelona."

He turned to watch the bishop squirm. According to some versions, he now faced Millán Astray and said, "I am a Basque, and I have spent my life teaching you the Spanish language which you do not know."

But that was not enough. "Just now, I heard a necrophilistic and senseless cry: 'Long live death.' And I, who have spent my life shaping paradoxes which have aroused the uncomprehending anger of others, I have to tell you, as an expert, that this outlandish paradox is repellent to me. General Millán Astray is a cripple."

He corrected himself: "Let's say it without any pejorative undertone. He is a war invalid. So was Cervantes. Unfortunately, there are too many cripples in Spain just now. Soon there will be even more, if God does not come to our aid. It pains me to think that General Millán Astray should dictate the pattern of mass psychology. A cripple, who lacks the spiritual greatness of a Cervantes, is likely to seek ominous relief in causing mutilation around him."

The general had heard enough. *"Mueran los intellectuales!"*
Death to intellectuals, he shouted. Falangists boisterously approved. Unamuno went on to explain: "You will win, because you have more than enough brute force. But you will not convince."
His words were prophetic.

Had it not been 1936 in Spain, this farce might have been remembered as a comic moment. But this was the end of Miguel de Unamuno, a sad end for the Basque who loved Spain. Franco's wife escorted him out of the hall where he was being booed, while the general's men angrily trained weapons on him. He lost his university position and spent the remaining months of his life at home, rarely going outside, isolated, ostracized, and guarded. He died in December.

A large number of Falangists attended his funeral. In the 1960s, Franco was still expressing his annoyance with Unamuno over the incident. But in the official school primer for the third grade level, from which all schoolchildren learned Spanish history and culture in the 1960s, only four Basques are mentioned: Ignatius Loyola, Francis Xavier, Sancho III, king of Navarra who fought the infidels, and Don Miguel de Unamuno. The second-level book mentions only two: Felix María Samaniego from Alavan Rioja, who, children were taught, traveled a great deal and "corrupted his soul" but "at the end of his life repented and died a good Christian," and Zumalacárregui, who died for Don Carlos. With none of the six was it mentioned that the man was Basque. About Unamuno, the primer said, "He was born in Bilbao in 1863. Professor and rector of the University of Salamanca for so many years, it could be said that Unamuno was a Salamancan. His style was proper, energetic, and impassioned."

IN DESPERATE NEED of support, the beleaguered Republic at last came to terms with the Basques on a statute of autonomy. Navarra, under rebel control, narrowly rejected the proposed autonomy. The other three provinces approved it by 459,000

votes in favor to 14,000 opposed. The statute even got the maketo vote. The results were approved by the Cortes on October 1,
1936, the day the rebels declared Francisco Franco head of state.

In accepting the statute, Aguirre had made clear that it was
only a "partial" victory, that the statute did not restore all the
autonomy of the Fueros and that more would be demanded
later. But for the moment, he pledged, "Until Fascism is defeated,
Basque Nationalism will remain at its post." Through horrors,
defeat, and exile, he would steadfastly keep that promise.

On October 7, a Basque government was installed with
Aguirre as *lehendakari*, leader. The vote for the thirty-two-year-
old Basque Nationalist Party mayor of Getxo was unanimous.

Even the leftist representatives of the Spanish Socialist Workers
Party and the Popular Front supported him. Explaining his youth,
Aguirre later wrote, "The oldest people of Europe had on that
day a 32-year-old head-of-government, as though to demonstrate
that the years do not age a nation that remains young in its faith
and hope."

He took his oath under the oak tree at Guernica, saying in
Euskera,

> *Humble before God*
> *Standing on Basque soil*
> *In remembrance of Basque ancestors*
> *Under the tree of Guernica, I swear*
> *to faithfully fulfill my commission.*

It was a historic moment, one that had been dreamed of for several generations: the lehendakari, heir to Sabino Arana's under
ground movement, standing in public, under the oak, pledging
in Euskera to serve a Basque government.

And that is the way it is remembered. But the event was
thickly veined with ominous signs. It is forgotten that the participants slipped into Guernica in secrecy, fearing an attack from

armed Fascists who had been spotted in the mountains less than thirty miles from Bilbao. Days before the ceremony, the government-elect had procured arms and ammunition to put down the rebellion, purchased with gold from the Banco de Vizcaya. During the ceremony, a lookout was placed in a tower to warn the participants in the event of an attack.

There is a dreamlike quality to the 1936 Basque government, the fulfillment of a historic longing that was to be crushed only nine months later in carnage the scale of which had never before been seen on Earth. Aguirre, a man said to have perfect manners, who never made decisions without listening to his ministers, gave the appearance of a "good guy" struggling against the Fascist enemy, who so clearly appeared to be "bad guys." Because the government lasted only nine months, snuffed out while still on its honeymoon, there was not time to go astray the way governments do, and so for decades it was remembered that in the worst of times there were nine months of good Basque government.

As soon as the Autonomous Basque Government was formed, it was ready with ideas for a budget, taxation, and extensive cultural and educational programs. For the first time in history, a Basque government ruled with a policy of promoting the Basque language. Even the Fueros of the Middle Ages had been written in Spanish, and Foral administration had encouraged the use of the Castilian language as a sign of culture and learning. But in 1936, the Basque Renaissance was in its sixtieth year. Ikastolas were well supplied with textbooks and dictionaries. In 1918, the Basque Academy of Language had been founded, and it was working on defining a standard Euskera from its eight spoken dialects. The new government's cultural policy pursued what was called the "Sabinian school of Bascology," following the linguistic ideas of Arana, which rejected Latin words and even Latin letters. *C* was changed to *k*, *ch* to *tx*, *v* to *b*, and *s* to *z*.

The Association of Basque Schools was formed with paral-

Official portrait from the swearing in of Aguirre as *lehendakari*. The oath, in Euskera, is printed on the portrait. (Sabino Arana Foundation, Bilbao)

lel organizations for Basque teachers and for Basque students. Publishing houses were established for nationalist books. In 1935, the Basque Nationalist Party published for the *Juventud Vasco de Bilbao*, the youth group headed by Aguirre, an official biography of Sabino Arana. The author, Ceferino de Jemein, presented in biblical Spanish the life of a saint. The darker sides of Sabino were carefully airbrushed. The book of some 200 pages spared no expense, from its green, red, gold, and chocolate Art Deco endpapers, to hundreds of photographs, etchings, and color reproductions of old Carlists, including several portraits of Tomás Zumalacárregui, numerous photographs of Carlist units in Vizcaya during the second war, documents and photos of Arana's life, a reproduction of Sabino and Luis's rough design for the ikurriña, and ending with 1930s photographs of rallies in support of the Basque autonomy statute.

Children who grew up in the 1930s in Basque Nationalist Party homes studied the Jemein book like a bible and revered the name Sabino Arana—not the troubling memory of the actual nineteenth-century man, but the Basque saint created in the twentieth century by Ceferino de Jemein and the Basque Nationalist Party. Anton Aurre, today president of the Sabino Arana Foundation, a key cultural wing of the modern Basque Nationalist Party, was born in 1933, in Aiangiz, a village near Guernica. Until Franco established his regime when Aurre was six years old, he lived in a completely Euskera-speaking world. "Sabino Arana was a constant reference. His photographs were around the house and there were wooden carvings of his likeness. As children, we use to do drawings copying photographs of him."

A flowering of Euskera poetry in the 1930s was led by José María Aguirre, known as Lizardi, who died in 1933, and Esteban de Urquizu, known as Lauaxeta, who worked directly for the Basque Nationalist Party. Euskera theater, traditional dancing, and Basque choirs became popular entertainment. Basque sports, not only the always popular pelota but regattas, wagon lifting, sheep fighting, tug-of-war rope contests, wood chopping—the entire array of ancient rural Basque sports, once again drew enthusiastic crowds. The Basque Nationalist Party published its own sports magazine, which was widely read throughout Spain.

But the Basque government had come to power at the outbreak of a war, and one of the primary challenges facing the new government was to ensure public order through the creation of a Basque police force, known by the traditional Euskera name, the *Ertzantza*. Telesforo de Monzón, the new Basque minister of the interior, was in charge of the force. Monzón, an aristocrat from Guipúzcoa, the same age as Aguirre, was one of the most hated figures among Basque haters, especially the Fascists. He was well known because he had been a Basque Nationalist Party deputy in the Cortes. The Fascists hated the idea of a Basque nationalist aristocrat—someone whose last name was a Castilian title, who had enormous landholdings in Guipúzcoa and an elegant family estate in Vergara, as well as an unmistakably upper-class bearing and accent, and yet was a nationalist of strong conviction, author of patriotic songs. In Basque nationalist circles, he was known as a pleasant young man who loved arguing about affairs of state.

Monzón organized the police very quickly, recruiting from among pelota players, boxers, and other athletes, mostly from Basque Nationalist Party families. Monzón created Spain's first motorized police force, under the direction of José María Pikazar, an aeronautic and electrical engineer who had studied police forces in Britain, France, Germany, and the United States. Pikazar recruited 400 men to do a kind of policing never seen before in Spain. Originally, they were to be issued patrol cars, but when the war made this impossible, many were supplied with fast motorcycles instead. Modeled after American police, they communicated by wireless radio. Dressed in brown leather jackets, caps, knee breeches, and high boots, armed with revolvers, they swiftly maintained order even when Vizcaya was on the verge of panic. Finally, their skills were enlisted in the war effort because they could intercept enemy communications on their radios and could rapidly dispatch orders to the front by motorcycle.

OF THE TWENTY-ONE major-generals on active service in the Spanish military, Franco was one of only four who were not loyal to the Republic. A squeaky-voiced, insecure little man, forty-four years old, Franco had an ability to lead and inspire that is hard to explain. Perhaps it was his confidence, his almost naive belief in his ability to prevail. Among his few admirable qualities, he had demonstrated great physical courage as a young officer in the endless Moroccan war. With a keen sense of the power of terror and little knowledge of modern warfare, he loved bayonet charges, because they were frightening. He was both ruthless and heartless, using fear as his favorite weapon. As a field officer, leading charges, mounted on a white horse, he was known for brutality both in Morocco and, in 1917, when he was in command of one of the units putting down a miners' strike in Asturias.

Franco had cunning rather than analytic intelligence, and an instinct for self-preservation rather than an ideology. He was capable of the most dramatic reversals, if they served his needs, fawning over Hitler when he thought Germany would win and then becoming pro-American to save himself. Acutely sensitive to symbolism, he wore clothes that reflected complex alliances and fantasies. When in the north, he often wore the red beret of Carlism, with the black shirt of fascism, and sometimes added a white admiral's jacket.

He had never been in the navy but had always wanted to be. Born in a military town in Galicia, he had been prevented by navy cutbacks caused by the "Disaster of 1898" from pursuing a naval career. His obsession with 1898 was typical of his generation of military. He talked about El Desastre regularly throughout his long life. It was for him a source of deep anti-American sentiments, as well as hatred for Basque and Catalan nationalists. In his 1960s school primer, the loss of Cuba and the Philippines is presented as an American plot. In the question section that follows this discussion, the student is asked: "What country caused the defeat in Cuba?" The United States, the student was supposed to answer.

In the winter of 1937, the campaign was going badly for the rebels, and the Vatican urged Franco to seek a negotiated peace. It was suggested that at the least, he might be able to make peace with the Basques, since they were such devout Catholics. Given the Basque history of negotiating, this might have worked. Many Basque nationalists saw the Republic as simply another government in Madrid. Luis Arana, Sabino's now aging brother, saw the conflict as the problem of foreigners, of Spaniards. Still sounding like the Carlist general Muñagorri, he asked, "What do we owe to this fight which is not ours, that is not about our race, that is not about our ideology?"

But Franco told the Vatican that he would not negotiate, since such an agreement would simply defer the problem. The only possible solution to the Basque problem, according to Franco, was the complete annihilation of Basque nationalists. Mola, commanding a northern army from Navarra, and German general Hugo Sperrle urged an assault on Bilbao.

Franco had courted the Germans, and they had sent troops, planes, and weapons. But German officers, including Sperrle, were not pleased with the way these resources were being used. Investigating Franco's failure to take Madrid in the fall of 1936, they found that he had little understanding of how to deploy ground forces in coordination with the air force that, thanks to the Germans and the Italians, he had at his disposal. Franco was a tactician for the nineteenth century, but there were to be no more calvary charges or officers on white horses.

As a condition for continued support, the Germans insisted on a consolidation of all German forces, known as the Condor Legion, under Sperrle's command. Once Franco agreed to this, a war machine of which he had little understanding arrived in Spain. It included the newest German bombers and fighter planes, tanks and motorized artillery, and an additional 12,000 troops, including armored, artillery, and air force units. A twentieth-century force arrived to fight a nineteenth-century civil war.

On March 24-26, 1937, the campaign was plotted by Francoist air force and ground troop commanders, Mola's chief of staff, and the Condor Legion's chief of staff, Colonel Wolfram von Richthofen, cousin of the World War I ace known as "the Red Baron." Richthofen explained to the Spanish how aircraft could be used to destroy the morale of the enemy before a ground assault. The commanders arranged for close coordination between ground and air forces and agreed that no attempt was to be made to spare civilians. Italian troops as well as Requetés,

Navarrese units, were included in the battle plan. Once again, Basques would fight Basques.

How were the Basques preparing for the first full-scale assault by a mechanized, ground and air, twentieth-century army?

In Guipúzcoa the militia that was formed clearly confused warfare with Hollywood romanticism. They armed themselves with revolvers—an almost useless weapon in combat—holstered to their hips, and many sported checked wool shirts and red bandanas. They were Basque cowboys going to war. When the rebels showed off the fire-power of their Italian airplanes and the heavy artillery from ships at sea and threatened to destroy the beautiful resort of San Sebastián unless the population surrendered immediately, the loyal locals raided the better hotels and took vacationing fascist sympathizers hostage, creating a standoff that saved the city. As warfare spread along the Bidasoa in view of the French side, the French Basques along the border rented telescopes, binoculars, and rooms on upper floors with a view.

But warfare does not stay picturesque for long and within weeks these same towns were crammed with refugees. In Hendaye, anxious parents went from hotel to crowded hotel looking for scraps of news from the besieged towns where their sons were fighting.

As the twentieth century came to a close, Juan José Rementeria, a tall, fit-looking Basque who wore a dark blue beret, was living in Guernica. Though he appeared to be no more than sixty-five years old, he was born in 1910, in the nearby town of Muxica. Coming from a Basque Nationalist Party family, he was one of the many who heard Aguirre's call to defend Vizcaya. He was given a single-shot, bolt-action rifle and five cartridges for ammunition. He never did learn the make of the weapon. He had no military training. "We should have had some training," he said, "but there was no time."

The Basque arms industry made small arms, grenades, and

munitions, but no bombs. The Basques avenged one of the first air attacks by dropping rocks on enemy troops.

"IF SUBMISSION IS NOT immediate, I will raze Vizcaya to the ground, beginning with the industries of war. I have the means to do so," declared Mola in a March 31 broadcast, the text of which was dropped in leaflets from airplanes. But he did not begin with industry. He began using artillery and aerial bombardment to destroy Durango, a rural town by the jagged, rocky gray crests of southern Vizcaya. And so began this new kind of warfare, a war waged against civilians. Durango was a town of ancient churches, rambling cobblestone streets with a river running through it lined by buildings with flower boxes. Once during the Carlist wars, it had served as Don Carlos' headquarters. This traditional town was attacked at 7:20 A.M. while the churches were filled for mass. The air raid lasted thirty minutes. Two hundred and fifty-eight civilians were killed. Franco's headquarters in Salamanca denied that the attack had taken place. But Durango was undeniably leveled. The Basques must have done it to themselves, headquarters explained to the international press. Communists must have attacked the churches and killed worshippers, they claimed.

The Germans were still displeased with their ally. After three days of attack, little ground had been taken. Mola proposed destroying the factories in Bilbao. The Germans asked him why he would do this, when he needed the industry and would soon capture it. Mola's reply to this pragmatic German question was redolent with all the festering hatreds of nineteenth-century Spain. First was the military resentment of Basques and Catalans: "Spain is totally dominated by the industrial centers of Bilbao and Barcelona. Under such domination, Spain can never be set right." Then came the Carlist hatred of urban industry: "Spain has got too many industries which only produce discontent."

It seems never to have occurred to Mola how a war machine

such as the one placed in his hands was built and maintained. Sperrle replied that he would only bomb industries under direct and specific orders from Franco. But Franco wanted to preserve the industry for his future use. While the commanders argued over targets, an air and artillery campaign of terror was moving across Vizcaya. Franco and Mola had expected a three-week campaign. But they had not understood the determination of Basque resistance nor the long Basque history as outnumbered guerrilla fighters. All the Basques could do was retreat, but they did so slowly and made every foot of territory cost rebel lives.

Franco was perplexed at why this dazzling new force, more power than he had ever imagined commanding, made such slow progress. The Germans too were perplexed. After Durango, Ochandiano was bombed. As the ground forces advanced, town after village was destroyed. The Germans were trying a new tactic of warfare that could later be used elsewhere in Europe. But it wasn't working. Basque history and character had not been factored into the German equation. To the Basques, the bombardment was new and it was terrifying, but it was not breaking their morale. To the Basques, this was a new variation on an old story—the invader, more numerous and better armed, trying to take their land.

Frustrated by the slowness of their advance, Mola and Franco's headquarters started talking about razing Bilbao. The army was bogged down, but the air force could chose its targets with impunity because the Basques had little defense against airplanes. At command centers, angry Spanish and German officers looked at maps to pick the town to destroy next.

The Basques, with their bolt-action rifles, having been pounded daily by artillery and aircraft, were in an increasingly disorganized retreat in the Guernica area. Franco, Mola, and the Germans agreed on the need to cut off the Basque retreat. But they wanted more than that tactical victory. They wanted to carry out Mola's threat, to symbolically "raze Vizcaya." Later, all parties tried to distance themselves from the decision, but given the scale of the operation, it is all but certain that the attack on Guernica, like all other attacks in the Basque campaign, was a joint decision of Franco, Mola, the Germans, and the Italians.

GUERNICA WAS, AND still is, a market town where the farmers of the region sell their produce on Mondays along the riverfront in the center of the medieval town of stone buildings. The Basque government had suspended the market because of the war, but the peasants had to sell their products. Not only did the attackers choose a market day, Monday, April 26, 1937, but they began their attack at 4:40 P.M. when the center of town was bursting with peasants displaying the first crops of spring carried in ox-drawn carts, with livestock, with shoppers from throughout the area, and with war refugees whose homes in other Basque towns had been bombed.

A church bell warned of approaching planes. There had been such warnings before, but Guernica had never been hit. One Heinkel 111, a new bomber just developed by the Germans for speed and payload, flew in low from the mountains. Since Guernica had no air defenses, low-altitude daylight bombing, the ideal situation for accuracy, posed no danger to attacking aircraft. The plane dropped its bombs and flew away and returned with three more of the new Heinkels. Then came a sort of deadly air show, displaying all that was new in German and Italian attack aircraft: twenty-three Junkers, Ju 52s, the old bombers that the Heinkels were to replace, appeared along with the four Heinkel 111s, three Savoia-Marchetti S81s, one of the new, fast Dornier Do 17s, a bomber so sleek the Germans called it "the flying pencil," twelve Fiat CR32s, and, according to some reports, the first Messerschmitt BF 109s ever used. This new fighter was a marvel of modern warfare, flying up to 350 miles an hour with bulletproof fuel tanks and a 400-mile range.

In the preceding months, only three of the old Ju 52 bombers, flying tight, low formation in the Vizcayan sky, their triple engines thundering, had terrified civilians below.

The Germans and Italians had unveiled their new modern air force with the market in Guernica as its only target. The bombers dropped an unusual payload, splinter and incendiary bombs, a cocktail of shrapnel and flame personally selected by Richthofen for maximum destruction to buildings. As people fled, the fighters came in low and chased them down with heavy-caliber machine guns.

At 7:45 the planes disappeared, leaving the blackened forms of the few remaining walls silhouetted against the bursting flames, which glowed into the night sky.

The cratered streets were cluttered with the entrails of bombed out buildings—blackened bricks and twisted wires and pipes. In the rubble were the charred corpses of people, sheep, and oxen. The Basque government estimated that 1,645 people were killed in the three-hour attack. Guernica's population was only 7,000, though between refugees and the market, there may have been another 3,000 people in town that afternoon. The only ones who had a chance to accurately count casualties were Franco's troops, who occupied the town three days later. Records of what they found have never been released. At first they said it never happened. Later, they admitted to possibly two hundred casualties. But given the intensity of the attack and the population of the town, the number of dead must have been far higher than the 258 deaths in the much briefer bombing of Durango.

Fortunately, four foreign journalists—three British and one Belgian—were in the area. George Steer, correspondent for the *Times* of London, filed a story that ran two days later in both his paper and the *New York Times*. The world was horrified—outraged at the ruthless massacre of unarmed civilians but also terrified at its first glimpse of the warfare of the future.

Pablo Picasso, commissioned to paint a mural for the Spanish pavillion of the 1937 Paris World's Fair, chose as his subject the horror of the Guernica bombing. Europeans began to realize that the Germans could attack their cities in the same way they did Guernica. George Steer pointed out that a similar raid could level the North Sea port of Hull or Portsmouth. Too late, the British government started to understand that the fate of the Basques was directly relevant to its own security. The Germans were only practicing in Spain. Even the Catholic Church in Spain showed signs of being less comfortable with their Fascist defenders after Guernica, and there was evidence of declining morale in Franco's troops.

From Franco's office a statement came explaining that due to bad weather, the planes under his command had been unable to fly on April 26, and therefore the attack could not have been theirs. As for the Germans and Italians, Franco's headquarters explained that no foreign aircraft were in the territory they held. He presented as proof a flight log, but it was for the wrong day.

It didn't work. There were thousands of witnesses. Franco arrived at an explanation. The Basques had dynamited and set fire to their own city, just as, according to him, they had done in Durango.

Franco's staff tried to give controlled press tours of the destroyed and occupied town. James Holburn, Steer's colleague who covered the Francoist side for the London *Times,* reported that the craters he inspected were caused by "exploding mines." But Franco's troops could not stop the weary survivors from talking. A London *Sunday Times* correspondent, in the presence of a Francoist press official, went up to an elderly man who was slowly removing bricks from the interior of his ruined home. He asked him who had done this and the man replied, "Italians and Germans." The press officer explained that the man was "a Red." Others told the same story, that the town was bombed for hours by Germans and Italians. "Guernica is full of Reds," was the only official explanation for this testimony. But one frustrated officer finally said, "Of course it was bombed. We bombed it, and bombed it, and bombed it and, *bueno*, why not."

George Steer was informed that if he were captured by Franco's troops, they intended to shoot him for the stories he had been writing. Steer started carrying a machine pistol with him though he later admitted that he never fired it and, like many of the Basque troops, no one had ever explained to him how to operate his weapon.

Even today there are people who remember what happened at Guernica. Anton Aurre says he remembers very well, though he was only four years old. He remembers it as a beautiful, clear April day.

> *I remember you could see the heads of the flyers. You could see they were German planes, see the numbers, the pilots, everything.*
>
> *Then there was a huge explosion. It was the beginning of the bombing. We could see the fire in Guernica. You could hear them machine gunning. They came in groups of three. I don't know how many or if the same ones kept coming back, but always three at a time.*
>
> *We could see the fires all night. The next day we went in to town. There were holes in the street. I could stand in them and they were higher than my head. The town was still burning in some places and there were corpses in the street.*

It was a warm spring, and Aurre's father was among the volunteers who buried hundreds of mangled and decomposing corpses. Anton remembers his father acting strangely and being told that his father was ill. All Anton remembers of this illness was that his father was very quiet and did not eat for a week.

Others remember that the incendiary bombs gave off a sapphire blue light when they exploded, that people were running through the streets screaming, fleeing the town and getting machine-gunned on the mountain slopes as the planes circled back, over and over again.

Juan José Rementeria was fighting in the defenses outside

Guernica, after the attack, the night of April 26, 1937, photographed by the Basque Government. (Sabino Arana Foundation, Bilbao)

Bilbao when he heard that Guernica was bombed. "We came back during the night. There was almost nothing left of Guernica and we took trucks and loaded survivors and their furniture and moved them to Asturias."

In 1970, Franco's government admitted for the first time that Guernica was bombed from the air. In 1998, the German government finally apologized to the Basque people, but the Spanish government never has, and it continues to deny Basques access to military records of the incident. In 1999, the Spanish legislature passed a resolution admitting that Franco had lied about Guernica.

THE BASQUES WERE still fighting. Rementeria went back to defend Bilbao. "Everybody thinks it was over with Guernica but it wasn't. There were a lot of fronts, we went to them and fought on."

In the rubble that was Guernica at the end of April 1937, the ancient stone bridge over the river remained intact, as did a few archways in the center of town. The rest was blackened heaps and collapsing walls. But at the edge of town where the mountains begin, a pillared nineteenth-century building still stood, with a straight oak tree in front. In the days after the bombing hundreds of homeless survivors, mostly women, gathered in front of the oak, sleeping on mattresses soaked from the effort to put out the fires. George Steer and other correspondents listened to their stories. "They conversed in tired gestures and words unnaturally short for Spain," Steer later reported. "And they made the funny noises of bombers poising, fighters machine-gunning, bombs bursting, houses falling, the tubes of fire spurting and spilling over the town. Such was the weary, sore-eyed testimony of the people of Guernica, and it was only later that people who were never in Guernica thought of other stories to tell."

The pillared building with the oak tree in front of it are

both still standing. Farther up the mountain, Juan José Rementeria can see the top of the tree from his apartment window.

Among the mysteries surrounding the attack is the question: Why Guernica? Many believe it was because of its symbolic importance. Yet the oak was not touched. Some theorize that the Requetés, the Navarrese troops, had asked the command not to damage that place. Or maybe it was just missed because it was at the edge of town. Maybe the Germans, not knowing Basque history, thought it was just a tree.

# 10: The Potato Time

*Silent and antisocial, if the Basques want to communicate
with others, they sing.*
*—Pío Baroja,* FANTASÍAS VASCAS

THE BASQUES HUNG ON, dug in around Bilbao, fiercely and futile-
ly defending every foot of ground. Unlike the Carlist sieges of
the last century, little olive oil was left, nor was milk or meat.
The only plentiful food was Mexican chick peas. In the old Basque
tradition, Bilbao controlled the import of Mexican chick peas for
all of Spain and when war broke out the warehouses were packed
with the nation's supply.

A British destroyer flotilla based in St. Jean-de-Luz, careful
not to compromise neutrality by carrying any implements of
war, tried to bring food into the city. The Basque government
procured a supply of grain and started making state bread, a
heavy, bitter, dark bread which offered a maximum of nutrition
by including all parts of the grain. The Basques were not accustomed to this type of dark whole wheat bread and it was popularly believed to be toxic. Among the alleged side effects, it was
said to cause miscarriages in pregnant women and madness in
men. But the ten-day food ration was a pound of rice, a pound
of chick peas, a pound of vegetables, and a half pound of cooking
oil per person. Bilbao was crowded with refugees from the cities
and towns already destroyed. Not only Guernica and Durango
but Eibar, Munguia, Muxica, Elgeta, Markina, Bolibar, Arbacegui,
Yurre, Castillo y Eleijabeitia, Amorebieta, Lemona, Fika, Rigoitia,
and Galdakano had all been destroyed or seriously damaged
from bombing. Many of the survivors had fled to Bilbao.

According to George Steer, domestic cats became a source

of meat. It had long been rumored that cat was a peacetime delicacy in the poorest neighborhoods of Bilbao. Steer even supplied the following recipe:

*First, the cat was caught, then laid in salt for twenty-four hours, then basted. A magnificent sauce of sherry and mushrooms and various spices was then prepared to drown the last carnivorous flavors of pussy, and the whole was said to resemble jugged hare, and even in the case of plump lady cats to give jugged hare points and a beating.*
—*George Steer,* THE TREE OF GUERNICA, *1938*

But the correspondent, who termed chick peas "the yellow menace" complained that by January 1937 cat Bilbaíno was not the same anymore. There was no longer any salt or sherry and anyone who could find mushrooms ate them immediately.

People looked to the sky, not only fearing attacks but hoping that the long awaited planes of the Republican air force would come to save them. Steer was convinced that those planes would have saved Bilbao. But they had come from Barcelona and bad weather had forced them to land in French territory. The French, respecting the neutrality agreement, would not allow them to continue. But the enemy planes came and dropped bombs regularly.

Only the Soviet Union and Mexico were willing to supply weapons and they could no longer reach Bilbao. The British and French were not going to enter this civil war but after Guernica their sympathies, and especially public opinion, were clearly with the Basques. Aguirre appealed through the Catholic Church for other countries to shelter Basque children. Britain agreed to take 4,000 children. France placed no limits at all on Basque refugees. These two countries, together with Belgium, Denmark, Switzerland, Mexico, and the Soviet Union, took in a combined total of more than 20,000 Basque children. The British Royal Navy assisted with the evacuation. The children were all vaccinated before they left, and each child was served coffee, milk, and a fried egg as they made their way to sea, saluted by the mournful honks of fishing boat horns. In England the children were installed near an airfield and needed to be constantly reassured that the incoming aircraft were friendly. At the sound of an airplane engine they would begin shouting "*bombas!*"

Unlike most of the loyalist governments in Spain, the Basque government functioned reasonably well, even in a democratic spirit, until its final day, an accomplishment widely credited to Aguirre. In contrast to the blood bath in other parts of Spain, the Basque government carried out fewer than 30 death sentences. The one great blemish on Aguirre's record occurred on January 4, 1937. The Condor Legion had briefly attacked Bilbao, and an angry mob retaliated by storming the municipal jails. The Basque government had sent a police force from the UGT, the Socialist Trade Union, to liberate the prison, reasoning that if they had to fire into the mob to avert a massacre it would not be as politically divisive as having their own Ertzantza police turning against the population. But the Socialists did not save the prisoners; instead they supervised the attack. Finally, Telesforo de Monzón arrived at the head of a column of motorized police at what was already a scene of carnage, with bullet-pocked walls and murdered prisoners lying by broken down doors. He calmly informed a UGT official that if he did not remove his men from the prison they would all be shot.

But 224 political prisoners had already been killed. Aguirre, usually known for his calm, was outraged and after an investigation of the massacre, had six UGT officials sentenced to death for failing to protect the prisoners. After that, Aguirre was reluctant to hold prisoners, and his government worked closely with the Red Cross arranging releases and exchanges. He unilateral-

The Compañia Fano, Batallon Otachadiano, fighting on the Elgeta front, Guipúzcoa, 1937. (Euskal Arkeologia, Ethnografia eta Kondaira Museoa, Bilbao)

ly released 113 women prisoners under Red Cross supervision, including Pilar Careaga, whom Franco would one day appoint mayor of Bilbao.

Among the Basque Nationalist Party families held by the rebels was Ramón Labayen and his mother. Separated from his wife and son, Ramon's father, mayor of Tolosa and Basque Nationalist Party activist, had already escaped from Guipúzcoa to France. Under a Red Cross-arranged exchange, a British destroyer went to Bilbao and took the prisoners held by the Basque government, while Labayen, his mother, and others held by the rebels were delivered to the St. Jacques Bridge over the Bidasoa. "I understood that it was scary," recalled Ramón, "that a lot of my father's friends had been killed." They walked across the two-lane bridge to the side with the tricolored French flag, and caped gendarmes led them down the curved road into Hendaye.

For two months 15,000 men had labored to surround Bilbao with barbed wire and trenches, clearing entire forests to deprive the invader of cover. They dug 124 miles of fortifications. The fortifications around Bilbao, the so-called iron ring built by Captain Alejandro Goicoechea, might have been formidable, had the captain not changed sides and turned the blueprints over to the enemy. By late spring 1937, artillery and air force were wearing down Bilbao's defenses. Most of the Basques in Bilbao, having never trusted Madrid and the Republic, believed that the Republican government had abandoned them. Fearing a Guernica-style destruction, the Basque army withdrew, and the enemy entered Bilbao unopposed, taking possession of its steel mills, armament plants, and explosives factories. When a priest in a Hampshire, England, refugee camp informed the Basque children that Bilbao had fallen, the young refugees were so upset that they attacked the priest with sticks.

Franco had achieved a great victory—at least according to Franco. His German allies, though pleased with the strategic importance of Bilbao's industry, wondered why Franco had needed a three-month full-scale campaign to seize a mere twenty-five miles of Basqueland.

In the next six months, the victorious rebels arrested 16,000 suspected Basque nationalists and executed almost 1,000 of them, while the Basque army, pushed into neighboring Asturias, fought on. Basques were arrested, even shot, for having a relative who was a Basque Nationalist or giving a meal to one. These arrests were triumphantly announced in the Fascist newspaper.

Finally, on August 26, the Basques surrendered. Mussolini, hoping to negotiate an end to the Basque front, had gotten Franco to guarantee that if the Basque army surrendered, military prisoners would be turned over to the Italians and no actions would be taken against civilians. Political leaders and soldiers, by agreement, were evacuated on two British ships under Italian escort. But under orders from Franco, his navy blocked the port, and after a four-day standoff, the Italians, having once again obtained Franco's guarantee of no reprisals, handed over the prisoners. Hundreds of executions followed.

Thousands of Basques fled to French Basqueland or to Cuba and Latin America. Aguirre and Telesforo de Monzón, after an emotional champagne farewell to their guard in Asturias, were flown to Biarritz in French Basqueland. The Basque government became the Basque government-in-exile, recognized by the United States, France, and Britain.

The Basque Nationalist Party decided that Sabino Arana should also go into hiding. Fearing the grave at Sukarrieta would be disturbed, the Basque government had his remains reburied in Zalla, but the location was a party secret. Young Ramón Labayen used to ask his uncle Doroteo Ziaurriz, a former party chairman, "Where is Sabino?"

"Shh. It's a secret," his uncle would tell him.

Some stayed. Franco's duplicity and the massacre of prisoners had, more than even Guernica, earned him a lasting animosity that would plague him for all his decades in power. Many Basque soldiers escaped to continue fighting. Juan José Rementeria continued battling for Catalonia along the Ebro and remained in combat until 1939 when there was no more fighting. Then he returned to Muxica, his rural village near Guernica. "When the war was over I went home. To Muxica. Some were shot. But I just went home." And he remained silent for the next thirty-six years until Franco died.

THIS WAS WHEN Basques learned to eat potatoes—or anything else they could find. There was little food for refugees in French Basqueland, and there was even less for those who stayed behind in Franco's shattered and bankrupt Spain. In St. Pée, Jeanine Pereuil, working in her family pastry shop across the street from the fronton, saw refugees come in and offer gold bridgework as collateral for bread.

The Basque refugees in French Basqueland established ties with Europe's other countryless nations, especially the Welsh, Bretons, and Flemish. Breton nationalists sent their newspapers to St.-Jean-de-Luz. But life changed dramatically with the German invasion of the Lowlands and France.

Fleeing through Nazi-occupied Europe, sometimes wearing a fake mustache or other disguises, Aguirre managed to get to New York, where he established a new headquarters. Monzón escaped on a ship out of Marseilles and arrived in the United States eleven months later.

Thousands of Basques from Spain had been deported to German labor and concentration camps. More than 2,000 Basques, along with captured combatants from the International Brigades, the foreign volunteers who fought for the Second Republic, were in a camp in the neighboring French region of Béarn. Many Basques were also among the estimated 20,000 Republican prisoners in concentration camps, notably Mauthausen in Austria, where thousands were executed. The preoccupation of the Basque government with these prisoners scattered through Europe led to relations with not only international relief organizations but the intelligence services of Britain, France, and the United States.

After an initial hunt for important leaders, the Gestapo searched among Basques principally for leftists, not nationalists. The Nazis had experienced some success in appealing to Flemish and Breton nationalism, claiming that by standing up for European racial purity, Nazism was defending the rights of these ancient peoples. Heinrich Himmler, a particularly virulent racist from a devout Catholic family, had discovered that Basques were devout Catholics who believed they were the original European race.

The Germans offered scholarships to the university in Munich for young Basques wishing to do research on the origins of their race. Ramón Labayen, then a teenager in St.-Jean-de-Luz, remembered a few Basques taking the scholarship. But though the Basques had often responded without scruples to any ruler who promised to recognize their autonomy, this time they were not fooled by these Germans who had been seen in cockpits over Guernica. Basques in France were experiencing German rule. In St.-Jean-de-Luz they saw the town jeweler, a World War I veteran, forced to wear a yellow star, which he defiantly pinned over his Croix de Guerre, France's highest combat medal. Labayen remembers a Jewish schoolmate whom French gendarmes took out of class and turned over to the Germans. Labayen never saw him again.

THE BASQUES FOUND themselves in a familiar circumstance. Europe was at war, and a crucial border ran through their homeland. The Germans, the French, and the Spanish watched the passes. But the Basques, knowing the footpaths, could approach and descend from the passes without being seen.

If one of the French underground units delivered to the Basques a shot-down flier, a political refugee, or a Jew, Basques could get him across the border.

Across the border was Spain, a nominally neutral country that, in reality, was Hitler's ally. Most of the cross-Pyrenees refugees who were caught by the Guardia Civil were taken to a camp at Miranda de Ebro on the southern edge of Basqueland. And many of the Basques, if caught, risked being shot.

But for the French underground, a more difficult border than the Pyrenees was between the two zones of France. The Germans had divided France into one zone under direct German occupation and another governed from the resort town of Vichy by a French puppet government under Marshal Philippe Pétain. Starting at Arnéguy—at the entrance to the Roncesvalles pass— the dividing line between these zones split Basse Navarre, headed north, then turned east to the Swiss border. The entire line was watched by German troops. The land west of the Roncesvalles pass, including all of Labourd, was in the German occupied zone, the same zone as Paris and northern France. A refugee could be taken from northern France to Paris and delivered to the Basques in St.-Jean-de-Luz and through the passes of Labourd without ever changing French zones.

Basques discovered that the pass near Sare had particularly lax sentries. Sleepily, the sentries, Austrians who had no enthusiasm for watching someone else's mountains, performed their rounds at the exact same time every day in exactly the same way. The Basques would move the refugees up the Nivelle Valley, past the St. Pée Gestapo headquarters in the large stone house across the street from Jeanine Pereuil's pastry shop, to the mountain village of Sare, up into the forest, where horses grazed on the rich, wooded pastureland. When the refugees had no more

GERMAN-OCCUPIED FRANCE

ENGLAND

English Channel

BELGIUM

GERMANY

LUXEMBOURG

Paris

OCCUPIED ZONE

SWITZERLAND

Atlantic Ocean

Vichy

VICHY ZONE

ITALY

St. Pée
St. Jean-de-Luz
Sare

Arnéguy

Valcarlos
Roncesvalles

SPAIN

Mediterranean Sea

©1999 Jeffrey L. Ward

trees for cover, and found themselves in fields like green domes next to the rocky crests, they were in Spain—Navarra.

For a time, the Basques were even helping Germans across, deserters, who went to a certain hotel to make Basque contacts. But then the Gestapo came, pretending to be deserters, and arrested the entire network of operatives, most of them never to be seen again.

Torture, execution, disappearance—the Germans made the risks clear. But to the Basques, it was an opportunity to go on fighting. To them, the current war was a continuation of the one they had already fought. The Americans had to be made to see that it was all the same fight, that Europe had to be purged of not just Hitler and Mussolini but Franco too.

The Basques, especially Aguirre, had confidence in the United States, with a mixture of an old Basque belief in Amerika and a new belief that the United States was the antidote needed to cure this ancient European sickness—the endless struggle among nations that had been both Basque and European history. It is interesting that this dedicated Basque nationalist saw assimilation, the ability to blend tribes, as America's strength. In May 1942, from his exile in New York, Aguirre added to the American edition of his autobiography:

*Hear me, American readers. Perhaps others have been quiet about this, but I am going to be brutally frank. This huge war, the most decisive and cruel in history, rests on you more than anyone. Dollars, war materials, tears, blood—in order to win, you are going to have to give more than any other people in the world . . . Everything depends on you, this new man that you are, symbolic fusion of all races and lands, all who can hope are hoping, those who will fall for the Cause, those who suffer for the Cause, and those who trust it is the holiest of Causes.*

*You will do it, you who encompass all the old blood in*

*your new heart. And on that day, the Tree of Guernica—a universal symbol—will again give shade to a land of freedom.*

A YOUNG Flemish Belgian Red Cross volunteer in Brussels, Andrée De Jongh, determined to resist the German occupiers, joined a small underground group with more conviction than skill. Soon the Germans had dismantled the group and arrested all its members except De Jongh and a man named Arnold Deppé.

Wanting to continue to resist, the two decided to establish a kind of underground railroad that could give shelter to Allied pilots shot down over northern Europe and return them to England. Before the war, Deppé had lived in St.-Jean-de-Luz, where he worked for the film company Gaumont. He knew a number of Basques who trafficked in contraband across the Pyrenees, and on several occasions during the Civil War, they had gotten him in and out of Spain. Deppé reasoned that he and De Jongh could get fliers to Paris and down to the Basque coast, to St.-Jean-de-Luz, where Basques could help them over the Pyrenees.

This was the beginning of "Operation Comet," or as it was more commonly called in the Resistance, *la ligne.* Operations began in May 1941, and by the time France was liberated in the summer of 1944, 1,700 agents had been involved in returning to combat 700 highly trained and valuable British, Canadian, and American fliers.

St.-Jean-de-Luz, a seaside town of a few narrow streets, a medieval church and sixteenth- and seventeenth-century stone houses, with bright-hulled tuna boats moored in the inner harbor and a curved beach along the oceanside, does not look like a place where many secrets could be kept. But numerous Resistance operations were centered there sponsored by the Communists, the Socialists, trade unions, the Free French of Charles de Gaulle, the American intelligence service known as the OSS, the Basque Nationalist Party, and the government-in-exile.

In St.-Jean-de-Luz, la ligne made contact with a refugee from Elizondo in northern Navarra, a smuggler who worked the passes. When in St.-Jean-de-Luz, he could be found at the Hotel Eskualduna. The informal café on the ground floor of the fine old stone corner building, even then was a popular meeting place, a place where someone could contact a smuggler.

All kinds of documents and information were passed through the Hotel Eskualduna by the owners Kattalin Aguirre and her teenage daughter Joséphine, called "Fifine," women of friendly but rugged demeanor and unmistakably Basque faces. They gave rooms and other help to Basque refugees in need. The Eskualduna became the central point of la ligne in Basque country.

One of the regulars at the café was a sturdy, thick-built Basque named Florentino Goikoetxea, whose name means "the house above." He was born in 1898 outside San Sebastián. His passion for hunting led to a deep knowledge of the land, which, in time, led to smuggling. Arrested by the Guardia Civil at the outbreak of the Civil War, he escaped to Ciboure, where he continued smuggling. La ligne recruited him as a guide to lead fleeing fliers through the mountains.

The fliers were usually taken from Brussels to St.-Jean-de-Luz by train. Most of them did not speak French and were accompanied by female agents who pretended to be strangers while watching out for them. At Bayonne or St.-Jean-de-Luz, the fliers had to slip out of the train station, past German inspectors, often through the men's room, which had a door to the street.

They were fed and rested, sometimes at the Eskualduna, which was near the train station, or at the Ocean Hotel by the beach. After nightfall Basque operatives took them to a nearby farm, from where Florentino Goikoetxea led them up along a small stream, climbing 1,600 feet in the dark over a mountain the Basques call Xoldocagagna, to an area of thick ferns. Then they would be led through a small pass to where the trail winds around to another pass and then down along a creek.

All this was done in complete darkness, because the Germans had ordered a total blackout at night. Stumbling in the dark off roads and paths, tripping over branches and into ruts or streams, is slow, exhausting work. It could take hours to gain a few miles. Finally arriving on the Spanish side, they would only be minutes by road from where they started in France. But now they were on the Spanish side and no longer in the sheltering darkness of the blackout. From a distance they would begin to see the lights of Irún and Fuenterabbía, even glimpses of the Fuenterabbía lighthouse at the mouth of the bay. But they had been better off back in the blackout. The lights on the Spanish side helped the Guardia Civil, in their black shiny triangular hats, to closely watch the road. The Basques would try to get the fliers to the Spanish side at about 4 A.M., at the end of the long night when the bored Guardia Civil were chatting or resting. Sometimes the Basques and their refugees would grope across a black and swift Bidasoa to rest at a farm, Sarobe, in a deep and winding valley. Fliers remember the good red wine, fine omelettes, and pungent sheep's milk cheese the farmer offered them. To avoid arousing suspicion, the fliers were often dressed in traditional Basque peasant shoes, rope-soled espadrilles. Now they could soak their bruised feet in salt water and get a change of shoes. But they always had to be ready to run, to jump out a window at the first odd rustle heard over the noisy rush of river water.

The Basques and their refugees walked for miles, dodging streetlights and main roads until they reached the town of Renteria, a few miles upriver from the ports of Pasajes. In Renteria, they got on the coastal tramway like any Basque commuter, hoping not to raise suspicion for the half hour it took to get to San Sebastián. They could rest in Hernani, a village on the southern edge of San Sebastián that is famous for its cider. The owner of a cider mill sheltered them. Or they could rest in San Sebastián at the home of Bernardo Aracama, a Guipúzcoan in his early forties. In 1936, Aracama had escaped the Francoists in Guipúzcoa and gone to Guernica. By chance, he decided to leave only hours before the bombardment had taken place, and he fled to Ciboure. In 1941, he somehow managed to get his papers in order and moved back to San Sebastián, where he worked as a garage mechanic.

The journey from St.-Jean-de-Luz to San Sebastián, today twenty minutes by highway, would take at least five hours—up to sixteen hours if the rivers were flooding with rain. The final destination of the Basque part of la ligne was the British consulate in Bilbao, which would then get the pilots back to England either through Lisbon or Gibraltar.

One night a German patrol on the French side opened fire with machine guns at shadows moving in the riverbed. The Germans captured a Basque smuggler, wounded in four places,

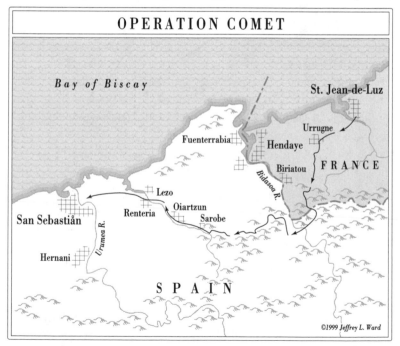

OPERATION COMET

Bay of Biscay

St. Jean-de-Luz

Urrugne

Fuenterrabia

Hendaye

Biriatou

FRANCE

Bidasoa R.

Lezo

Oiartzun

Renteria

Sarobe

San Sebastián

Urumea R.

Hernani

S P A I N

©1999 Jeffrey L. Ward

and took him to the hospital in Bayonne. Not knowing that their prisoner was Florentino Goikoetxea, they placed him under light guard, while at the Hotel Eskualduna, the regular crowd was whispering frightening scenarios. Would the Germans be able to identify Florentino? Would they interrogate him? Could they get him to talk? The Gestapo could learn every Basque name in la ligne. The operatives decided that the only solution was to free Florentino before the Germans grew suspicious, while he was still just another casually guarded Basque smuggler. To communicate with him without the Germans knowing, the oldest of Basque tricks was used: Euskera. An operative visited him in the hospital and said, *"Florentino, bihar zure bila etorriko dira, arraltsaldean,"* a sentence that aroused no curiosity from the guards but means: "Florentino, tomorrow afternoon, they will come to get you."

The next day it took three people and a truck exactly two minutes to get Florentino out of the hospital. He was then taken through the back roads of Labourd until hidden at a safe house, where he remained until the Liberation. He had personally escorted 227 pilots, mostly Royal Air Force, to safety.

Many were not as lucky as Florentino Goikoetxea. Juan Manuel Larburu's farm in Hernani, supposedly safe in neutral Spain, was a rest stop for fliers until Larburu was turned over to the Gestapo in March 1944, only months before the Liberation, and deported to Germany, where he disappeared.

The final operation of la ligne before the liberation of France carried documents, a captured list of Gestapo operatives in France and Belgium who were escaping to Spain. The Basques got the list to the British to be used in the hunt for war criminals, which the Basques assumed would take place after the Allied occupation of Spain.

In 1944, when combat shifted to French soil, the Basques fought in small units attached to Allied forces. A Basque unit landed in

Normandy on D-Day, and Basques fought in the liberation of Paris, insisting that the ikurriña fly among the victorious flags when de Gaulle entered the capital. They also fought with the French resistance, especially FFI, the Forces Français à l'Intérieur, and in small guerrilla bands in the Pyrenees.

Aguirre, wanting the Basque Nationalist Party to have its own unit, formed a battalion of 200 men commanded by a veteran of the Basque Army, Kepa Ordoki, a stonemason from Irún. Ordoki had commanded a battalion in the defense of Bilbao, had been taken prisoner and sent across the border to a camp in occupied France. Escaping, he became an expert at sabotage. The Germans captured and tortured him and were about to execute him, when he escaped again.

The new unit Ordoki commanded was called the *Gernika Batalloa*, the Guernica Battalion. Sixty percent of its troops were combat veterans from the Civil War.

After the Allies landed in Normandy and even after Paris was liberated, the Germans left behind a force of 25,500 troops in the southwest of France, mostly dug in so solidly along the Atlantic coast that their concrete bunkers can still be seen there today. De Gaulle attached considerable importance to flushing out this rear guard that was able to remain supplied by the Franco-controlled Basque ports of Spain. As the front shifted to Belgium and into Germany, FFI, the Guernica Battalion, and Moroccan volunteers fought the last battles in France.

Suddenly, from their bunkers German soldiers would hear a cry in a strange language, "Gora Euskadi!" and look through their concrete fortifications at an attacking army, at last with modern weapons in their hands, waving a red, white, and green flag, singing an indecipherable hymn, "*Eusko gudariak gera*," We Are the Basque Fighters.

Once more the Basques, outnumbered, had waited to take their revenge, attacking the last of the rear guard. Driving the

Germans from their bunkers and fortifications was their vengeance, but the Basques also believed that they were at last beginning the final great campaign of World War II. Franco would now go the way of Hitler and Mussolini.

April 14, 1945, three weeks before the end of World War II, the Guernica Battalion led a joint attack on the last Germans in the Gironde, the Bordeaux wine region on the Atlantic coast. With their former comrades of the Spanish Nationalist Union, a Communist Republican unit on one flank and the Moroccans on the other, they led an attack on 4,000 Germans of the Festung Gironde, fortress Gironde. The Germans were entrenched in Pointe-de-Grave, a point of land guarding the entrance to the mouth of the Gironde, the river that leads to Bordeaux.

Basques always said Mass before going into battle. Standing on a grassy field, bareheaded for prayer, Kepa Ordoki addressed his troops after the service: "The hour of battle has arrived, to defeat the enemy, to let the people of France know that the Basques know how to fight and die for freedom. Those of you who are veterans, take the young with you to victory. Avenge the dead of Euskadi. These are the same Germans who caused the deaths at Durango and Guernica. Do not forget that France will be proud of your example. *Gora Euskadi askatuta!*"

Long live free Basqueland!

Like medieval warriors, they unfurled their colors, the ikurriña, fastened their helmets on their heads, shouted back *"Gora Euskadi!"* and, singing their battle hymn from 1937, an ancient language of an ancient warrior people rolling over the budding vineyards, they began a fifteen-hour assault.

Liberated France wanted to give the Croix de Guerre, to the soldiers of the Guernica Battalion. But the Basque veterans refused, insisting instead that the medal go to the ikurriña itself. Only forty-two years after Sabino Arana's death, the secret flag of his underground organization received full French military honors. When the medal was presented to President Aguirre by the commander of the Foreign and Moroccan Mixed Regiment, he told the Basque leader, "When we go to liberate your country, I will meet you under the tree at Guernica."

Basque soldiers saying Mass before a battle, photo by David Seymour, 1937. The Ikurriña is in the foreground and pinned on some of the uniforms. (Magnum Photos, Inc.)

# 11: Speaking Christian

*And like the Basque poet who saw the immaculate snowflake
disappear the instant he held it in his hand, I found myself
with all my dreams turned to foam at the moment I possessed
them.*
—*José Luis Alvarez Enparantza, a.k.a. Txillardegi,*
HAIZEAZ BESTALDETIK *(Beyond the Wind), 1979*

FRANCO, FOR THE most part, was a successful liar. Though few
people completely believed his explanations of Guernica, subsequent generations of Basques, having grown up going to
Franco's schools, often believe the Guernica death toll to be far
less than the staggering numbers asserted by witnesses and
accepted by historians in the rest of Europe. One of Franco's
most successful lies was that through his cleverness, he had out-
maneuvered Hitler and kept Spain out of World War II. Then,
according to him, he seduced the Americans. Even today,
Spaniards of Republican families who grew up hating Franco
but attending his school system believe these myths.

In reality, Franco had desperately wanted to get into the
war. The war machine the Germans and Italians had shown him
stretched his military imagination to its limits. At the outset of
World War II, it did not even occur to him that other nations
might possess the military power not only to stop but to defeat
the Germans. Certain of German victory, he hoped for a share
of the war booty. He was especially interested in gaining more
of Morocco at France's expense. But the Germans thought that he
was an ineffective general and that his army was poorly equipped
and backward. After the Civil War, the Spanish economy having
collapsed, hunger and unemployment were widespread, and the
Germans reasoned that if Spain were an ally, Germany would

have to feed its people, arm them, train them, even, as the Germans had done in the Civil War, fight for them. Hitler repeatedly spurned Franco's offers.

The two met on October 23, 1940, at the train station in Hendaye, which is about 100 yards from the border, the St. Jacques Bridge over the Bidasoa. The meeting resembled a comic encounter from Charlie Chaplin's film *The Great Dictator,* which was made the same year. Hitler and the German command were kept waiting, stiffly pacing in the train station. Franco's slow chugging train arrived, depending on whose version is believed, either eight minutes or one hour late. There were rumors of an attempt on Franco's life by grenade-throwing Spanish anarchists. No such attack took place, though a plot may have existed. Franco, mortified at being late, fumed and ranted, threatening to fire the officer responsible for his travel arrangements, but recovered in time to step down on the Hendaye platform, tears of joy glistening in his eyes. The Caudillo, as Hitler addressed Franco, was evidently overcome at the moment of meeting the man he addressed as the Führer.

Franco made his case for entering the war. Hitler talked of his war problems. Franco talked of his supply needs to ready for war. The two conversations rarely intersected. Hitler began to grow irritated. Franco, to show a knowledge of war strategy, suggested, as an aide had told him, that once England was defeated, the British would still fight on from Canada. The Führer did not find this an interesting point and, hopping to his feet, announced with notable agitation that it would be pointless to continue the conversation.

From this meeting, Franco let it be widely known in Spain that he, their Caudillo, had held off the Nazis at Hendaye, that they had come threatening to take over Spain, and he had masterfully negotiated Spanish neutrality. According to Franco, Hitler had said, "I am the master of Europe and, as I have 200 divisions at my orders, there is no alternative but to obey."

There is no record of this remark, and German records show that Hitler and his divisions wished to stay far away from Spain. Hitler's only known comment on leaving the Hendaye meeting was *"Mit diesem Kerl ist nichts zu machen,"* You can't do anything with this character. Later, he said to Mussolini of his meeting with Franco, "I would rather have three or four teeth pulled, than go through that again." Curiously, another time, on the subject of the Hendaye meeting, the Führer muttered something to an adjutant about "Jesuit swine."

It was one of many times that Franco was saved by luck. Had he succeeded in persuading Hitler to let him join the Nazi war effort, Spain would have been overrun by the Allies in 1945 as the Basques had hoped. But as it was, Spain was a neutral country, albeit one that supplied raw material and armaments to the German war effort. The Wehrmacht fought with Spanish-made cartridges, rifle barrels, engines, uniforms, and parachutes. And they also fought with a Spanish volunteer division, the Blue Division, whose veterans continued, even years after Franco's death, to proudly display the iron crosses they had won from Germany.

Franco had personally assisted in the escape to Spain of Léon Degrelle, the wanted Belgian SS officer about whom Hitler had reportedly once said, "If I had a son, I would want him to be like Degrelle." In 1949, Franco did the same for wanted SS colonel Otto Skorzeny. The United Nations reported after the war that between 2,000 and 3,000 German Nazis as well as many more war criminals from the Vichy regime lived in Spain. The U.S. government estimated that Nazi holdings in Spain were worth $95 million in late 1940s dollars. The war criminals whose records la ligne had smuggled over the Pyrenees to the British were now safe and comfortable and continued to live openly in Spain, giving interviews to Western press expressing Nazi ideology, even after Franco's death. Many prominent war criminals died in luxury in Spain in the 1970s and 1980s. In 1994, when the German government sought to prosecute Otto

Ernst Remer, Hitler's security chief, for preaching racial hatred, he fled to Spain. The Spanish court ruled that since there was no such crime under Spanish law, he could not be extradited. He died in a Costa del Sol resort in 1997.

THE BASQUE NATIONALISTS claim that after the Civil War, during Franco's World War II neutrality, 21,780 Basques were executed. The figure has never been verified. In San Sebastián, by the graceful curve of the world's most beautiful urban beach, was a prison where Franco's men shot Basque nationalists almost every day until 1947.

Immediately after the Basque provinces had been taken, Franco outlawed the Euskera language. The Basques were told to "speak Christian." Vizcaya and Guipúzcoa, the "traitor provinces," were singled out for special punishment and lost all rights of self-rule. Navarra, a very loyal province, still had some fiscal autonomy.

In the summer of 1944, when large numbers of armed Republicans, especially Basques and Catalans, neared the Spanish border, many in Madrid believed that the invasion was about to begin, that Franco would soon be overthrown. But units such as the Guernica Battalion decided to finish the war for France first, thus gaining both the sympathy and availability of the Allies to help them in Spain. In October 1944, a group of Communist Republicans did invade and were defeated.

In March 1945, Don Juan de Borbón, the pretender to the Spanish throne, denounced the dictatorship as an ally of the Axis and called on Franco to step down and make way for a constitutional monarchy.

Ever since the conference at Yalta in February 1945, when the Allies had promised democracy to the countries controlled by the Axis powers, Franco had started a frantic and largely successful project, revising history. He would never again admit that he had wanted to enter the war or that he was a German sympathizer. He claimed he had only 26,000 political prisoners. That

The Basque government-in-exile meeting in midtown Manhattan in 1944. Aguirre is in the center at the end of the table and Telesforo de Monzón is on his left. (Sabino Arana Foundation, Bilbao)

did not include those in his forced labor camps. Still, two years earlier the government had confessed to 75,000 political prisoners, none of whom had been released.

To the French, British, and Americans, Franco's Spain was a pariah nation. Despite constant overtures by Franco, it was to be excluded from the United Nations, NATO, the Marshall Plan, and later, the European Economic Community. In effect, it was shut out of the postwar Western world. But it was not invaded. Spain was not to be liberated. The policy of President Franklin Roosevelt, stated in 1945, was that the United States would not interfere in Spain as long as it was not a threat to world peace. On the other hand, he said, "I can see no place in the community of nations for governments founded on fascist principles." Ostracism but not intervention. In 1946, a Polish diplomat tried to make the case that Franco was "a threat to world peace" because German Nazis in Spain were building an atom bomb. This might have led to an invasion, except that the diplomat had no evidence to support his charge.

But the Basques, most Republican exiles, even many in the Franco government, were convinced that the end was near. In July 1945 the Basque Nationalist Party had created an intelligence service to keep the United States informed on events in Spain, in preparation for the invasion. Convening his government in New York in late 1945, Aguirre told his cabinet, "We will return to our country, this year."

The government-in-exile returned to Basqueland, to Bayonne, and even reorganized the cabinet in preparation for its new responsibilities after the anticipated liberation of Spain. In Spanish Basque country, ikurriñas were turning up unexpectedly on public monuments. Someone was painting *EUZKADI,* the forbidden word from the forbidden language, on walls in very large letters. Statues of the regime's heroes, such as General Mola, were dynamited.

Then the Basque government made a decision that would change the landscape of Basque politics for the next two generations.

The government-in-exile contemplated three options: Should it continue an armed underground resistance? Should it organize mass protests and other types of political resistance? Or should it disarm and concentrate on international diplomacy? Putting its faith chiefly in the United States and going against millennia of Basque history, the government-in-exile chose the third option.

The United States and the Basque nationalists, according to Aguirre, were allies. All the way back to President Woodrow Wilson, who had mentioned Basques and Catalans as examples of nations struggling for the right to self-determination, the United States had been friendly to the Basque cause. The Basque Nationalist Party and the OSS had worked hand in hand. The Guernica Battalion had received American training and weapons.

Now, in 1947, the Basque government had no more money to maintain an armed force. The United States, Aguirre believed, would be its defender. The veterans dispersed, some settling in France, some in Latin America, some in the United States. A few refused to accept Aguirre's decision and slipped into Spain to fight and, in most cases, were killed. Many would never return to their native provinces. Kepa Ordoki died at the age of eighty in 1993, in Hendaye.

While Telesforo de Monzón was living with his wife in St.-Jean-de-Luz growing raspberry bushes, Franco was summering in San Sebastián, eating, according to legend, with the silverware his troops had stolen from the Monzón estate in Vergara. But the Basque government was confident that Franco, the left-over dictator of a destroyed alliance, could not hold out much longer, with his country impoverished and isolated. Basque shipbuilding was barely functioning, Altos Hornos de Vizcaya had laid off half its work force, and trade unions were calling general strikes. The Franco government responded by sending thousands of Guardia Civil and police to Bilbao.

Then salvation came to Franco from unexpected places such as Prague, taken over by a Communist coup in 1948. The world was being divided into Communists and anti-Communists, and Franco was a long-standing anti-Communist—one of his few consistencies. The two Germanies declared separate capitals in 1949. In June 1950, the United States went to war in Korea. Two months after the Korean War began, the U.S. Congress authorized $62 million in credit for Franco's anti-Communist Spain. The following year France removed the diplomatic status of the Basque government office in Paris, expelling Basques from the city they had helped liberate and turning the building, near the Eiffel Tower, back into the Spanish Embassy.

THE COLD WAR rescued Franco's regime at a desperate last moment. While the rest of Europe had been recovering from the destruction of World War II, Spain was becoming poorer. In 1950, Spanish meat consumption per capita was half what it had been in 1926. While telling Spain how he was standing up to the Americans, Franco made it clear in Washington, that he would make any kind of deal they wanted. In 1953, the newly elected president, Dwight Eisenhower, sought a military presence in the southwestern flank of Europe. This produced the Defense Pacts of September 1953.

Franco made these agreements seem to Spaniards like far more than they were. In Spain it was believed that the wily Caudillo had at last duped the United States into supporting him with friendship, money, and development projects. The moment was brilliantly satirized by Luis Garcia Berlanga in the film *Bienvenido, Mr. Marshall,* in which a small Spanish town, confusing the Defense Pacts with the Marshall Plan, feverishly prepares for the arrival of Mr. Marshall and all the gifts he will bestow. When the small entourage of Americans arrive, they drive through the town without stopping.

The pacts gave the United States a bomber base near Madrid, in Torrejón, and other air bases near Zaragoza, Seville, and Morón de Frontera, as well as the Rota navy base in Cádiz. In exchange for allowing a foreign power to establish bases that were potential nuclear targets next to Spanish cities, Spain got $226 million in assistance, but most of it was of little value. The only developmental assistance was for roads, port facilities, and ancillary defense industries that the Americans would need to operate. They did give military equipment, but only used and dated leftovers from World War II and the Korean War.

But the pacts were of enormous symbolic importance. The

Basques were stunned by the betrayal. Aguirre, himself a passionate anti-Communist, accepted the Cold War logic that the United States feared an unstable Spain, but he complained that the move was a "weakening of moral force in the fight against totalitarianism."

Other Basques, however, especially younger ones, were furious. Xabier Arzalluz, today the most powerful Basque politician, was a young law student in Zaragoza at the time. "People of our generation are bitter," he recently said. "I have great empathy for Americans. But not for the government, not for the State Department. I feel the same way about the British." Arzalluz remained loyal to the Basque Nationalist Party, but many of his contemporaries began to question their support. "They thought the party was bourgeois, old and passé," Arzalluz recalled. "When America signed an accord with Franco, young people didn't believe that we were fighting Franco anymore."

The Basques were not the only ones of his generation angered by the pact. An eleven-year-old in Seville, Felipe González, vowed that he would never set foot on U.S. soil. In 1977, preparing to be elected prime minister of the new Spanish democracy, he reneged and visited Washington, D.C.

What the pacts had meant was that Franco would survive, though he always remained somewhat of a pariah. In 1959, concerned about the well-being of his bases, Eisenhower visited Spain. According to accounts of this visit, he was uncomfortable and distant, but he was photographed giving the Caudillo the famous Ike smile, and that was the photo Franco needed to show Spaniards. Eisenhower did seem to be impressed by the huge welcome the Spanish gave him, not seeming to realize that it had been staged by the Falange, the last vestige of the fascist Europe he had defeated.

BUT, THE NEW generation's disenchantment with the Basque Nationalist Party had not begun with the Defense Pacts.

José Luis Alvarez was born in 1929. Sabino Arana would not have considered him a Basque. His grandfather was not only a Liberal but a maketo—an engraver from Madrid who had moved north at the time of the Second Carlist War, setting up a lithograph shop in Tolosa. José Luis's father was born in the shop and later moved the family business to San Sebastián, where José Luis was born.

Growing up in the 1930s, José Luis heard Euskera all around him. He heard his Basque mother speaking it with the neighbors.

"What does that mean?" he would ask her.

"I heard it everywhere," he said. "It seemed to be something that I lacked. Something that was ours. I felt robbed. Cut off from my country."

Soon no one was allowed to speak it. He remembers the prison by the beach where Franco's troops shot people every day. A teacher he knew from the neighborhood was taken there. By 1946, he considered himself a Basque nationalist, but a nationalist without a movement and no idea of what to do.

"I didn't know anyone who was a nationalist. Or who said he was a nationalist. I had an uncle who was executed in Madrid in 1942. I don't think even he was a nationalist."

He found a Basque grammar book in the Guipúzcoan dialect and started studying. Eventually, he was able to get secret language lessons from a teacher who said he was from the Basque Nationalist Party.

In 1949, he went to Bilbao to study industrial engineering. His studies gave him the contacts to arrange intense language instruction and soon he was writing in Euskera for an underground publication. But he still had not had any contact with the Basque Nationalist Party.

In 1950, he was arrested in San Sebastián for belonging to an underground student movement. He spent one month in prison. "We couldn't do anything political but we felt we had to do something," he said. He and his small group reasoned that they needed to make contact with members of the Basque Nationalist Party. But where were they? In hiding, it was always said. José Luis thought a friend of his brother's might be one of them. Carefully José Luis and his group asked questions and in time were able to meet with actual representatives of the fabled Basque Nationalist Party.

The young Basques were utterly disappointed.

"We had the impression that they were waiting for Franco to die, or waiting for the Americans to invade. Characteristic of youth we did not take easily to the idea of waiting."

In 1952, five of them decided to start their own underground movement, organized into small cells. At first there was one cell in San Sebastián and a second in Bilbao. A cell was often no more than three people, making it difficult for the Guardia Civil to penetrate the organization. A cell might be exposed but not the organization.

They named their group ATA, an acronym for Aberri Ta Askatasuna, Homeland and Liberty. But they were Guipúzcoans. In Vizcayan dialect, they later discovered, *ata* means "duck." So after six years of being a clandestine duck to Vizcayans, in 1959 they changed their name to ETA, the acronym for Euskadi Ta Askatasuna, Euskadi and Liberty. As with Arana's Basque Nationalist Party, July 31, Ignatius Loyola's Saint's Day, was chosen as ETA's official founding date.

ETA, the second choice, was a brilliant label. To someone who does not read Euskera, any text in Basque appears to be peppered with the initials because *eta* is also the conjunction that means "and." The sculptor and inveterate punster, Jorge de Oteiza, at ninety his pale eyes still sparkling with mischief, sometimes referred to ETA as Y—the Spanish language word for "and." ETA appears to mean many other things. Once ETA began its anti-Franco activities, the Guardia Civil desperately tried to decipher the three letters. One infamous Guardia Civil beat prisoners for hours trying to get them to confirm that it stood for a Greek letter and to explain what that meant.

THE ORIGINAL ETA members considered themselves intellectuals and published an underground journal called *Ekin,* meaning "to persist" or "to act." Their stated goal was an independent Basque nation recognized as an equal in the community of nations. But their primary activity was promoting the forbidden Basque language. That, at least, was to be the first step. José Luis explained, "Well, we were the children of petit bourgeoisie."

There was important work to be done by intellectuals. They recognized that to have a just nation, the teachings of Sabino Arana had to be revised. The racial definition of a Basque was not acceptable. Racism was to be purged from Basque nationalism, as was the Aranist commitment to the Catholic Church. ETA reverted to the original Basque definition. A Basque is an Euskaldun, someone who speaks Euskera. Instead of genealogy, last names, and earlobes, it was fluency in the Basque language and culture that would determine who was and was not Basque.

According to ETA, "Euskera is the quintessence of Euskadi. So long as Euskera is alive, Euskadi will live."

Franco always had contempt for the impact of culture and so frequently neglected to repress writing and art intended as a protest against him. In 1957, José Luis was able to get his first novel published in Euskera under the pseudonym Txillardegi. The name came from the San Sebastián neighborhood where he grew up. Txillardegi writes in a seductively lyrical style that seems to burst uncontrollably into free verse from time to time.

The novel *Leturiaren egunkari ezkutua* (The Secret Diary of Leturia), was a milestone in Basque literature, presenting the first Basque antihero. Until then, literature in Euskera had been about Basque history and Basque tradition, about the great deeds of Basques. But Txillardegi's novel was about the human condition—about love, grief, and suicide—a novel in Basque rather than a "Basque novel."

By the end of 1959, ETA had between 200 and 250 members, and they were studying armed liberation movements. Of particular interest was the Tunisian liberation movement of Habib Bourguiba. They were also interested in a favorite of the Basque Nationalist Party, Menachem Begin's Irgun, which had used violence to drive the British out of Palestine during the fight to create a Jewish state.

But regardless of their models, violent activism was primarily directed against walls and statues. Their signature became *Gora Euskadi.*

Though the structure of separate cells helped to protect them, it also made it difficult to control the organization. The members had agreed to meet once every year, but some years the annual meeting never got organized.

In addition to the appearance of *Gora Euskadi* on more and more walls, ETA bombed an elevator at the Guardia Civil headquarters in Vitoria. Spanish flags were burned. On July 18, 1961, a train carrying celebrators to a ceremony in San Sebastián for the anniversary of the 1936 coup d'état was derailed by ETA. Though the operation was carried out with great care to avoid casualties, the message was clear: The Spanish enemy celebrated in Euskadi at their own peril.

Madrid's response was equally clear—a massive sweep, arresting, torturing, and imprisoning more than 100 Basques. Among those arrested were Txillardegi and the other five leaders of ETA. But they were released after short sentences. The Spanish were not infiltrating and destroying ETA. They were simply avenging the derailment. ETA would avenge the retaliation. An eye for an eye came to define the relationship between ETA and the Spanish.

Once released from prison, the leaders crossed the border

and established operations in France, from where ETA, it is believed, has been directed ever since.

ENEMIES OFTEN become mirror images of each other. Franco was obsessed by his hatred of communism. Each family with its small property being a basic element of the Basque sense of order, communism is anathema to most Basques as well. While the Basque Nationalist Party, from Arana to Aguirre, had been resolutely anti-Communist—the Guernica Battalion had been created to separate from Communist fighters—the new generation was increasingly drawn to Marxist ideology. Franco's venom had made communism appealing to those who hated him. What could be more anti-Franco? And Aguirre and the nationalists, it seemed to young Basques, were not sufficiently anti-Franco.

Much of this process happened through the Church. Franco was pro-Church, so young anti-Franco Basques, following the negative logic, should have been anti-Church. But the Basque clergy provided an important source of language study, having always been the guardians of the language. For centuries, clerics had been the only writers of Euskera, and during the 1950s, while the Basque language was becoming increasingly rare, more than 80 percent of the rural clergy in Vizcaya and Guipúzcoa were Basque speakers. These priests became an undercover source for the preservation and dissemination of Basque culture. Paradoxically, a large number of these priests, publicly denounced by Franco as "separatist clergy," in further defiance of the Caudillo, not to mention the pope, were also embracing Marxism.

Marxism was moving ETA farther from the Basque Nationalist Party and closer to workers' movements. In 1960, the unexpected death from heart failure of fifty-four-year-old José Antonio Aguirre dramatically accelerated this process. Aguirre died in Paris, and his body was brought to St.-Jean-de-Luz, to the home of Telesforo de Monzón. ETA had called Aguirre "our beloved leader," and its members were among the mourners. Aguirre, partly a product of the dramatic times he lived through, but also through his own eloquence, had been a universal symbol for Basque nationalists—the lehendakari who, like his government, had died young and would be remembered uncritically. His replacement, Jesús María Leizaola, a San Sebastián-born academic ten years older than Aguirre, had none of the first lehendakari's charisma.

Forgotten by a new generation, if they had ever known, was Leizaola, the young student who had been marched from Bermeo in handcuffs for sixteen miles by Guardia Civil for having shouted, *"Jaungoikua eta lagizarra;"* Leizaola, the young defender of the church in the first Republican Cortes, who was punched in the face in mid-debate by an angry Socialist; and the Basque Government's Minister of Justice who had risked his own safety to preserve order in Bibao until the final day of retreat. It is indicative of Leizaola's standing that it was always rumored that Aguirre's most unpopular decision, the 1947 disarming of nationalists, had been Leizaola's idea.

Whereas the Basque Nationalist Party was a conservative movement led by the heirs of Vizcaya industry, the young ETA movement wanted to recruit among workers. Occasional illegal factory worker strikes were the only visible form of resistance to the regime. And Basque labor had a small measure of power because Basque industry was vital for Franco's hopes of economic recovery. With the help of U.S. credits, Franco was trying to rebuild industry, restoring Vizcaya at the same time he was singling it out for persecution. In 1956, 70 percent of all pig iron and 60 percent of all steel produced in Spain came from the province of Vizcaya.

ETA would not have been able to recruit among workers if it had not rewritten Aranism. Their new nonracist definition of Basques was essential since many of the workers were of non-

Basque origin. To be a Basque, they had only to learn the language and embrace the culture, which many did. And even the ones who didn't, posed no ideological problem for the new nationalists. Asked who is a Basque, Txillardegi recently said, "A Basque is someone who speaks Basque. But there are Basques who don't. It is something imposed by Madrid. They are victims."

A workable definition of who is a Basque also became more important because Franco had a policy of populating Basque country with people from other parts of Spain. By the time of his death in 1975, more than 40 percent of the population of the Spanish Basque provinces had no Basque parent.

Guernica's medieval streets had been rebuilt with 1940s brick architecture, occasionally adorned with a surviving archway. It is an odd-looking town because of its uniform 1940s style, set on a medieval street plan. Older residents say that the original city before the war had straighter streets, as though the loss of antiquity had been compensated for with a more antique-looking street plan. The people here who are old enough to remember the war still speak of only two sides: the Reds and the Fascists. Many of the people who moved in after the town was rebuilt were considered to be the latter. Still, if they were open to Basque culture, if they learned the language, then, as far as ETA was concerned, they could become Basques, and, more important, they could become Basque nationalists. By the 1970s, only about half the members of ETA had two Basque parents.

More than a cynical calculation, this was a necessary reform. After all, even Txillardegi was an Alvarez whose family had come from Madrid.

TERMS SUCH AS *national liberation, class struggle, revolution* were heard increasingly. Under Leizaola, the Basque Nationalist Party began openly denouncing ETA as "a Communist organization."

Txillardegi struggled to master his own creation until 1967, when the clandestine network of cells managed only its fifth

meeting in eight years, consisting of two encounters which together were called Assembly V.

By this time there may have been as many as 450 members.
The second of the encounters was held on Easter week, 1967, in
Guetaria, Guipúzcoa. The assembly published a document titled
"The Official Ideology of ETA." According to this document,
ETA was now "a Basque socialist national liberation movement"
defining its nationalism as "revolutionary nationalism" that would
fuse the Basque people and their struggle for national liberation
with the working-class struggle for "social liberation." One
moment ETA appeared to be Basque nationalist, but the next, it
was supporting Spanish workers against a Basque bourgeoisie.
It was a complex blend of Marx, Mao, Fidel Castro, and Sabino
Arana—Miguel Unamuno's worst nightmare, ideologies run amok,
ism heaped on ism.

Assembly V changed the entire leadership. A new generation that had never known the Basque government or the
Second Republic, that had been born in the hungry years of the
1940s and never experienced anything but the grinding stagnation of the Franco dictatorship, took over ETA. The man who
presided over the assembly by unanimous acclaim was Txabi
Etxebarrieta.

Born in Bilbao in 1944, Etxebarrieta was the author of
much of the revolutionary theory of the new ETA. While he was
being elevated to the executive committee of the new armed
wing of the organization, the older Txillardegi and most of the
other founders left or were forced out. "It was a sad period in
my life," said Txillardegi. "I just didn't believe in this."

In the 1960's, in Basqueland, Txabi was a name much like
Che in Latin America. He was the most popular leader ETA ever
had, a man of clear intelligence with a vision—a plan for Basque
independence through selective violence and close alliance with
social causes and labor unions. But more than an intellectual, he

was a man of action, ready to test his physical courage in the fight for his beliefs. Txabi was an anti-Franco revolutionary.

He earned two distinctions. He was the first ETArist to kill, and he was the first ETA leader to be shot down by the Guardia Civil.

Following Assembly V, ETA became more active. The Guardia Civil began a practice of spot checks along the roads. On June 7, 1968, a Guardia Civil stopped a car in Guipúzcoa that happened to have Etxebarrieta and a colleague inside. The two opened fire and killed the Guardia Civil, a man named José Pardines. Later, Etxebarrieta was tracked down and killed. It was still the same pattern: an eye for an eye between ETA and the Guardia Civil. Only the nature of the acts was escalating. Txabi had counted on this, believing that provoking Guardia Civil would in turn provoke Basques, and eventually a general uprising would be provoked. Next would be ETA's turn.

# 12: Eventually Night Falls

*Baina gaua dator, joan dira sapelaitsak, eta trikuak,*
*Marraskilo, Zizare, Zomorro, Armiarma, Igel,*
*Erreka utzi eta mendiaren pendizari ekiten dio,*
*seguru bere arantsetaz nola egon baitzitekeen*
*Gerlari bat bere eskutuaz, Espartan edo Korinton;*

*Eta bapatean, zeharkatu egiten du*
*belardiaren eta kamio berriaren arteko muga;*
*Zure eta nire denboran sartzen de pauso bakar batez,*
*Eta nola bere hiztegi unibertsala ez den*
*azkeneko zazpi mila urteotan berritu,*
*ez ditu ezagutzen gure automobilaren argiak,*
*ez da ohartzen bere heriotzaren hurbiltasunaz ere.*

Eventually night falls, the eagles disappear and the hedgehog,
Frog, Snail, Spider, Worm, Insect,
Leaves the river and walks up the side of the mountain,
as confident in his spines
as any warrior with his shield in Sparta or in Corinth;

and suddenly he crosses the border, the line
that separates the earth and the grass from the new road;
with one step he enters your time and mine,
and since his dictionary of the universe
has not been corrected or updated
in the last seven thousand years,
he does not recognize the lights of our car,
and does not even realize that he is going to die.

—*Joseba Irazu Garmendia, a.k.a. Bernardo Atxaga,*
TRIKUARENA *(The Hedgehog)*

ON AUGUST 2, 1968, Melitón Manzanas, a hated San Sebastián police captain, was returning to Villa Arana, his three-story home in Irún within walking distance of the French border. As he approached the steps to his house, he heard the words, "Melitón, look who's killing you."

He fumbled for a sidearm, but with his wife listening on the other side of the door, seven bullets were pumped into his body. This was "Operation *Sagarra*." In Euskera, *sagarra* means "apples," as does *manzanas* in Spanish. ETA humor.

It was ETA's second killing and first planned assassination. Txabi was avenged.

The target was well chosen. Others had been considered, even attempted, but the victim, Manzanas, was as loathed as Txabi had been loved. In Basqueland the vengeance was viewed with satisfaction.

The regime responded on cue. The assassination occurred on a Friday and Franco declared a state of siege throughout Basqueland on Monday. It lasted for months, and thousands of Basques were arrested and tortured. Some were sentenced to years in prison. Once the state of siege was under way, the Basque Nationalist Party said through one of its publications, for the first time since 1947, that it was not opposed to the use of violence.

The repression culminated with the December 1970 trials in Burgos. The Burgos trials, show trials of sixteen alleged ETA members charged with "military rebellion, banditism, and terrorism," were the kind of disaster for Franco that ETA members had always dreamed of provoking. From the courtroom they shouted, *"Gora Euskadi!,"* and sang the hymn "Eusko gudariak gera." ETA had returned Basques to their image of the 1930s and 1940s—the heroic Basques, standing up to fascism. The one new addition was an occasionally shouted slogan: *"Iraultza ala hil!"* Revolution or Death, a line borrowed from the Cuban Revolution. International intellectual celebrities such as the Catalan painter Joan Miró declared their support for ETA. After three ETA members were condemned to death in Burgos, demonstrations broke out, not only in Bilbao and Pamplona but in Barcelona, Seville, Oviedo, and Madrid. The governments of Sweden, Norway, Denmark, West Germany, France, Belgium, the Vatican, and Australia petitioned the Spanish government not to carry out the sentences.

Franco's close advisers convinced the aging and confused Caudillo, after considerable resistance on his part, that it would be a blunder to carry out the death sentences, and he reluctantly commuted them to life imprisonment.

As IN MOST PLACES in the world, in Basqueland the late 1960s was both the worst and best of times to be attending a university. Franco had barred public universities from the "traitor provinces," but there were two private universities: Deusto, run by the Jesuits in Bilbao, and the more prestigious University of Pamplona, run by the Opus Dei, an elite conservative Catholic lay order. To attend the public university system, most Basques had to leave, go to Madrid or Zaragoza.

However, it had always been Franco's policy, while repressing the Basques, to nurture Basque industry. This meant that a few university facilities teaching such subjects as economics and engineering had to be available in Bilbao. The economics school in Bilbao was called Sarriko. The government did not want a university in Basqueland full of dissident students studying literature, history, and political science, but those who were interested in engineering, steelmaking, or banking could go to school in Vizcaya.

By 1968, Franco's plan had clearly failed. Many young Basques had decided to study economics. Txabi, the singular hero of the student body, had been an economics graduate from Sarriko. Deusto, across the river from the center of Bilbao, was known as a breeding ground for militant Basque nationalism.

But Sarriko students thought the radicals of Deusto were too moderate, and said they "hid behind the skirts of the Jesuits."

"Txabi was a strong model, he still is," said Joseba Irazu, who, like many Sarriko students of the late 1960s, was an unlikely economics student. He had chosen the school largely because he wanted to stay in Basque country, and he had chosen economics because it was taught there.

Joseba Irazu Garmendia was born in 1951 in Asteasu, a village of stone-walled Basque houses tucked into the velvet green mountain slopes of Guipúzcoa. Although only twenty miles inland from San Sebastián, it was then an isolated community of 1,000 people that waited for two Spanish newspapers to be delivered once a day by donkey. Joseba grew up speaking Euskera at home with his carpenter father and his schoolteacher mother, who had been expelled from the school system because she was Basque. In Asteasu, most people spoke Euskera in their houses, but once they passed the front door, they switched to Spanish.

The new teachers, the ones who had replaced teachers like Joseba's mother, were pro-Franco. Joseba described his teacher as "Fascist but sensible." The sensible Fascist once made him hold out his fingers to beat the tips with a stick after Joseba had been overheard speaking Euskera. But the teacher did not do this very often, because he remembered his predecessor, who, after beating the fingertips of two husky Euskera-speaking boys, was tossed out the schoolhouse window by them. "We have a guerrilla tradition," explained Joseba.

By the late 1960s, when Joseba decided to study economics at Sarriko, Basque life and especially the Basque language were changing. In the 1960s, with limited U.S. help but still largely in isolation, Franco had finely been able to move the Spanish economy—by subsidizing Basque industry. After centuries of being highly competitive in the world, this industry had now become absurdly overblown. Instead of the cheapest steel in Europe, the Basques now produced some of the most expensive. The government was covering the high cost of production and guaranteeing a price-controlled Spanish market. Like Franco himself, this false economy was certain to collapse, but the end was not in sight. For now Spain, especially northern Spain, was enjoying some relief from years of misery.

Without the crushing pressure of economic collapse, the Basques, defiant again, were expressing themselves through culture. "For years the Basque society had been underground like a potato," Joseba said. "And in the 1960s a new Basque country was born."

Traditional folk festivals that had been banned after the Civil War were being celebrated once again, and traditional dances and music began reappearing. In 1960, three ikastolas, the first since the Civil War, were opened. While studying economics, Joseba for the first time heard songs, ballads of political protest, in his language.

Singers such as Benito Lertxundi from Guipúzcoa, and a number of singers from the French side, including the mayor of Cambo, Michel Labéguerie, sang songs that every student knew by heart, in a style the Cuban Revolution had learned from Joan Baez and popularized with all the leftist movements of the Spanish-speaking world. Because Franco did not understand the impact of 45 rpm records, college campuses had stacks of Lertxundi's songs of Basque nationalism sung in Euskera.

"Only 10 percent of the students spoke Basque," Joseba said, "but everyone knew how to say strike in Basque—*greba*."

The most significant cultural advance of the 1960s was that the Basque Academy of Language at last realized its dream of unifying the Basque language. Although the earliest record of written Basque is from the third century, it remained mostly an oral language until the twentieth century. The reason for its slow development as a written language was not, as Unamuno had suggested, that agglutinating languages are unsuitable for literature. The problem was that Euskera varied so much from one region to another. The local dialect worked well for talking to a neighbor. It asserted intimacy, membership in a community. But Spanish, the universal language, was preferred for writing something down to be read by a large number of people.

Seven distinct dialects of Euskera are spoken: one from each of the seven provinces, with an eighth in eastern Navarra known as Alto Navarra Meridionale. Many of the differences stem from pronunciation. *Dut*, from the verb "to have," becomes *det* in Guipúzcoa and *dot* in Vizcaya.

The aspirated *h* is the most unique phoneme in Euskera. That slightly aspirated "ha" on the *h* separates Euskalduns from Spanish speakers. The Spanish call Hondarribia *Fuenterrabía*, because they cannot say the *h*. Yet neither can all Basques. In the Roncal Valley, near Roncesvalles, the *h* becomes a *k*, and in another valley *h* is pronounced like a *g*.

Generally, Basques can understand each other, though there are moments, such as Txillardegi's call for clandestine ducks, when the meaning is entirely changed. Vizcaya and Soule, the two geographic extremes of Basqueland, are also the linguistic extremes of Euskera. The geographically central dialects, especially Guipúzcoan, are more easily understood by most Basques than Vizcayan or Souletine. But even Guipúzcoan, which is not only from a centrally located province but also from the province with the largest number of Euskera speakers, is not a universal Basque. Without a common written language, a Basque writer had a minuscule readership—only Euskera readers of the author's native province. In 1571, a Bible was published in Euskera with a prologue that said, "We should try to find the most common language possible." But such a universal Euskera did not exist. Some authors wrote in several dialects. The first novelist in Euskera, the late-nineteenth-century romantic Domingo de Aguirre, was from the Vizcayan port of Ondarroa but tried to increase his readership by writing some of his novels in Vizcayan dialect and others in Guipúzcoan. Even after the Basque Academy of Language was founded in 1918 with the stated goal of finding a common written language, it took decades to develop it. Impatiently, Xabier de Lizardi, one of the most influential Basque writers of the early twentieth century, wrote poetry in a unified language of his own invention. But most Euskera readers found it difficult to understand.

In the 1960s, the Basque academy established a common written language, which was called Batua. The twenty-four-member academy, each member representing a different linguistic tendency, tried to identify the word forms that were most commonly used. This often led them to the Guipúzcoan version. They also favored the older version over the contemporary, but rejected words and forms that were no longer in use.

AT THE AGE of twenty, Joseba Irazu for the first time read a novel in his mother tongue. He began meeting with underground groups, learning how to write in the secret language.

But campuses were busy places in the 1960s. "I am not proud of it, but I didn't learn anything at university. We were always on strike," said Joseba. Militants from the Basque Nationalist Party were the first to take over a Bilbao radio station. ETA members on campus soon did the same. But neither group was as active at Sarriko as the Communists. The Maoists emerged there as a highly organized group. Their small armed faction occasionally bombed a factory. "Cultural meetings" were held in which "the anticolonial struggle" and Che Guevara were discussed.

The police would sometimes enter the campus with helmets and clubs. The students did not fear them the way they did the Guardia Civil. The Guardia Civil rarely came onto the campus, but when it did, students disappeared, a terror technique learned from its onetime ally, the Nazis.

With his healthy Basque distrust of doctrines, Joseba steered around most of the radical groups. When the Maoists asked, he did translate their political tracts into Euskera. But he joined nothing. When he says now that he didn't learn anything, he means in the field of economics. But he and an entire generation of innovative and talented writers learned how to write in their native language while studying other subjects in the universities of the late 1960s. It was their revolution.

Teaching Euskera was not allowed, but the Basque Nationalist Party and ETA offered "cultural events" that amounted to courses in Batua. Joseba's teacher was a Basque Nationalist Party activist who, in between cultural events, more than once helped take over the radio station.

Joseba, who had always wanted to be a writer, at first found it difficult to imagine working in the secret language of his parents. That began to change when he met an infirm poet, old before his time, named Gabriel Aresti. Born in Bilbao in 1933, Aresti did not grow up speaking Euskera and was one of the first *Euskaldunberri*, literally, "new Basque speaker," a non-Euskera speaker who learned the language through adult education. He went on to become one of the most influential writers of the new language. Although not a nationalist in the political sense—he was closer to the Spanish Communist Party than the nationalists—he was a passionate lover of Basqueness. His 1964 collection of poems, *Harri eta Herri* (Rock and People), earned him the affection of nationalists and a summons before a disapproving tribunal. But he also greatly expanded the language through such projects as translating the poetry of T. S. Eliot.

Joseba began writing poems and short stories and publishing them in underground magazines, using the name Bernardo Atxaga to protect his true identity. Aresti, having read some of the stories, sent a note telling him that there were only five real writers in Euskera. "If you keep away from the purists you could be the sixth."

By purists, he meant the "Sabino school," which rejected all Latin words, denied the evolution of the language, and pretended that a purely Basque language existed. Many of Arana's invented words, such as *Euskadi,* had become established in the vocabulary. But there was heated debate about whether such creative linguistics should continue. Linguistic political correctness is one of the oldest controversies in the Basque Academy, of which Aresti was a member. The academy wants Euskera to be a usable, not necessarily a pure, language. Where Spanish words have become common usage, the academy kept them in Batua; modern computer terms have been adopted from the English language. "Batua is a unification of the written language," said Juan San Martin, who was secretary of the academy in 1968 and a close associate of Aresti. "The only new language came from Sabino Arana, who made up words. We do not invent words. We are opposed to invented words."

Gabriel Aresti died in 1975, the same year as Franco. The poet was only forty-two. Aside from his work, he left behind the young writers he influenced, the most important generation of writers in the long history of the Basque language.

> *No one is a prophet*
> *in his own time.*
> *Again I have come*
> *to the idea,*
> *if I had no wife or children*
> *with pleasure*
> *would I die*
> *because Basque rock*
> *would ponder my words.*
> *—Gabriel Aresti,* NERE MENDEAN,
> *(In My Time), 1967*

FRANCO GREW OLDER, his regime looking every year more like something dusty and Baroque in a tasteless out-of-the-way museum. But he did not fall from power. There in Spain, in the 1970s, was Europe's remaining 1930s strutting dictator.

It never went smoothly, but Franco always managed to survive. What small resistance to his regime that he was unable to quell by force served only as an embarrassment to a regime that, in the eyes of the world, never would achieve respectability. In spite of ETA and the Basque nationalists, Franco could vacation in San Sebastián without incident. In September 1970, he attended the pelota national championships. Joseba Elósegi, captain of the only Basque unit to have been in Guernica the day of the bombing, ran out to the fronton, set himself on fire, shouted *"Gora Euskadi askatuta!"* and leaped from the wall almost fifteen feet, landing in front of Franco.

When he recovered from his burns, Elósegi was sentenced to seven years in prison. He had been in prison before. Franco's troops had condemned him to death in 1937, but he had escaped to France. The Nazis had imprisoned him, but he had escaped again. In 1946, he had been arrested for flying the ikurriña from a church during a Fascist celebration.

Shortly after the Elósegi incident, U.S. president Richard Nixon arrived in Spain. Accompanying him was his secretary of state, Henry Kissinger, whose impression was that the entire country was "waiting for a life to end so that it could rejoin European history." Nixon had come to Spain hoping for a reception as large as Eisenhower had gotten, and Franco obliged him. But the long motorcade from the airport, with the cheering crowd, both paid and unpaid, appeared to have tired the seventy-eight-year-old Franco. When Nixon sat down for talks with him, the aged Caudillo dozed off, leaving the president to talk with an adviser. Reportedly, Kissinger nodded off as well.

As though he feared denting the myth of his own indestructibility, Franco did little to arrange a succession. He had played a cunning game with the heir to the throne, Don Juan, spurning his attempts at establishing a constitutional monarchy. When the pretender's son, Juan Carlos, was ten years old, Franco had gotten Don Juan to agree to remain in exile while permitting Juan Carlos to be educated in Spain. Juan Carlos's education, administered by Franco's most ardent followers, was ostensibly to groom him for monarchy.

Though he hated Don Juan, who had called for an end to the regime in 1945, Franco liked Juan Carlos and thought he could make a respectable figurehead of no great weight who would not interfere with the Caudillo's henchmen. But for years the Caudillo refused to name him as successor, and when he finally did, in 1969, he made the announcement suddenly, without warning the prince. But young Juan Carlos was not to be a true confidant. The only one Franco entrusted to fill in, should he fall ill, the man who was to look after things once Franco died, was the ever loyal Admiral Luis Carrero Blanco, who had worked his way up from an undersecretary in 1942 to prime minister in June 1973. ETA called him "the Ogre."

BY THE END of 1973, ETA had allegedly killed six people, though not all of the killings were claimed by or ever proved to be done by ETA. Since 1968, the Guardia Civil and police had killed 14, wounded by gunshot 52, and arrested without trial 4,356 Basques. Between 1956 and 1975, the regime declared eleven states of emergency. All but one of them were in Basque country. Five of them were exclusively in Basque country. Random arrests were whittling down ETA's small ranks. The number of active ETA members in 1973 was a fraction of the estimated 600 in the late 1960s.

And yet ETA's scenario was not unfolding. Basques were not rising up in revolution in the face of stepped-up repression, and if they did, Spaniards were clearly not going to follow. Kissinger had been right. The country was just waiting for the death of one man.

Following the Burgos trials, ETA started developing a new plan. Its commandos reasoned that if they could kidnap a Spanish official, he could be traded for a number of their imprisoned colleagues. But it would have to be a high official, not some unguarded diplomat who might be easy to grab but would not be important enough to obtain the release of a large number of prisoners.

In late 1972, two ETA operatives in Madrid were told by an informant that the Ogre, Admiral Carrero Blanco, went to Mass at the Jesuit church of San Francisco de Borja on Calle Serrano every day at the same time in his black Dodge, accompanied by two police officers—sometimes only one.

"Operation Ogre" was born. ETA commandos began to stalk Carrero Blanco. They knew the movements of the guard, of the chauffeur, and of the Ogre himself. He was easy to get close to inside the church. But the longer they stalked him, the more they thought about killing him. A kidnapping would gain them back some imprisoned militants, but assassinating the man they saw as "the symbol of pure Francoism" would have far-reaching political repercussions.

Later, one of the commandos said, "Everyone knew that the Spanish oligarchy was counting on Carrero to assure a convulsion-free transition to Francoism without Franco." The more they pondered the quarry within their sights, the more they realized that this was the target, the man who could keep Francoism alive. Even killing Franco, who surely would die soon, would not strike the blow that this assassination would. This was more important than liberating prisoners.

But also, a kidnapping would be much more difficult than assassination. The church was in an area of embassies and consulates and many guards. After June, when the admiral became prime minister, his security increased and kidnapping seemed even more difficult. The ETA commandos contemplated a shooting, then turned to the idea of an explosion detonated by electric cable from a distance. Then they realized that since the black Dodge stopped at the exact same spot every morning, they could dig a shallow tunnel and place high explosives in the spot, detonating it from a distance without anyone ever seeing them.

On December 20, 1973, another of Franco's show trials, public exhibits of injustice that perpetuated Spain's low standing among Western nations, was to begin. This was to be a trial of trade unionists. Carrero Blanco went to Mass as usual, parking his car at 9:30 in the usual place. One hundred and sixty-five pounds of dynamite sent the car several stories into the air over the top of a building. According to one immediate and popular joke, the admiral had become the first Spanish astronaut. *"Una bache mas, un cabron menos,"* One more pothole, one less asshole, was another popular comment.

The ETA commandos had covered their retreat by shouting about a gas explosion, and Franco's staff, either out of confusion or fearing his rage, had initially told the Caudillo that his closest associate really had died in a gas explosion. Franco repeatedly muttered, "These things happen" and went into a deep depression. By the next day's cabinet meeting, he understood what had really happened, and staring at the admiral's empty chair, he wept.

It is difficult to say to what extent the dynamite on Calle Serrano changed Spanish history. Carrero was replaced by Carlos Arias Navarro, a brutal leader, notorious for his war crimes during the Civil War. But Arias Navarro was unable to hold power. Would Carrero Blanco have done better?

Whatever is the judgment of history, at the time the assassination was widely seen as the end of Francoism. The stagnating nation felt exhilarated. Leaders such as Felipe González, Communist chief and Second Republic veteran Santiago Carillo, and both Basque and Catalan leaders began secretly meeting to plan for a transition to democracy.

By September 1975, ETA was suspected of a total of thirty-eight killings, whereas during the same period the police and Civil Guard had only killed thirty-three Basques. On September 27, Franco had five political prisoners, including two accused ETA members, shot by a firing squad of Guardia Civil volunteers. The Spanish Basques went on strike. The French Basques demonstrated in Bayonne. An angry crowd set the Spanish Embassy in Lisbon on fire. The French government protested the executions. Swedish prime minister Olaf Palme called the members of the Spanish government "murderers." Mexican president Luis Álvarez Echevarría, of Basque ancestry, himself notorious for suppression of student demonstrations, asked for the expulsion of Spain from the United Nations. All the leading European trade unions called for the boycott of Spain, fifteen European countries withdrew their ambassadors, and Spanish embassies faced demonstrations around the world. But Franco was still alive, still in power, still killing.

THE PLAZA DE ORIENTE in Madrid is an oval-shaped area in front of the Royal Palace. The streets around it are short and lead in seemingly random directions, but whichever direction is taken, ending up in the plaza is almost inevitable. On October 1, 1975, a crisp fall day with a bright blue sky, anyone milling around those little central Madrid streets felt helplessly sucked into the plaza by a growing crowd that looked like a cross section of Spain. Many were well dressed, though some looked like workers. The elderly, the ubiquitous amputees from the Civil War, and the newly emerging middle class and teenagers, even some children, were there. Overhead in the flawless cornflower blue sky, a plane circled, trailing a red-and-yellow banner that said, "*Arriba España*," Forward Spain.

Suddenly, what seemed to be an eighty-pound man, a frail and bald figure with uncertain steps, appeared on the palace balcony almost as though he had drifted out there in his confusion. A thousand right arms stiffened and snapped straight out at forty-five-degree angles, repeating the Fascist salute over and over again while shouting in unison, "Franco! Franco! Franco!"

Under the "Forward Spain" banner, as if the past forty years had never happened, the Europe of the 1930s was alive in Madrid. The elderly man spoke in his wheezing, squeaky voice of the grave menaces to society: the Freemasons and the Communists. The voice was difficult to hear, but was anyone there who had not heard all this before? The crowd responded with their mantra and their stiff arms, and Franco weakly raised his two shaking arms in reply, then drifted behind a curtain, never to be seen by his public again.

# Part Three

# EUSKADI ASKATUTA

*Ideas, at least profound ideas, develop very slowly and, even though geocentrism may have been in theory rejected, it has not been eclipsed and is still among our most deeply implanted concepts. Geocentrism and centrism, for that matter, remain at the foundation of Western thought, seeming to us almost the natural thing to think, or, at least, to feel; that that which is ours is the center of whatever thing. However, this idea of the center is not natural but cultural, and the image of the universe coming from it seems to be caused by an erroneous perspective.*
*—Joseba Sarrionaindia,* Ni ez naiz hemengoa,
*(I Am Not from Here), 1985*

# Slippery Maketos

*Bilbao drinking water is agreeable and abundant.*
*—José Antonio Zamácola, 1815*

*There is a lot of money here [in Bilbao]. What difference does*
*it make if there isn't a glass of fresh water?*
*—Sabino Arana, 1897*

ABOUT THE FAMOUS Basque delicacy, baby eels, José María Busca
Isusi wrote, "I believe that only in our country have people dared
to prepare and consume a dish which resembles a bunch of
worms." It is a Basque habit of mind to imagine that everything
Basque is uniquely Basque, but Busca Isusi was mistaken. Aside
from the fact that there are people in Mexico who do not hesi-
tate to eat real worms by the plateful, Basques are not the only
ones who eat the wormlike baby eel. A baby eel is called an *elver*
in English, *angula* in Spanish, *pibale* in French, and *txitxardin,*
which means "wormlike," in Euskera. Elvers appear in all European rivers that flow to the Atlantic and Mediterranean, and a
number of other peoples, notably Atlantic French, enjoy them.
But what disturbed the Basques in the 1990s was the terrible
discovery that the Japanese eat them too.

The small creatures, actually smaller than most worms, turn
up in Basque rivers every winter, and became associated with
Basque winter holidays, such as carnival. For centuries they were
scooped out just above the mouths of Guipúzcoan rivers. Six
Basque families in Aguinaga, on the Orio River only a few miles
from San Sebastián, became the principal suppliers in the world.

Elver fishermen waited for nightfall before dragging the
river, because the elvers stay on the bottom, resting during the
day. Eels avoid light. At night, the fishermen would haul up a

fine weave of white squirmy creatures, which they then kept alive in their own freshwater tanks for about a week until the elvers' backs mysteriously turned dark. Since a dead eel will not turn color, the dark color ensures that the eel was taken live. This issue took on added importance as the rivers grew increasingly polluted and inhospitable to delicate little elvers.

Like all eel, elvers must be cooked live or shortly after death to maintain an agreeable texture. The fisheries are very secretive about the exact process, maintaining that this is where the real quality of the product is determined. The chief defense of an eel is its slipperiness, which comes not only from its smooth skin—the scales are ingrown—but also from glands that secrete a slime, which must somehow be removed. Plunging them in salty lukewarm water after cooking is part of the process. Then they are wrapped in cloth to be kept moist.

The elvers are sold all over Spain and exported fresh, frozen, or canned to France and Latin America. The Basques usually prepare them in olive oil, garlic, and peppers. The recipe stays the same, but the servings have gotten smaller every year.

In the 1980s, when the Orio and other rivers turned green with surfaces that were sometimes foamy and other times dark and pearly, the catches were so meager that it was widely believed the eels were dying out. The price tripled, and the Aguinaga fisheries could still not meet the demand.

That was when one of the old established Basque family-owned companies, Angulas Aguinaga, decided it was time for an alternative. It turned from the Orio to the Japanese for technology to convert surimi into a substitute elver. Surimi is the white flesh of bottom-feeding fish that has been pressed into blocks on factory ships. At one time it was made from Atlantic cod, but when that was overfished, Pacific pollack took its place. Japan's Nichirei Corporation designed machines for Angulas Aguinaga that force the surimi out, spaghettilike, into the shape of elvers.

A touch of squid ink tints the backs dark. Angulas Aguinaga, which has no Japanese on its staff, produces the substitute elvers in a factory in the Guipúzcoan industrial mountain village of Irura. It sells 500 tons of these fake angulas, which it calls *gulas*, in a good year.

"It's a completely natural product," asserted Angulas Aguinaga sales director Juan Carlos Souto Ibañez, although the list of ingredients on the package includes Monosodium Glutamate E-415. Souto Ibañez further asserted that unlike angulas, gulas are cholesterol-free.

What they are not is eels, and they have neither the same taste nor texture. Visually, the main difference is that there is no face. The two black specks that are eyes and the thread line of a tiny mouth on one end are missing. In the Basque provinces, where it is widely believed that it is the Japanese who are making gulas in Irura, discriminating consumers sift through their sizzling earthenware casserole with the traditional wooden fork that is always provided, and search for faces before they eat. Some Basques do not even trust this test. Against all logic and

An *angulero*, an angula fisherman in Aguinaga, on the Orio in the 1920s. (Kutxa Fototeka, San Sebastián)

evidence, persistent rumors are heard that "the Japanese are painting fake faces on gulas."

Souto Ibañez points out that his company deliberately left off the faces and changed the name to gulas, so that they could not be accused of perpetrating a fraud.

"It's a swindle," José María Otamendi, director of a traditional elver fishery, El Angulero de Aguinaga, nevertheless declared. Although gulas were selling for $16 per pound instead of the $40 per pound for elvers, he asserted that this was still "very expensive for some unknown fish."

Back in the days when Angulas Aguinaga was fishing real elvers and was really in Aguinaga, Otamendi had worked for the company. But once it changed its product, he left and returned to his own family's business. In hip boots by the swirling tanks of the busy family elver pound, he said, "It is hard work, but it is a tradition. It is what my grandfather did and my father and my son."

Since the Orio River, which twists past the stone houses of Aguinaga, is a suspiciously bright green-gray color, and its banks are peppered with bits of trash, the companies started supplementing their dwindling catch by buying French and British elvers. But, Angulas Aguinaga claimed to be saving the eels and even asked the European Community to ban elver fishing.

Then, in the early 1990s, the angulas started coming back.

Eels have always puzzled man. Until the 1920s, no one had been able to identify reproductive organs in the creatures, and it was often supposed that Aristotle had been right when he stated that they somehow were created out of the mud. An eighteenth-century Italian had claimed to discover an eel's ovaries, but the scientific world did not accept his finding for another seventy years simply because no one had ever seen an eel egg. If eel eggs could have been found, no doubt the Basques would have eaten them too.

In the twentieth century, the surprising discovery was made that the eels in the Orio were not Basque at all. In fact, all of the European eels and all of the American eels, a related species but with approximately ten fewer vertebrae, are born in the middle of the Atlantic, in the deep, warm, algae-laden waters off Bermuda known as the Sargasso Sea.

The tiny, newborn, oval-shaped creatures then begin a journey, like salmon in reverse, to the river of their parents' adulthood. By the second summer they pass the Azores and have grown to five times their original size, but are still only a quarter the size of a tiny river elver. In the fall of the third year, they reach the Orio River and continue to grow, until they become angula size by the winter.

Most of this process is still unknown. Once a full-grown eel leaves a European river, it seems to vanish in the depths, and the cycle has never been entirely traced. So it was not known why, later in the 1990s, the eels began to disappear from the rivers once again. Was it pollution? Aguinaga fishermen had been saying for years that most of the elvers that they didn't catch quickly, died in the green Orio. Or were they just taking too many of them? Every elver that is eaten is one that will not grow into an eel and swim back to the Sargasso Sea to reproduce.

And yet the Basques had always taken huge quantities of elvers. In 1775, a British naturalist on a trip to Bilbao said that elvers were caught "by the millions." A French naturalist, Louis Roule, made some calculations based on early-twentieth-century train records from Landes, the region on the other side of the Adour, and found that in 1906, between 100 and 150 million elvers were shipped by train.

By THE LATE 1990s, the Basques were growing desperate. In Hendaye an elver shop operated near the St. Jacques Bridge border crossing, selling in either pesetas or francs. The shop was only open in the winter, Thursday, Friday, and Saturday. Soon it was sold out by Friday. Eventually it was only open one day a week. The shopkeeper's father had bought the antique building in a *viager* contract, a French arrangement in which the owner is paid a lifetime salary and the payer inherits the property. The owner had died early enough so that the house had been a bargain, and with no real overhead, the son was able to be in the angula business. But after a while he did not even have enough for a full day. The storefront looked like an empty fish shop with a long refrigerated display counter inside containing only one cloth-covered shallow crate.

The son even tried selling "white elvers" for half price, which, since the price had soared to more than $100 a pound, was still not a bargain. White elvers were ones that for one reason or another had died before they got to the tanks and had been cooked already dead—the mushy ones that are usually culled from the bunch. No, most Basques would rather eat a gula.

In time, most Basque rumors prove to be at least partly true and eventually companies developed—Basque companies, not Japanese ones—surimi elvers with two dots for eyes. On close inspection by those with good enough eyesight, there is still no mouth.


IN 1998, trout and eel from the Bidasoa River were examined by the Navarra government, and although northern Navarra is thought of as one of the more pristine parts of Basqueland, the fish were found to contain high levels of heavy metals, especially copper.

But was that the real problem? All peoples are a product of their history, and Basque history has always been about defending their birthright against outsiders. And so, after centuries of scooping up every baby eel they could find, and after more than a 100 years of dumping industrial refuse in rivers, the Basques discovered the real problem with their prized elvers.

Once again, it was the Japanese. In the winter, articles began appearing in Basque newspapers saying that the Japanese were paying high prices and buying up all the angulas. One paper, *La Semaine du Pays Basque*, a popular weekend tabloid in French Basqueland, trying to be fair, ran the headline, "The eel, which are a delicacy to the Japanese, are disappearing from the estuaries because of pollution."

BERNABE RAMA was born in Bilbao but speaks no Euskera. His father was from Andalusia and, being unemployed, came to Bilbao in 1945 to work as a laborer, on roads, construction—whatever he could find. Bernabe does not consider himself a nationalist or Basqueland a nation. But like many others, he uses the word *inmigrante*, an internal immigrant, to describe outsiders like his family.

Bernabe is the head chef at the Restaurant Bermeo, a leading traditional Bilbao restaurant. Asked for his angulas recipe, he referred to a twenty-year-old book of standard recipes. His only change was that where the old recipe had indicated angulas for four people, he crossed it out and wrote "for six."

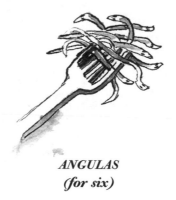

*ANGULAS*
*(for six)*

*600 grams angulas*
*4 cloves garlic, sliced*

*a few slices of guindilla*
*enough olive oil to cover the bottom of a casserole*

*Put the casserole on a high flame with olive oil and sliced garlic.*
*When the garlic starts to change color, work in the angulas and*
*guindilla slices. Keep the casserole constantly moving for 30 sec-*
*onds. Then remove it. It is essential that the dish be served very*
*hot, but not overcooked.*

# 13: The Great Opportunity

*This is the best opportunity Spain has had in a century.*
*—Felipe González, interview with the author, September 1981*

FRANCO DIED SLOWLY, torturing himself and Spain for more than a month, while aides and ministers, the fawning court, tried to get everything signed and readied for the fight to perpetuate their rule without their Caudillo. Finally, his daughter insisted on disconnecting the various tubes of an elaborate life-support system. On November 20, 1975, he died, leaving behind a written statement warning: "Do not forget that the enemies of Spain and Christian civilization are on the alert." While black armbands were seen on the streets of Madrid, Catalans discreetly uncorked champagne at home, and Basque youth less discreetly danced in the streets of Euskadi.

Juan Carlos became king and head-of-state, in accordance with Franco's wishes. He further fulfilled Franco's wishes by appointing Arias Navarro head-of-government. The first phase of what is known in Spanish history as "the transition" was largely a struggle among various members of Franco's regime. Arias Navarro tried to build a stable government but, by July, had given up and resigned. Juan Carlos next appointed another figure from the Franco years, a former civil governor, suave and sphinxlike forty-three-year-old Adolfo Suárez.

The new thirty-seven-year-old king, tall, handsome, and silent, known more for skiing than politics, was a mystery. The extreme right wing had never trusted him. Franco had been warned that this prince who never talked was waiting for his sponsor's death to dismantle the regime. But Franco's opponents believed, as did Franco, that he was a harmless puppet. The Spanish public believed he had few thoughts of his own and could be manipulated by anyone close to him. Juan Carlos jokes, in which the king was portrayed as an idiot, were in fashion.

One of the new king's first acts was sending a representative to French Basqueland with the task of contacting ETA, assuring them things were going to be very different, and inviting them to negotiate peace. But nothing about Juan Carlos's demeanor, public image, or initial public acts had given ETA cause to trust him, and they dismissed the offer as insincere.

The last Franco year had broken all records since the 1950s for repression of Basques. The first post-Franco year, which began with Arias Navarro, was barely an improvement. His minister of the interior, Manuel Fraga Iribarne, another figure from Franco's dictatorship, but one with an image as a reformer, was now disappointingly Francoist. The participants in demonstrations were brutally attacked, and though the number of arrests was drastically reduced, the sixteen Basques killed by Guardia Civil and police in 1976 was barely an improvement over the eighteen in 1975.

Spain had an opportunity at last to catch up with European history, to become a democracy and rejoin the West. As head-of-government, Suárez tried to please the forces pushing for democracy while keeping his old Francoist colleagues and the military content enough to restrain from forcibly overthrowing the government. The rightists wanted a tough policy toward the Basques, and throwing them to the Guardia Civil seemed a small price to pay for persuading the unhappy right wing not to derail the entire process. Even displaying the ikurriña remained illegal.

ETA was not waiting to see how the transition turned out. According to Spanish authorities, ETA killed eighteen people in 1976, starting with a Guardia Civil who tried to remove a booby-trapped ikurriña. At this point, ETA had divided into two groups. The killing was done primarily by a group called *ETA militar*. In an underground publication they identified three types of people they intended to kill: Franco-supported mayors, police collaborators and informants, and law enforcement officials who attempted to remove ikurriñas.

The second group, *ETA politico-militar*, began the post-Franco era with a new tactic: They would kidnap people for high ransoms. On January 11, 1976, they captured industrialist Francisco Luzariaga, who suffered a heart attack during the kidnapping and was released. Two days later, they took another hostage but released him after a month because it became clear that the victim's family were Basque nationalists.

All of this might have made ETA unpopular if the Guardia Civil was not at the same time engaged in its tactics of tearing down ikurriñas and disrupting folk festivals. On August 18, the Guardia Civil attacked a Basque song festival in Guernica because of the presence of ikurriñas.

The Basque Nationalist Party was having its own transition. Leizaola took a teaching position and faded into obscurity, while the newly invigorated old party, led by Xabier Arzalluz, an emotional man from an old Carlist family, at last dropped its insistence on loyalty to the Catholic Church. But the old slogan *Jaungoikua eta Lagizarra*, God and the Old Laws, has remained. Letters in the party still end with *un abrazo en JeL*, an embrace in JeL, when written in Spanish, or in Euskera, *JeL beti gogoan dogula*, always remember JeL.

When the Basque Nationalist Party demands the return of the Fueros, it is not asking that the legal code of 1526 be put back into place with its statutes on everything from a woman's place to the purity of cider. Nor does the party demand complete independence, something the Basques have not had since the Romans. What it wants is the restoration of the ability Basques had under the Fueros to enact their own laws.

But the first order of post-Franco business for the Basques was an amnesty for political prisoners. The amnesty movement,

Gestoras Pro-Amnistía, attracted many of the most prominent Basques, including not only stubborn longtime activists like Joseba Elósegi but also soccer stars and artists. The sculptor Eduardo Chillida, whose massive abstract work in stone, wood, or steel had become renowned in the international art world, designed the movement's logo.

In hindsight, the fact that it took two years to achieve a general amnesty for those imprisoned for resisting Franco—two years of demonstrations, petitions, and negotiations to decriminalize opposition to the dictatorship—was one of the early signs that the new Spanish democracy would not be entirely different from the old regime. Guardia Civil attacked peaceful demonstrations for amnesty and on several occasions shot and killed demonstrators.

Another sign was the fate of Eva Forest, a Catalan mother of three who had run a Madrid organization called Solidarity with Basqueland. She had been jailed and tortured in 1974 for the crime of interviewing the ETA commandos who had killed Carrero Blanco and then publishing the interview in Hendaye under the name Julen Agirre "from somewhere in Southern Euskadi." Police had discovered a draft of the manuscript in her apartment in a random search. The charge was "necessary collaboration," meaning presumed guilt by circumstance. After the death of Franco, the Spanish continued to hold, interrogate, and torture her. The story is all the more remarkable because Spain was desperately trying to gain acceptance in Europe as a budding Western democracy and freeing Eva Forest was becoming a European cause célèbre. She was finally released in 1977 without ever having been brought to trial.

Freeing Eva Forest was one of many steps in slowly, one group at a time, obtaining the release of political prisoners. Arzalluz showed a new tough leadership, insisting, in line with Basque public opinion, on a total amnesty that would include all

ETA members. The last of the imprisoned Basques were released in December 1977. For a few days, Spanish jails held no Basque political prisoners.

In January, a new round of arrests began.

In 1977, the new democracy that was to end Spain's isolation in Europe was launched with general elections to a two-house parliament, the Cortes. One month before the elections, the ikurriña was at last legalized when the Basque Nationalist Party demanded the right to use it as their party symbol. Adolfo Suárez, the former Franco technocrat, became the first elected prime minister. His party won 34 percent, and Felipe González's Socialists came in second with 28 percent. But in the Basque provinces, the parties demanding autonomy from Spain, led by the Basque Nationalist Party, won a clear majority, including ten Senate seats. One of the new Basque Nationalist Party senators was the fiery Joseba Elósegi.

The combination of amnesty and elections had brought many Spanish Basques home from exile. Dolores Ibarruri, La Pasionaria, still dressed in black, returning from the Soviet Union, held her first political rally in Bilbao to the tune of "*Eusko gudariak gera*" and, at the age of eighty-two, won back her old seat as a deputy from Asturias to the lower house of the Cortes. Born in 1895, only three years younger than Franco, she had outlasted him. "I said they shall not pass, and they haven't," the octogenarian Communist deputy insisted defiantly.

Even Sabino Arana was back, his body returned to its grave in Sukarrieta.

Telesforo de Monzón was also back. In 1971 he and Txillardegi, along with thirty-five supporters, had taken refuge in the cathedral in Bayonne and began a hunger strike. After three days, the sixty-seven-year-old Monzón suffered a heart attack and was hospitalized, but he still refused to take nourishment.

In 1977 he was still alive and back on the Spanish side, as militant as ever.

THE TIME HAD arrived for what Madrid thought of as the next step toward democracy and what the Basques thought of as the next battle: the drafting of a new Spanish constitution. The hard history of Spain, the divisions of the nineteenth century, lingered on. When Felipe González said that Spain had the "best opportunity" in a century, he was referring to recapturing the opportunity the Liberals had missed after the Second Carlist War to build a liberal democracy. But to the Basques it was the best opportunity in a century to restore the autonomy that the Carlist Wars had taken away from them.

When work began in Madrid on a new constitution, two things became clear very quickly. A broad consensus existed that for Spain to have a peaceful future, it had to allow regions—especially Basqueland and Catalonia—a measure of autonomy. But it was equally clear that the Basques were not going to be left to choose the nature of that autonomy. There would be no return to the autonomy of the Foral system. The constitutional committee did not include a sampling of the parties in the Cortes, but rather a group of seven parliamentarians, including one Catalan and no Basques.

In the language of the 1978 Spanish constitution, Basque or Catalan is referred to as "a nationality," but only Spain is a nation. It states: "The Constitution is founded on the indissoluble unity of the Spanish nation, the common and indivisible fatherland of all Spaniards, and recognizes and guarantees the right to autonomy of the nationalities and regions of which it is composed and solidarity among them."

Spain has had numerous constitutions since the one General Espoz y Mina placed on a chair and ordered shot in 1812. But the 1978 constitution was the only one that ever declared the Spanish language the sole official language of Spain.

The constitution was to be ratified by popular vote. Arzalluz and the Basque Nationalist Party called on Basques to abstain from the vote. But Monzón believed it would make a stronger statement if Basques showed their disapproval by voting no. He argued, "We cannot accept the Spanish constitution because we are not Spaniards." But to most Basques, this was an argument for abstention rather than the participation of casting a negative vote.

The constitution was approved by a majority of Spaniards, but not by Basques: While only 11.3 percent of Basques followed Monzón and voted no, more than 40 percent of Basque voters abstained and others cast blank ballots. The constitution was not approved by a majority of voters in any of the Basque provinces. But against the will of the Basque "nationality," the new constitution became the law of the "nation." Any further discussion of Basque independence would be questioning "the indissoluble unity of the Spanish nation" and therefore would be unconstitutional.

With the breakup of the state declared unconstitutional and the military given the right, in fact, the constitutional obligation, to intervene if a government violated the law of the land by compromising the indissoluble unity of the state, lawmakers believed that they had given enough assurances to the military to be able to proceed with demands for regional autonomy.

The constitution called for the establishment of seventeen regional entities including Ceuta and Melilla in Africa, which have a combined size of thirty-two square miles. The next smallest is the Balearic Islands in the Mediterranean, and the third smallest is the Autonomous Basque Community of Euskadi. The constitution did not specify the nature of regional government. Each region proposed, subject to Cortes approval, its own idea of what a region should be. New Castile, which includes Madrid, was not interested in autonomy. To no one's surprise, the Basques and the Catalans wanted more autonomy than anyone else.

To the dismay of many Basques, Navarra became a separate

region. Conservative, pro-Spanish elements in Navarra had pushed for a region apart from the three Basque provinces, but whether or not this was the will of the general population was a long-standing debate. In 1981, the so-called politico-militar wing of ETA made a Navarrese referendum on rejoining the Basque region one of its conditions for a cease-fire. Madrid never responded to that item.

The many differences accrued from several historic periods have separated Navarra from the other three Basque provinces in Spain. Going back to Roman times, the Romanization of the Ebro Valley had made Navarra, by most definitions, only half Basque. The area south of Pamplona is not culturally Basque, and "Spanish" political parties—what the Basques call, not without a slight sneer, *Españolistas,* Spain lovers—win a far higher percentage of the vote in Navarra than they do in the other Basque provinces. The split over the Kingdom of Navarra, the split over the Carlist Wars, the split over Franco and the Civil War—two separate histories have driven these people apart.

Opinion polls in Navarra indicate that only a minority of Navarrese consider themselves Spanish, but a somewhat smaller minority consider themselves Basque. The majority of modern Navarrese think of themselves as simply Navarrese. But the Navarrese speak Euskera and fit almost any definition of Basque—except theirs. If the seven provinces were to be united today, a separatist movement might emerge in Navarra.

The Basques and the Navarrese in their separate regions, the Autonomous Community of Euskadi and the Foral Community of Navarra, had the same reference point: the Fueros. They each wanted something as close to that ancient condition of semi-independence as they could get. This was far more than anyone else was asking for. Even the Catalans hesitated at the kind of fiscal autonomy the Basques demanded.

The Basques and Navarrese did not get the kind of separate Foral state they wanted, but they did get their own local governments, their own parliaments, their own school systems and highways, all of which were paid for by their own taxes. The only tax restriction was that the total tax package be the same as that in the rest of Spain. The statute of autonomy for the three provinces barely passed, getting an affirmative vote from only 54 percent of eligible voters. It is impossible to say how many Basques would want complete independence from Spain, since such a plebiscite would be unconstitutional and has never been held. But within the Autonomous Basque Community, a clear majority votes in every election for nationalist parties that proclaim as a goal more independence from the Spanish state.

Carlos Garaikoetxea became the first lehendakari since Aguirre. Like all of the subsequent ones, he was handpicked by the Basque Nationalist Party. The party, both conservative and nationalist, has been able to dominate elections and control the Basque government, making Xabier Arzalluz, the party boss, the single most powerful Basque in the Autonomous Basque Community. Part of Garaikoetxea's appeal was that he was a Navarrese from Pamplona, and his leadership was supposed to bring the two Basques together. Ramón Labayen said, "We thought it would be a good gesture for the people of Navarra, but it turned out that the people of Navarra didn't give a damn for the gesture."

Still, for the Civil War generation, there was a sense of triumph in March 1980 when Garaikoetxea stood under the oak tree in Guernica and took the same oath as Aguirre: "Humble before God, standing on Basque soil, in remembrance of our ancestors, under the tree of Guernica . . ."

For an instant, those who had been there in 1936 could almost feel that the terrible four decades that followed had never happened, had been reversed, somehow erased. Except that Garaikoetxea did not speak mother-tongue Euskera as Aguirre had. An entire generation had grown up under Franco not speaking Euskera, and the Basques were very aware that one of the great challenges before their government was to bring back the language of the Basque people. Garaikoetxea was an Euskaldunberri. He had grown up speaking only Spanish but was now learning Euskera. In his four years as lehendakari, he achieved fluency.

The first time the Spanish army was officially to meet the lehendakari, the officers initially said they would not salute him. They were persuaded that the salute was all in the name of upholding the constitution with its sworn loyalty to the king. But then Garaikoetxea had to be persuaded to salute in return.

To BASQUES WHO wanted autonomy, the "autonomous regions" were a parody of their dream, and, once again, many young Basques were blaming the Basque Nationalist Party. In 1978, the year of the constitution, Monzón had broken with the Basque Nationalist Party to form a new, more militant group solidly behind ETA that attracted young Basque voters. It was called Herri Batasuna, Popular Unity. In 1979, Monzón was arrested, along with most of the principal figures in Herri Batasuna. The Basque public reacted with a strike that virtually closed down Guipúzcoa. The leaders were all released except Monzón, who was charged with "apology for terrorism." Telesforo de Monzón, his spirit unchanged but his body feeling the wear of almost fifty years of nonstop political resistance, went on another hunger strike which almost killed him. But that same year, there was another round of parliamentary elections, and this time Herri Batasuna won three deputy's seats and one in the Senate at the expense of the Basque Nationalist Party. Monzón had to be released to take the seat he had won in the Cortes, the same seat he had occupied in the 1930s for the Basque Nationalist Party. To be precise, he was released to reject his seat, since it was the policy of Herri Batasuna candidates to refuse to take the Madrid seats to which they were elected.

Only months later, a prosecutor ordered Monzón arrested after he outlined the Herri Batasuna position to the foreign press. His health deteriorating, he fled to France to avoid arrest, and in March 1981 he died in Bayonne. Many of his poems, although not of great literary value, became popular songs that are still sung. Herri Batasuna, the only party that is openly supportive of ETA, has consistently garnered 15 to 20 percent of the Basque vote, though the parliamentarians elected to Madrid always refuse to take their seats.

Telesforo de Monzón could have lived a comfortable aristocrat's life in Vergara, eating with his own silver. But that was not the life he chose. He managed to be arrested one last time, when his funeral procession from St.-Jean-de-Luz was briefly stopped by Spanish police on its way to the family home in Vergara.

AFTER MARCH 1980 the Basques had a government and a legal flag, and signs went up along the Ebro to tell motorists when they were entering and leaving the Autonomous Basque Community of Euskadi. But establishing regions did not silence the demands of the Basque Nationalist Party, nor the guns of ETA, which grew even more active while support for Basque nationalist political parties remained solid.

All of this perplexed, frustrated, and infuriated the Spanish military. The military, and particularly the Guardia Civil, tend to be family careers passed on from father to son, and after more than a generation in power, the transition years were not happy ones for those military families. Their power had been greatly reduced, hemmed in by a Ministry of Defense that was part of a popularly elected government. The 65,000 Guardia Civil were taken out of direct military command and made answerable to the Ministry of Interior. They were also badly demoralized by ETA attacks and their complete isolation in Basque country. Increasingly, they asked not to be stationed in Basqueland, and each year hundreds of those who were stationed there requested transfers.

From the military point of view, the politicians had given

away far more than they should have—and still the Basques were not satisfied. The prime minister, Adolfo Suárez, was called "a traitor." By 1980, rumors of a military coup d'état, persistent since the resignation of Arias Navarro, were one of the main topics of political gossip in Madrid. Many leaders, including Felipe González, warned of the danger.

Between 1978 and 1980, ETA killed as many as eighty people in a year, the most violent period in its history. In the same period, police and Guardia Civil broke up demonstrations almost 600 times and in the process killed forty-one people. In 1979, Amnesty International sent a team to Spain that reported on the use of torture in Madrid, Barcelona, and Bilbao.

The increasingly restless military was acting in odd and troubling ways. Groups of right wingers, popularly known as *incontrolados*, attacked Basque nationalists, killing thirty-five people during this period. But were they really uncontrolled as their name suggested? In November 1980, someone walked into a small, dark, crowded bar, the Bar Hendayais, on a narrow street that dropped down to the bay in central Hendaye, and sprayed the drinking customers with machine gun bullets, killing two, both French citizens, and wounding ten others. The bar, said to be popular with Basque nationalists, was only a few minutes from the border, the St. Jacques Bridge, and three Spaniards were intercepted at the crossing by Guardia Civil. After a phone call to Madrid, they were taken to Irún and released. The attack was claimed by an unknown group called the Basque-Spanish Battalion.

Felipe González's Spanish Socialist Workers Party joined with the Communists and the Basque Nationalist Party in demanding to know if the government was sponsoring this Basque-Spanish Battalion.

The atmosphere became even more tense in January, when Suárez suddenly resigned from the government without explanation. Was he trying to pacify an angry military that had turned against him? He wouldn't say.

On the same day as the resignation, ETA kidnaped José María Ryan, an engineer at the Lemóniz nuclear power plant. During the nuclear power controversy of the 1970s, no proposed nuclear plant anywhere was more bitterly opposed than the one in Lemóniz. In 1977 an ETA commando was killed attempting to attack the construction site. In 1978, ETA blew a twelve-inch hole in a steam generator at the site, killing two workers. By the time the project was abandoned in 1982, it had been the object of not only constant demonstrations, several with more than 50,000 participants, but also 250 attacks, primarily by ETA.

Lemóniz was part of a project undertaken by the Franco regime to provide power for Basque industry. A series of three reactors had been planned on the Deba River, none of which was ever completed. Given the unpopularity of nuclear energy in Europe at the time, only a military dictatorship could have contemplated a nuclear power program in Basque country. Lemóniz, which was dangerously close to Bilbao, a city too large to evacuate in the event of an accident, was begun in 1972, but the new democracy had to face the combined forces of ETA and a suddenly liberated ecology movement with thousands of backers. Though Arzalluz and the Basque Nationalist Party supported the plan, which was contracted to companies controlled by the old families of Vizcayan industry, their stance was always unpopular.

In addition to the distrust of the technology itself, which was common to many Europeans in areas where plants had been installed, there was a political issue. Basques were supposed to control their own energy system, but no one believed the Spanish would let them run a nuclear plant autonomously. Nuclear power implied centralized authority, and not only Basque but Galician, Catalan, Breton, Wallonian Belgian, Scot, and Welsh nationalists were among the fiercest antinuclear activists in Europe.

At the time of the Ryan kidnaping, the Spanish king and queen were scheduled to visit Basque country, and, in keeping with tradition, they were to meet with the Basques at the Batzarre-txea, the meeting house by the oak of Guernica. The royal couple flew to Vitoria, which had become the capital of the Autonomous Community. Defying protocol, the Basque government organized no official welcome. While the king reviewed Spanish troops, Herri Batasuna activists sang "Eusko gudariak gera."

When the king delivered his speech in the Batzarretxea in Guernica, he was again outvoiced, by the elected Herri Batasuna delegation singing the Basque hymn. The Basque Nationalist Party disapproved and wanted the Herri Batasuna delegation silenced, but it also made it clear to the king that the only rela-tionship with the monarch that interested the party was not the one in the constitution but the Foral relationship which was now unconstitutional.

The mood in Spain was growing darker with each event.

Three days later, Ryan's body was found in Vizcaya, blind-folded and shot dead. The killing of the engineer was deplored by most Basques. But instead of capitalizing on a tragic public relations victory, Madrid reacted the way it always did to ETA violence. An ETA militant, José Arregui, held incommunicado for ten days in prison, died. The gruesome wounds on his corpse testified to the ten days of torture that had killed him. So instead of widespread condemnation of the Ryan killing, Basqueland mobilized a general strike to protest the military's killing of an ETA member. Five policemen were arrested and several govern-ment figures resigned over the Arregui killing.

To a few extremists in the military and the Guardia Civil, the insult to the king followed by the government turning against them, arresting defenders of Spain's honor, was too much to en-dure. In December they began to work on a plan of action.

IN THE GENRE of horror movies, a common ploy at the end of the film, after the monster has been vanquished, is for it to suddenly rise up one more time from the muck. That was the role of Guardia Civil lieutenant colonel Antonio Tejero in the history of Franco's Spain.

On February 23, 1981, while the Cortes in Madrid was installing a new government, twenty armed Guardia Civil entered the legislative chamber, fired rounds into the ceiling, and ordered everyone to the floor. There was Tejero, the officer who, in 1977, had been relieved of his command in San Sebastián for refusing to accept the legalization of the ikurriña, up on the speaker podium, pistol drawn, in his Guardia Civil uniform with its tricornered nineteenth-century hat and his long, full, nineteenth-century mustache, giving orders. The old Spanish monster was back for one more try. It was the twenty-fifth attempted military coup d'état in Spain since 1814.

The Basque government prepared to go back into exile. Garaikoetxea, at the time suffering from a sneezy bout of hay fever, was moved to the pollen-rich mountains near the border, ready to cross over.

But the coup failed. It may have been more than one coup. The relationship between the Guardia Civil action, the army's Brunete Division, which was to move on Madrid, and various other military actions at the time has never been completely clarified. King Juan Carlos, the commander in chief of the armed forces, is credited with talking the military officers out of backing the rebellion. But some of the plotters claimed that the king knew of the plot and that they had acted believing the king was behind them. It is not known if he had ever indicated support, or if he even knew of the plot. But its success would have been unlikely without his backing, and, in the end, it was the king's lack of support that caused these officers to back down.

Whether the king had or had not been involved in the plot, the coup's failure was a resounding success for him, for the military, and for the Guardia Civil. The king, presented as the man who talked down the coup, gained a prestige he had never had before. The Juan Carlos jokes ended. So did rumors of military coups.

Most political leaders took February 23 as a lesson that the military and Guardia Civil needed to be kept happy. Not only the government, but Felipe González and his opposition Socialists, people who had spent their lives opposing the Guardia Civil and the military, suddenly responded sympathetically to their viewpoint and with increasing hostility to Basque nationalism. New antiterrorism laws were passed, giving the government the right to close down publications charged with "apology for terrorism," a crime which was upgraded from misdemeanor to felony.

Tejero and General Jaime Milans del Bosch received thirty-year sentences, a third leader was sentenced to six years, and eleven others were sentenced to less than three years. But Spain was to have its transition to democracy without purging a single figure from the Franco era, without prosecuting a single one of the many crimes these men had committed over forty years. The democracy would be built without purging the ranks of the military, the Guardia Civil, or even the operations of prisons.

The nations of western Europe had learned the same lesson as the Spanish politicians. They had almost seen their neighbor return yet again to the 1930s. In the future Spain would be encouraged and not criticized. There would no longer be discussion of its human rights record. Spain would be welcomed into the ranks of Europe. A great effort would be made to move forward its request for membership in the European Economic Community. The West would also persuade Spain to join NATO, thereby integrating its troublesome troops into the Western alliance.

Even ETA was changed by the coup. The Spanish government's frustrating two year negotiation with ETA's politico-militar wing suddenly bore fruit. The members of politico-militar saw that they would be defenseless if the military overthrew the democracy, and concluded that continuing to attack the current Spanish state would be too dangerous for the Basque people. In exchange for an amnesty and release from prison of its members, ETA politico-militar dissolved. But that did not end the violence because other branches of ETA were still active. There is always a splinter group. In time the Spanish government has come to feel that no matter what it negotiates with ETA, a dissident group refusing the accord will always emerge.

IN THE HISTORY of the Spanish "transition," there is no more dramatic change than the metamorphosis of Felipe González between the 1981 coup d'état and his election as prime minister the following year. After the coup attempt, the coming-to-power of the man all of Spain simply called Felipe was seen as inevitable. The youthful Socialist lawyer-turned-underground-labor-organizer was to be a political leader. The man who used to leap onto the back of trucks, dressed in corduroys and leather jacket, and talk to the workers had somehow vanished. The new man in the dark suits was still youthful and charming, but gone was the lawyer who defended civil rights. He became a firm advocate of repressive antiterrorist laws, arguing that other democracies, faced with terrorism, had done the same and therefore it was a democratic thing to do.

Felipe had been an active member of the Socialist International, a protégé of Germany's Willy Brandt, and a young friend of France's avuncular François Mitterrand, who was also about to come to power. Felipe had headed the Socialist's committee on Nicaragua that had taken a critical stance in favor of the Sandinista rebels and against U.S. policy. Asked, in a 1981 interview, in what sense of the word was he a Socialist, he replied, "In all senses of the word—except in the Communist sense." One political maneuver, in preparation for power, was to resign from the Spanish Socialist Workers Party and refuse to come back until it struck the word *Marxist* from its party charter.

Asked if he was concerned that power might have a corrupting effect, he insisted that there would be no temptation for him to abuse power because the constitution provided a system of checks and balances that would prevent it.

The Socialist Party slogan for the 1982 election was *Por Cambio*, For Change, and although little change was being offered, the Spanish, even many Basques, could not help but feel excited about the prospect of someone taking over the government who had not been a part of, who had in fact opposed, the thirty-six-year dictatorship. After so many years of morose stagnation, nothing more than forward motion was a thrilling prospect. Begoña Aretxaga, later a Harvard anthropologist, was in her native San Sebastián at the time. "I was excited in spite of myself, even without believing," she recalls of the 1982 election. "The legitimacy of the government depends on the continuous exercise of an act of forgetting."

# 14: Checks and Balances

*In people's lives and in social history there is always a first mistake, a little mistake, which happens almost imperceptibly, a momentary slip-up, but this first mistake creates others, and these mistakes follow each other, accumulating little by little, one on top of another. Eventually, this creates a growing and fateful error.*
*—Joseba Sarrionaindia, NI EZ NAIZ HEMENGOA,*
*(I Am Not from Here), 1985*

FRENCH POLICY TOWARD "the Basque problem" has always been to keep it in Spain. As long as the problem stayed in Spain, ETA members could stay in France. The French government's support of Spanish Basque refugees had long helped to keep peaceful relations between Paris and French Basques. But after the death of Franco, French foreign policy changed. Being an enemy of Spain no longer gave a Spanish refugee automatic legitimacy in France. Since the Spanish government was no longer unquestionably the villain, Basques were no longer unquestionably the victims. Political refugee status and work permits for Spanish Basques were no longer automatically granted. Increasingly, French police rounded up Basques, not all of them ETA members, for questioning, broke into homes, and searched without warrants. Suspected ETA members were arrested and sometimes spent months in prison without being charged with a crime. In 1979, the French government ended political refugee status for newly arrived Basques. But it still refused to extradite Basques to Spain.

In 1980, an international conference on terrorism sponsored by the Council of Europe meeting in Strasbourg concluded, to the approval of human rights groups, that suspects should not be extradited to countries that practiced torture. The two examples cited were Turkey and Spain.

In May 1981, Mitterrand was elected president of France. The following year, on October 28, 1982, Felipe González came to power in Spain expecting a special relationship with France, since the president was his old colleague from the Socialist International. To his great frustration and disappointment, Mitterrand would not cooperate. To head his law enforcement team, González chose as minister of interior a fellow Andalusian of his generation, a forty-two-year-old son of a policeman of Carlist sympathy, José Barrionuevo. The day the new government was announced, *El País* noted that Barrionuevo was "considered by those who know him as a man capable of imposing authority because he knows how to legitimize it."

The new Socialist government was to be "tough" like past regimes, but unlike its predecessors, it would operate by the legitimate rule of law. Yet on December 15, with the new Spanish Socialist government only two weeks old, Barrionuevo announced that he was reviewing antiterrorist policy. The result was the Socialists passed laws limiting the right of an accused to legal assistance and giving police the right to hold prisoners incommunicado—without access to lawyers and without presenting them to a court—for up to ten days. Known in legal language as the suspension of habeas corpus, this is considered a violation of basic rights in all Western law because it gives law enforcement the liberty to commit even worse crimes. That is exactly what happened with Spain's new antiterrorist laws. Suspects detained under these new laws were routinely beaten and tortured, and then released in a few days without ever being charged. Journalists were arrested and convicted of "insulting the Spanish government and the King." Especially targeted was the pro-Herri Batasuna paper *Egin*.

*Egin*, meaning "to act," began publishing in 1977 with small investments from 25,000 backers. As the constant object of government repression, the paper gathered a following. The Spanish government's attempt to shut it down seemed to be almost a reenactment of the Franco era. In 1983, an *Egin* columnist, Sanchez Erauskin, became a popular hero when, while serving time on charges of insulting the king, he used a hunger strike to force the government to reclassify him as a political prisoner. The editor of the paper, José Felix Azurmendi, was regularly arrested by the González government. Columnists, journalists, even people who were quoted in articles, were arrested and sometimes convicted for insulting the government or "apology for terrorism."

THE NUMBER OF Basque prisoners in Spanish prisons began rising steadily, with more than 100 arrests in some months. It was becoming apparent that government by Felipe, despite his endearing smile and years of antifascism, was not going to offer an improvement in human rights.

In 1983, Amnesty International, after sending observers to Spain, reported: "The torture and ill-treatment of detainees, principally people detained under anti-terrorist laws, continues to be Amnesty International's main concern." The observers found that 691 people, mostly in Basque country, had been arrested under the antiterrorist laws, and gave examples of prisoners who had been tortured. In replying to the report, Barrionuevo said, "At this point it should be noted that it is normal for terrorist groups to accuse the authorities of torture and ill-treatment as a way of interrupting incommunicado detentions and hindering police investigations." He went on to say that harsh measures were "justified by the grave threat that is posed by terrorism."

Barrionuevo went to the legislature and got approval for a project costing almost $100 million. Called ZEN or Zona Especial del Norte, it was intended to transform the politics of the Basque region by winning support for the Guardia Civil and National Police and turning the population against ETA. Among the proposed techniques to accomplish this was the planting of false stories in Basque newspapers. After Basque municipalities passed measures against the plan and it was condemned by the Basque government, ZEN was quietly dropped—at least as far as is known.

Other plans proceeded, including sending more Guardia Civil to Basqueland and transferring Basque prisoners to special prisons outside Basque country, where they could be held by Guardia Civil instead of the usual prison guards.

González was faced with a decrease, not an increase, in ETA activity. But the government encountered constant accusations from the opposition Alianza Popular, the Popular Alliance Party, that the Socialists were soft on terrorism. The Alianza Popular was an alliance of former Francoist factions headed by former Franco minister Manuel Fraga Iribarne. When the government proposed laws suspending basic civil liberties, Fraga said they were not enough, that Basqueland should be put under a state of siege, the way Franco used to do, suspending all civil liberties. Fraga once said, "When the innocent blood of citizens is running, a government should prefer to have blood on its hands than water like Pilate."

ON OCTOBER 16, 1983, two Basque refugees, José Antonio Lasa and José Ignacio Zabala, were kidnapped in France. No one claimed responsibility for the kidnapping, and neither the two men nor their bodies were ever found.

On December 4, Segundo Marey, fifty-one, was sitting in his home in Hendaye, shoes off, watching *The Benny Hill Show* on television, when two hefty men broke in and took him, still in socks, to a mountain hideaway in Spain. The Red Cross received a note that Marey could be exchanged for four Spanish policemen being held by the French government in connection with an unsuccessful attempt to kidnap a Basque.

The four policemen were released, and Marey was found near the border, fifteen pounds lighter after ten days in captivity. A note was found in his pocket saying, "You will have more news from GAL." GAL, it was to be learned, was a Spanish acronym for Antiterrorist Liberation Groups. It appeared to be an extreme right-wing vigilante death squad that attacked Basque militants in their safe refuge across the border. Still, the Marey case was odd because he seemed to be nothing more than a furniture dealer without any known political involvements.

On December 19, GAL struck again, killing a Basque refugee, Ramón Oñaederra, in a Bayonne bar.

It was widely rumored in Basqueland that GAL worked for the Spanish government. After the Oñaederra killing, Arzalluz came out and said it. "I am personally persuaded, although I cannot prove it, that the GAL and that 'dirty war' have ties to government measures in Madrid."

This was vintage Arzalluz. The head of the Basque Nationalist Party was always making wild accusations and later admitting that he had no proof. His party lived in terror of his next statement. Herri Batasuna made the same allegation as Arzalluz, but it too was always making accusations against the Spanish state. Another rumor was that wealthy Vizcayan businessmen sponsored GAL. There were always rumors in Basqueland.

The killings went on. The brother of the most wanted ETA leader was killed. The French state became more concerned about terrorism in Basqueland now that it was spreading to their provinces. In September 1984, after a series of meetings between the two governments, France agreed to extradite to Spain seven alleged directors of ETA. More extraditions followed. ETA responded with a campaign against French interests in Spain, not in France. ETA has always tried to keep the war out of France so that commandos would have a border to escape across.

On November 20, 1984, Santiago Brouard, a pediatrician, was killed in his Bilbao office by GAL. Brouard was the perfect go-between, both a respectable professional and a well-known leftist nationalist who had once gone into exile rather than betray a wounded ETArist he had treated. At the time of his killing, he had been trying to arrange negotiations between ETA and Madrid. The public outrage over this assassination seemed to slow down GAL activities. Or was it a more cooperative France that made the difference? In 1986, France increased the number of Basque extraditions to Spain, even though it had been documented that Basques turned over to the Spanish on previous occasions had been tortured.

In 1986, after killing perhaps twenty-seven people, GAL vanished.

In 1987, the Madrid magazine *Tiempo* conducted a poll in which 52 percent of respondents said they believed the Spanish government had been behind GAL. But in what may offer a more telling insight into Spanish democracy, 51 percent approved of GAL's killings.

WHERE WAS THE system of checks and balances that González had confidently predicted would prevent his abuse of power? For five years he was able to govern without any such impediments. Then the mystery of GAL began to unravel. After a traffic accident, incriminating documents were found in the car of José Amedo, a senior Spanish policeman. It appeared that he and another high-ranking officer, Michel Domínguez, had traveled frequently to French Basqueland with false identification papers. Arrested by Spain and wanted in France, the two confessed. Their 1989 trial, inevitably labeled "GALgate," resulted in sentences of 108 years for both of them for organizing GAL and its killings.

GAL agents turned out to be mercenaries: an assortment of right-wing French military left over from the Algerian war, underworld hitmen from organized crime in Marseilles, former Portuguese colonialists, and Italian neo-Fascists. Once, in 1984, the French had even caught a GAL operative and identified him as a former member of the OAS, an infamous right-wing French military group from the early 1960s Algerian independence war.

He was known to have been working for the Spanish government since Franco's time.

Citing security concerns, Barrionuevo refused to make any comments on the case. He was widely thought to be the true author of GAL. The Amedo and Domínguez trial revealed that the two convicted GAL organizers had operated with money from the Ministry of Interior. Felipe González insisted, even in the 1990s, when the trail finally led to Barrionuevo, that he himself had known nothing about GAL. Although a member of his own party in Vizcaya as well as several GAL members implicated González, no one was able to mount a successful legal case against him. González claimed that the case was being pursued as a political attack against his party, which may be true, but would still not establish his innocence.

Barrionuevo's undoing was that early Marey kidnapping. The reason Marey was taken was that the GAL kidnappers had mistaken him for an ETA suspect named Mikel Lujúa. Once they realized that the shivering victim carried away from his television was not Lujúa the terrorist, but Marey the furniture dealer, they contacted the number two Spanish law enforcement official, Rafael Vera, the director of state security. Vera called police officials in Bilbao, who consulted with Julián Sancristóbal, the civil governor of Vizcaya, who in turn got approval from Barrionuevo to try to exchange Marey for the four Spanish policemen.

Barrionuevo, Vera, and Sancristóbal each received ten-year prison terms, and nine other defendants received lesser sentences. The prosecution had asked for sentences of up to twenty-three years, the penalty for belonging to an armed terrorist group under Barrionuevo's antiterrorist laws. But the judges ruled that the prosecution had failed to prove that GAL was an armed terrorist group.

THE EXACT NUMBER of law enforcement officers in Spanish Basqueland is a state security secret. The Guardia Civil, which admits to 5,000 officers there, also has an undisclosed number of Basque-speaking undercover agents, as does the National Police. According to the Spanish government, there are about 15,000 uniformed police, including Basque police, Ertzantza, who are patrolling the 2.1 million inhabitants in the three provinces of Euskadi—more than seven police officers for every 1,000 citizens. This makes Spanish Basqueland the most policed population in Europe, although the ratio is probably similar in Navarra and may be even higher in the three French provinces.

One of the reasons for the high numbers of police is Madrid's lack of confidence in the Ertzantza. "The Ertzantza are reluctant to go to certain lengths," explained an adviser to the Spanish government. The Spanish government claims that the Guardia Civil and National Police have an arrest record four or five times higher than that of the Basque force. This is not necessarily an accomplishment, considering that most of those arrested are released after a few days without ever having been charged. According to Gestoras Pro-Amnistía, the Basque human rights group founded to campaign for amnesty after the death of Franco, in the twenty years since it achieved the 1977 general amnesty, 8,000 Basques have been imprisoned for political reasons, and the majority of them never had trials. Most human rights monitors believe Gestoras Pro-Amnistía's estimate to be extremely conservative.

The Basques do not credit their police force with gentleness. The Ertzantza has created tough antiterrorist units. Human rights monitors have found that all three groups practice torture, though they use different techniques. Josu Barela, head of Gestoras Pro-Amnistía, said, "What is worse? Do you want to be nearly asphyxiated with a plastic bag by the Guardia Civil, interrogated all night by the National Police, or threatened with death by the Ertzantza?"

More cases of psychological torment than physical torture have been found among those held by the Ertzantza. But Barela said, "We often find that physical torture does not leave victims as damaged as psychological torture. We often find that people who have hardly been touched physically are the most scarred." Insomnia, unreasoned fear, low self-esteem, a deep sense of guilt are among the symptoms.

The Ertzantza, from its inception, had been concerned about its public image. The Basque government had turned to Ramón Labayen to design a uniform for the new Basque police force. Ramón's passion is toy lead soldiers. He designs them, creating his own molds. For the new Ertzantza's uniforms, his only instructions had been to make them look as different from Spanish uniforms as possible. Labayen gave them red berets.

For all its Basqueness and its bright berets, the public had always been a little distrustful of yet another police force. When the new Basque security force began training, rumors spread that the Israelis were doing something in Alava. The Israeli-Basque connection, mostly imaginary, was a chronic topic of rumors.

Basque youth called Ertzantza *cipayos,* a pejorative used in the Indian independence movement for Indian troops that served the British. Armed with sticks and rocks, groups of youth called *encapuchados,* hooded ones, because they wore ski masks, staged seemingly disorganized attacks. The Spanish government believed that they worked with ETA, but in early 1998, ETA leadership publicly denounced them as "very young people ready to do anything," who interfere with ETA's overall strategies.

The Spanish government has always seemed to be either unwilling or unable to distinguish among widely diverse Basque groups. But in fact everyone was starting to look alike. Few faces were seen. ETA commandos wore knitted ski masks to conceal their identity. Then, in the 1990s, pro-ETA demonstrators began wearing them too—perhaps to show solidarity with the commandos, perhaps because the police started videotaping demonstrations, perhaps because the rebels in the Chiapas region of Mexico had popularized ski masks as a revolutionary symbol.

An ETA commando. Ertzantza officers on the street. (Both courtesy of the photography archives of *Egin*, Hernani)

Guardia Civil and National Police also began wearing masks to protect themselves from being singled out for reprisals. The Ertzantza's antiterrorist units adopted the same practice. Judges and court officials started wearing them too, for especially controversial sentencing.

In March 1996, Felipe González's Socialist Workers Party was defeated. Manuel Fraga's Popular Alliance, originally an alliance of Francoist politicians, had changed its name to the Popular Party, the PP, and came to power with José María Aznar as prime minister. The PP, with its Francoist roots, had promised to take a harder line with the Basques than had the Socialists. In spite of muzzling the press, imprisoning thousands, and engaging in torture, kidnapping, and murder, the González government was still vulnerable to the accusation of being "soft on Basques." To demonstrate the sincerity of its stance, the new government decided to have the entire twenty-three-person directorate of Herri Batasuna arrested.

During the election, in which each party had an allotted television airtime, Herri Batasuna had used its time to run a video from ETA. This party again won its usual 12-15 percent of the Basque vote and two seats in the Madrid legislature, which it again refused to fill, along with hundreds of offices in the Basque legislature and municipalities. The video had shown three men, faces concealed in ski masks, who, having been identified as ETA members, explained the demands of the organization for an independent Euskadi. This tape was a response to the Spanish government's often-stated view that "nobody knows what ETA wants."

Aznar's camp was divided on the impending arrests. Some thought that it would be a mistake to isolate Herri Batasuna, which represented almost 200,000 people; and it would be more useful, they thought, to try to win over its supporters. They also worried that other European countries would strongly criticize the new government for attempting to silence a legal political party that had the backing of voters.

Nevertheless, the twenty-three were arrested by masked men in front of press cameras. On December 1, 1997, the Supreme Court of Spain, also with masks on, sentenced the twenty-three politicians to seven years each.

Successive Spanish governments have learned that it is easy to ignore criticism from human rights groups. Numerous human rights groups have regularly protested the practice of torture in Spanish prisons, but they have also, often in the same reports, protested the violence and intimidation of ETA. The Spanish government does not deny the existence of torture, which is frequently corroborated by prison doctors. It has prosecuted and convicted officers and then sentenced them to two or three months in prison. A 1997 United Nations Human Rights Committee report on Spanish torture noted that when the Spanish government was confronted with allegations of torture, it often did nothing; and in cases where it did take legal action and obtained convictions, the torturers were "often pardoned or released early, or simply [did] not serve the sentence."

"The prisons are worse now than under Franco," said Eva Forest, human rights advocate and former prisoner. "Torture is more directed, more institutionalized. The Franquistas [Francoists] were not only not purged from the system, they have been promoted."

The Spanish government counters by repeatedly claiming that ETA has killed more than 800 people since Txabi killed the first Guardia Civil. But in that period of time, the Guardia Civil and others answering to the Spanish government have killed hundreds of Basques. Some have been presumed guilty and shot down in the streets, often in an alleged act of self-defense that none of the witnesses could verify. Some have died of "accidents" while in custody.

The persistent reports on Spanish abuse by human rights groups have little impact because European governments do not respond to them. What the Spanish government fears is condemnation from Western democracies, especially those of Europe. Their nightmare is condemnation from the broadest European forum, the Council of Europe. Founded in 1949, this was the first pan-European political organization.

Outside Spain, despite years of continuing human rights reports, it is widely believed that arbitrary arrest and torture in Spain are things of the past. No one noted the paradox when in October 1998 a Spanish judge, Baltazar Garzón, requested the extradition of Chilean leader Augusto Pinochet for the torture and killing of Spanish citizens during his rule. The irony was even underlined when aged Franquistas, unpunished and unrepentant, showed their support for Pinochet by a rally in which they gave the Fascist salute. Garzón indicated that his quest for justice to be served to torturers might not even be limited to Chile. He was considering Argentina, Brazil, Bolivia, Paraguay, and Uruguay. Garzón was unmoved by the argument from these

South American countries that they could not bring the crimes of the past to justice without provoking a military rebellion that would end their struggling new democracies. Nor did he appear deterred by the fact that regimes had often attempted to justify these crimes by saying they were fighting dangerous terrorists. Both arguments have been standard fare for Spanish governments.

*El Mundo*, a conservative Madrid daily, was among the many enthusiastic voices of support for Garzón's new approach. *El Mundo* and Judge Garzón were both key players in uncovering the GAL. *El Mundo* broke the story, and Garzón built an impressive case alleging that Felipe González was the director of GAL, which the Supreme Court refused to hear, citing a lack of evidence.

*El Mundo* excitedly termed Garzón's new policy of pursuing human rights cases in Latin America as "justice without borders." But an older concept that might be termed "justice within borders" seemed forgotten. Neither *El Mundo* nor Garzón had showed much concern for human rights abuse by Spanish officials unless they were Socialists. Even as the Spanish judge moved to try a Chilean leader for his regime's abuses, the fact that Spain had not brought to trial a single perpetrator of the many crimes committed in the thirty-six-year dictatorship was never raised in Spain. Neither the politically motivated arrest of at least 8,000 Basques, nor the fact that the majority of these victims were tortured while under arrest, that hundreds were killed by law enforcement, and that political leaders and journalists were jailed, has provoked the kind of legal scrutiny of the GAL scandal.

Garzón was concerned with torture in South America, not in Spain. Basque victims have tried taking their complaints to Garzón with little success. Enkarni Martínez, who was arrested in 1994 because her husband was not home when the police came to arrest him, went to Garzón with more than thirty bruises still evident on her body. "I was tortured from June 5 to June 8, 1994.

When they set me free, I went to the doctor to be examined. As soon as they read the results of the tests they were alarmed and ordered my immediate hospitalization. . . . If not for the test, they told me, I could have lost my kidney. I denounced it all in front of Judge Garzón. I told him, 'Do you want me to show you the marks?' He replied: 'No. No. No.'"

THE SPANISH GOVERNMENT, along with the Madrid press, have successfully dominated Spain's and the outside world's view of Basques. The Spanish celebrate the great Basque soccer players and bicyclists, the great Basque cuisine. The adjective *Basque* on a restaurant in Spain implies quality. Traditional Guipúzcoa taverns, selling fermented cider from barrels, salt cod omelettes, and steak, are being imitated throughout the country. Atxaga, whose writings have been translated into Spanish, has a large following. Massive Chillida sculptures are planted like great iron Basque anchors on the wide boulevards of Madrid. Yet the first thing Spaniards think of as Basque is what the Aznar government estimates to be seventy ETA commandos and their 800 killings, without much reflection on what 15,000 police were doing to thousands of Basques.

The Basques provoke a deep insecurity in Spain. The legal charge that Basques have "insulted" the country is one expression of that insecurity. Spain has never gotten past 1898, the year of "the Disaster." The centennial of it was an enormous event: Bookstore windows were filled with new books on 1898; the newspapers ran special feature series; television had special programming. The Spanish still feel theirs is a country that has failed or is somehow unworthy of nationhood. This is why the government so fears a condemnation from European governments.

But European governments accept without question the Spanish government line that ETA, whose primary demand for several decades has been negotiation, refuses to negotiate. In

1998, the U.S. State Department placed ETA on a short list of thirty "terrorist" organizations for whom it is illegal to provide funds. Neither the Irish Republican Army nor the violent Corsicans were on the list, but ETA was, along with Egypt's Holy War, Iran's Mujadeen, Peru's Shining Path, which had killed thousands, and the Khmer Rouge, which had murdered a million Cambodians.

One recent study by Iñaki Zabaleta found that 85 percent of all articles on Basques in the U.S. press made a reference to terrorism. The outside world knows little of the 2.4 million Basques except those seventy faceless commandos. The Spanish government has learned, as did Franco, that international opinion can be managed.

The standing of ETA among the Basques is difficult to measure. In recent years there have been huge demonstrations against ETA violence. But there have also been significant demonstrations of support for ETA. ETA is not trying to be popular. It is trying to cause the breakdown of the status quo. Practices such as extorting money from Basque businessmen and killing Basques thought to be collaborating with the enemy were always certain to be unpopular. A campaign unleashed in the mid-1990s to assassinate local PP officials, Basques who belonged to the ruling party, both angered and mystified fellow Basques, who saw this as purposeless violence. Just when the Guardia Civil was becoming demoralized and receiving hundreds of requests for transfers out of Navarra and Euskadi, it was suddenly being ignored while small town mayors were instead becoming targets.

The PP, aside from the tragedy of seeing their colleagues murdered, coldly found the new ETA strategy to be to their advantage. The killing of PP officials, especially when they were Basque, was extremely unpopular with Basques. Charles Powell, an adviser to Aznar, said, "These attacks have enabled us to play the victim. The victim! Here we are the party in power, but we are also made to look like the victim. That is not a bad political position."

The great majority of Basques had grown weary of the violence. If a vote for Herri Batasuna—renamed Euskal Herritarok, We, the Basque People, after the jailing of its leaders—is a vote supporting ETA, that would still mean an overwhelming majority of Basques are not ETA supporters. But there may be many ETA supporters who do not vote for Herri Batasuna, including some who do not vote at all, while, on the other hand, not everyone in Herri Batasuna supports ETA violence. Patxi Zabaleta, an Herri Batasuna representative in the Navarra legislature, said, "HB is divided on armed struggle. Some think it's not furthering political goals. But at least ETArists are people who sacrifice for what they believe. They are not mercenaries like in GAL."

Herri Batasuna was finding that most of its supporters were angry young people, children of workers and farmers, often not even of Basque racial origin. These supporters were typically between eighteen and twenty-five years old. Once they turned thirty, they began to drift away from the party. "Once people start settling down, HB is seen as far from the problems of daily life," said Zabaleta. "Self-determination is not the bread and butter of daily life."

The Basque Nationalist Party has been unambiguous in its condemnation of ETA violence. While various Spanish governments discussed, debated, agreed to, and refused to negotiate with ETA, no government ever showed interest in negotiating with the nonviolent Basque nationalists who represented the largest portion of Basques. Not only did they refuse to allow a referendum to test the popularity of Basque nationalism, but they would not enter into talks with the Basque Nationalist Party on increased autonomy. It is only the tiny violent minority to whom they responded.

According to Arzalluz, "The problem is that there are people in Madrid who only want a victory. If auto-determination was negotiated, if Spain let Basques go their way—not independence but freedom to go their way—ETA would disappear."

JUST WHEN ETA seemed cornered and the Spanish government was plausibly claiming that the commandos were few and unpopular, ETA changed the rules of the game. In September 1998, it announced that it had decided to unilaterally and unconditionally give up violence.

The Aznar government, caught completely by surprise, at first tried to do what it always had done with ETA announcements: dismissed it as insincere. But in spite of the government's refusal to respond, ETA kept to its word. Local elections were coming up, and the government began to realize that the PP would not be forgiven for ignoring this opportunity. So, for the first time since the transition, the Spanish government began talking to Basque leaders about their demands. It still refused to talk with ETA or even Herri Batasuna. But Aznar met with Arzalluz and leaders of other Basque nationalist parties.

Conservatives, leftists, and moderates—all the Basque nationalists told him the same things, the same things ETA had been saying. They wanted the Guardia Civil to leave. Beyond that, they all wanted the relationship of Basqueland to Spain to be revised. The constitution had to be amended.

Things got even worse for Madrid. The Catalans and the Gallegos, the people of Galicia, informed the government that they too wanted the constitution to be revised. Twenty years earlier, the constitution had been ratified without a majority in these regions either, and time, it seemed, had silenced no one. This was the first instance in many years when Basques, Catalans, and Gallegos were united. If things continued this way, regional parties might soon make up a decisive block in the legislature.

For as long as its rulers had been calling it Spain, this had been Madrid's fear of the Basques, that they would lead a movement that would quickly unravel the entire Spanish state. Government officials and Españolist intellectuals started appearing on television asserting that Spain did exist. "Spain is a country. It has been one for a long time," declared one Madrid supporter.

France had been far more clever than Spain in its repression, using economic forces more than military. France did not tolerate regional economic powers like Vizcaya. Today, France could lose Brittany, the Basques, and Corsica and still be the same country, possibly even save some money. But without the Basque and Catalan provinces, the two most productive regions, Spain would become an impoverished third-world nation.

Faced with ETA's cease-fire, Madrid almost immediately revealed its Achilles' heel, the Aznar government went to the Council of Europe and asked Europe not to become involved in the peace process. Madrid then retreated to talking of not "rewarding terrorism." But Basques, Catalans, and Gallegos were not going to be satisfied with that posture. While the government struggled for a lofty position, shunning the wayward, violent Basques who had not turned in their weapons or in any way repented for their years of violence and 800 victims, José Antonio Ardanza, the retiring lehendakari, a resolutely undramatic politician, suddenly came to life in the way lame-duck politicians often do. "It would be nice if everyone who committed acts that caused pain to others asked for forgiveness," he said. But then he pointed out that no one had ever apologized for the thirty-six-year Franco dictatorship, nor for the violence against Basques after Franco's death, nor for GAL.

Nonviolence would be a new tactic, an anomaly in Basque history. All of Basque history is violent. Nationalist literature praises violence and men of violence. Sabino Arana's first writings on Basque nationalism were an analysis of four battles. "Violence is not for the fruit it will bear. It is a consequence, an expression," said Patxi Zabaleta.

To the conservative businessmen of the Basque Nationalist Party, an end to violence would mean a greatly enhanced ability to attract foreign investment. To the left, it would mean more friends and supporters.

If ETA could control its ranks and keep its non-violence pledge, it would in time disappear. But could Spain exist without ETA? In order to have a Spain, did there not have to be enemies? This was why Franco, trying to perpetuate his rule with his last breath, insisted that "the enemies of Spain" must not be forgotten. And why the PP always claimed to be the party that fought better and harder against the enemies of Spain.

What was to be done with the soldiers of the Reconquista, the warriors against "the enemies of Spain"? How would Spain justify its huge armed forces, Guardia Civil, and police if it no longer had enemies? Why was a Guardia Civil needed?

ETA was, after all, a necessary evil.

IN JANUARY, a cold wind from the mountains drifts into San Sebastián. Sudden icy sprays of rain are followed by blinding white sunlight. With the weather that way, San Sebastián families like to make *cocidas*, a bean dish that is between a soup and a stew. Different areas have their own cocidas. A Labourd cocida, known as an *eltzekari*, is sometimes made with duck or goose fat. But a good San Sebastián cocida uses pork fat and has to have a ham bone. Heavyset, tough-looking housewives go to the market at the end of the medieval section of town to buy split pigs' feet and the stump of a ham. They test the patience of the shopkeeper, choosing just the right stump—the leftover bone and foot. Some want it old and dried and very cured, some less cured, some saltier, some less salty. After choosing the optimal old foot, they insist it be cut exactly as they specify. Some want three pieces, some four. Certain pieces short, others longer. One woman wanted the dried foot, hard as a weathered tree stump, split vertically. The shopkeeper sighed and then whacked it fiercely with a heavy hatchet for a few minutes until it split.

January 20, at the heart of cocida season, is the Saint's Day of Sebastián. The bars put out their best *pintxos,* the city's bar snacks. Angulas are traditional for this day.

Gastronomic societies march through the streets. There is considerable debate about the origin of this institution known as a *txoko,* which means "a cozy place." Though San Sebastián is the city most known for them, some theorize that the first of these gastronomic societies began in nineteenth-century Bilbao as company social clubs, possibly even inspired by the British. They try to be exclusive, voting on new members, restricting kitchen entry to members. Originally, most of these gastronomic societies did not allow women even to enter their clubhouse. Now some will allow them to come to dinner, but since only members are allowed in the kitchen, the women cannot cook. Only a very few allow women members. Txoko members periodically get together and cook feasts in what are usually professional-quality kitchens. The wine cellars are restocked every year with a pilgrimage to the Rioja.

The seventy-five gastronomic societies in San Sebastián are considered important enough that the mayor is expected to eat in each of them at least once a year. Constant meals at these men's clubs was one of the things Ramón Labayen said he liked least about being mayor of San Sebastián.

On Saint Sebastián Day, half of the members of the local gastronomic societies dress as chefs in white with toques, aprons, and even towels on their hips. These potbellied chefs pursue the other half, who are wearing Napoleonic military uniforms. Throughout the evening, groups of chefs pursue Napoleonic soldiers through the streets. The soldiers in tall cylindrical hats beat drums, and the chefs, led by a conductor-chef using a giant knife, spoon, or whisk for a baton, clank out the same on their barrels. The seemingly vexed soldiers then pound even harder and more elaborately on their drums. Only to get a flat echo from the barrels at the rear of the column.

When Napoleon's troops occupied San Sebastián, Basque citizenry taunted them by following behind and beating on barrels. But then, when it was daring, it was mostly women doing it. The festival lasts from midnight on January 19 until the following midnight. The chefs pass around bottles and get progressively red faced and bloated looking, but both chefs and soldiers beat out their rhythms and responses with great seriousness.

By 10:30 P.M., the crowds go into the restaurants to eat *txangurro a la Donastiarra*, San Sebastián-style stuffed spider crab. The dish is all in the stuffing, since the crab is a leggy but scrawny animal that many cultures have ignored because it requires a gastronome's heart and a surgeon's hands to extract its meat.

*TXANGURRO A LA DONASTIARRA*

*Use sea water, or else water with salt and yeast. Once the water boils, put the crab in for 15 minutes. After it has chilled, remove all the meat from the legs and the center, and whatever water is there, to pass through a food mill.*

*The preparation is as follows: put some olive oil in a skillet with minced onion and a finely minced clove of garlic; when they start to brown add a glass of wine (some prefer brandy), reduce and pass through a food mill with a little white pepper, a teaspoon of English sauce and a little mustard, according to taste, and a couple of spoonfuls of previously prepared tomato. When all this is reduced, add a spoonful of bread crumbs. Once*

*you have made the preparation, add the crab meat, and when all this is seasoned, put it in the shell and add a little butter just before serving and a little more bread crumbs and slip it into the oven.*
       *—Nicolasa Pradera, 1933*

ON SAINT SEBASTIÁN NIGHT, 1998, by the central market at Nicolasa Pradera's famous old restaurant, the contemporary chef-owner, Juan José Castillo, from Bermeo, surveyed the crab dishes coming out of the kitchen. Meanwhile, the chefs and soldiers were marching through town saluting the police station and various other institutions. When they came to Casa Nicolasa, Castillo ran out to the balcony and bounced up and down on his toes, waving his arms to the drum cadence in unconcealed boyish glee as his waiters ran below distributing bottles of champagne. Then he suddenly decided it was too cold for champagne and ran downstairs to distribute coffee and brandy, then charged back up to his balcony to listen some more.

As the gastronomes got increasingly merry and plodding, toques and high Napoleonic hats starting to slide to one side, another group began to form. They were marching for amnesty for political prisoners—accused ETArists in Spanish prisons around the peninsula. Each one carried a sign on a stick showing a photo of a prisoner. Many of the demonstrators were relatives of these prisoners, but rather than carry photos of their own family members, the group shuffled their signs, each carrying one selected by random to make the point that they were not asking for amnesty for a relative, but rather for freedom for all Basque political prisoners.

Among those carrying a sign was a professorial-looking man in a blue duffel coat with his white hair disarranged in the clear winter night's air.

It was Txillardegi, whose son was among the twenty-three

sentenced to seven years in prison for being on the board of directors of the Herri Batasuna party.

In 1997, the *New York Times* asked Felipe González how it was possible that GAL could have come from within his government without him ordering it. He replied that the state, after thirty-six years of dictatorship, might still have elements that he could not control. "People don't want to understand that we inherited a state apparatus in its entirety from the dictatorship," said the man who is credited with leading his country to democracy.

"There is always a first mistake," wrote Joseba Sarrionaindia, a Basque writer accused of being an ETA member, currently in hiding.

# 15: Surviving Democracy

*The Basque language is a country, almost a religion.*
—Victor Hugo, on a visit, 1843

IN 1998, a Spanish-speaking customer came into Jeanine Pereuil's gâteau Basque shop in St. Pée. With worry lines tightening on her face, the woman ordered a cake, custard filled, and before Jeanine could wrap it, began to describe the latest attack by ETA. Simply to prove it could strike anywhere, ETA had killed a PP politician and his wife, both in their midthirties, in the distant Andalusian city of Seville.

"And they had three children," said the customer.

Jeanine shuddered, as she often did when she contemplated Spanish Basqueland, a few miles away. She had been seeing the refugees from there all her life. "But they do have some wonderful things," she said with a sudden smile, and began talking about dances and folk celebrations she has seen there, traditions that were vanishing from her province.

In the French provinces, two schools of thought compete: One watches the development of the Autonomous Basque Community of Euskadi with envy, wanting the same cultural and economic opportunities for Labourd, Basse Navarre, and Soule. The other sees the Spanish provinces full of menace and tragedy and fears that French Basqueland could go the same way. Many French Basques feel both ways.

Most French Basques will say that they feel they have more in common with a Guipúzcoan or a Vizcayan than with a Frenchman from the other side of the Adour. The Vizcayans and Guipúzcoans say that they feel they have more in common with a Basque from St. Pée or St.-Jean-Pied-de-Port than with a Spaniard from the other side of the Ebro.

But on the other hand, one side has experienced French history and the other side Spanish. The Spanish Basques suspect, as do many Spaniards, that the people north of the Pyrenees are a bit frivolous and insincere. The French Basques, like the French, suspect that the people south of the Pyrenees, Basques included, are a bit barbarous, dangerous, and not to be trusted.

In Mauléon, the quiet capital of Soule, Maïte Faure sells traditional fabrics. A popular item is off-white cotton with colored stripes—originally indigo but now often red and green—a motif copied from the canvases that used to protect cows from flies. By long-standing tradition, there are always seven stripes, one for each province. "I am proud to be French," she said. "I don't trust the Basques over there. They say we are all Basques, but I don't think they include us." She paused for a moment and smiled. "On the other hand, at the age of fifty, I am suddenly taking up traditional Basque dance."

This seeming non sequitur referred to the fact that the Basques in Spain, at last free of dictatorship, are pursuing their Basqueness with such remarkable energy and limitless ambition that it is waking up the sleepy Basques who have lived in peace in France. Excitement about the growth of Basque culture on the Spanish side inspired Faure to learn dance.

The 212,000 people in the French Basque provinces represent less than 9 percent of Basques. But they have played an important role because, though they have not had the prosperity of Guipúzcoa and Vizcaya, neither have they had the political turmoil. The little provinces of Labourd, Basse Navarre, and Soule have been the safe haven of Basqueland, where refugees could go, where troubled Basques from the other side could find shelter. But what would the role of French Basqueland be in a peaceful Euskadi? If the seven provinces were ever united, the situation of the French Basques would be similar to what it is now under France: Neither the population, nor the money, nor the power would be in their provinces.

A belle epoque postcard from Biarritz.

THE BASQUES WERE among the inventors of beach resorts. Biarritz, like San Sebastián, is one of the oldest beach resorts in the world. In 1892 on a visit to Labourd, Pierre Loti, the French merchant marine officer-turned-novelist, wrote, "Poor Basqueland, such a long time intact, like some sort of little Arabia, protected by loyalty to its ancestral traditions and by its language that no one can learn, and here it is, vanished just like that. In just the last few seasons, tourists, who seemed not to know about it, have made the discovery."

Since then, French social programs have greatly expanded both tourism and retirement to the Basque provinces. In Loti's day, the Basques had only to stave off an invasion of the wealthy. But six weeks guaranteed vacation and early retirement pensions have made tourists and retirees the basis of the economy in coastal Labourd, which the French tourist industry insists on calling La Côte Basque.

Ugly white housing, of a design that speaks of nothing so much as quick construction and easy cleaning, much of it occupied only from May through October, is marring the outskirts of the beautiful ancient port of St.-Jean-de-Luz. Tourism is moving into Basse Navarre, and in Soule locals wish it would come their way too because their farms cannot compete with agro-industry, and traditional crafts cannot compete with Asian factories.

Soule, where fewer than 14,000 people live in quiet villages surrounded by mountainsides patched with small cornfields, is the forgotten province. It has always been that way. On May 5, 1789, on the eve of the French Revolution, when Louis XVI presided over the États Généraux, Soule, neighboring Béarn, and also Brittany were the only parts of France that were not represented. Soule had not been making a political statement. It simply could not raise enough public funds to send someone to Paris. Mauléon, Soule's capital, has a shady main square with a fronton court, where a few dozen people might pass at the busiest time of day. This is called the lower town. The upper town is built along the ramparts of a medieval castle. Why don't tourists visit the castle? locals wonder. Without them there is only the corn crop, and a few sheep. Little is left of the town's main business, making espadrilles.

In the thirteenth century, the king of Aragón commented on the curious hemp-soled cloth shoes, tied at the ankles, worn by recruits from the Pyrenees in the army of the Crusade. In nineteenth- and early-twentieth-century Mauléon, the identical shoe was still being made and sold throughout Basqueland. In the famous photo of Sabino Arana behind prison bars, he is wearing espadrilles. Even in the early twentieth century, every morning, the now quiet town of Mauléon would fill up with about 1,000 espadrille workers. One plant made soles, another made fabrics, and women, often working at home, sewed them together.

In the 1950s, when Maïte Faure's father died, her mother had to support the family with the only work available for women: sewing espadrilles. Strapped to her palm almost permanently was the small circular metal guard for pushing the thick needle.

In the 1980s, the handmade espadrille started to lose its market to the less expensive factory-made one from Spain, and then an even less expensive one from China. In 1981, France imported 3 million pairs of Chinese espadrilles. About eighty people still work on espadrilles in Mauléon, because no local would wear one from China or anywhere else if it was not handmade. The last traditional textile plant for espadrilles is outside town, and a few artisans still hand sew them. But the population of Mauléon is in decline, as people leave their Euskera-speaking world for employment on the French-speaking coast or in Paris.

Sabino Arana in prison wearing espadrilles. (Sabino Arana Foundation, Bilbao)

WHILE THE SPANISH wanted the Basques to be the engine of their economy, the French provinces were of little economic significance to planners in Paris. The French, with coal, iron, and waterways to build great industrial centers in the north and east, could afford to let their Basques, ports and all, languish in benign neglect. The French state offered French services to the Basques and few opportunities for development. French schools were provided, were obligatory, and did not allow any language but French. Many Basques heard the French language for the first time at age five when it was forced on them in school. Under French administration, Basque culture had suffered a slow erosion over 160 years, but between 1965 and 1970, Euskera experienced a sudden, powerful blow: Television was introduced to rural France. For the first time in history, the French language was commonly heard in the homes of Basque farmers.

Daniel Landart, born in 1945, the son of Labourdine farmers, saw the disintegration of Euskera in his family. "During World War I my grandfather went to war and wrote my grandmother in Basque. During World War II my father was deported to a German labor camp and wrote my mother in French. They always spoke in Basque, but they wrote in French."

Having grown up before television, no one spoke anything but Euskera in Landart's home. But the language was forbidden in school. Some teachers let children speak Euskera during recess, but others were more strict. One teacher would force the student, caught in the act of speaking Euskera, to stand by the door holding a broom until he could catch someone else speaking it. The newly betrayed Euskaldun would then be given the broom until he caught someone else. The one holding the broom at the end of the class had to write fifty times, "I will not speak Basque."

Landart said, "This created an atmosphere of denunciation and fear among us. The one who was denounced remained angry at the denouncer for life. It divided us."

As a teenager, Landart could speak Basque, but he could only read and write in French, the language of his education. At sixteen, he began to teach himself to read in his mother tongue, starting with French Basque writers, because the dialect was easiest for him. In time, he was writing in Euskera. He wrote a sixty-four-page book of poetry and short stories and published 1,000 copies at his own expense. The 300 copies he sold in local markets paid the cost of publication, and the rest he gave away. Some of the poems have since become popular songs. He later wrote a novel and several plays, but the book for which he is best known is *Aihen Ahula,* (Weak Root), an autobiographical account of his search for his own culture. It is a search that many French Basques have been undertaking.

THE PERCENTAGE OF Basques throughout the seven provinces who speak Euskera depends on whose definition of a Basque is used. The official definition is someone residing in Basqueland. The Basque government considers any citizen of its three-province region to be a Basque. But polls have shown that Basques have wide disagreement on the definition. Juan San Martin of the Basque Academy of Language said, "This is not a relevant debate in the Basque language. It only speaks of Basque speakers. Someone with a Basque name from Basque country who does not speak Basque is a Basque, but he is not an Euskaldun. And in Basque culture, being Basque is not significant. It can't even be said."

Taking into account the entire population gives little Soule, which has attracted few outsiders and, for that matter, has few locals, the highest percentage of Basque speakers, and gives Labourd, where retired Parisians have taken up residence by the beach, and Navarra, where half the province is no longer culturally Basque, the lowest ratios of Basque speakers. In all seven provinces, retirees and Castilians included, 37 percent of people speak some Euskera, but only 25 percent are completely fluent. This would mean that slightly more than 600,000 people speak fluent Euskera, though more than 800,000 speak some Euskera. Among that additional 200,000 are many people who are in the process of learning the language.

But what is of deep concern is that while the percentage of Euskera speakers is dramatically rising on the Spanish side, it is declining on the French side. Basques hold their territory by language, and there is a risk of completely losing the French Basque provinces. This would be the first significant loss of Basque territory since the late Roman Empire.

Until the abolition of the Fueros, Euskera was surviving far better under Spanish rule than under the French. In the mid-nineteenth century, when Hugo found the Basque language to be almost a religion, it was spoken by only about one-third of the population in the French provinces where he was visiting, whereas in 1867, more than 96 percent of the residents of Guipúzcoa spoke Basque.

In Spanish Basqueland, the number of Basque speakers declined under Franco and has risen to twentieth-century heights since his death. Despite the seventy commandos and the 15,000 police, this is one of the best moments Spanish Basques have ever had. Vizcaya, Guipúzcoa, and Alava, home to almost three-fourths of the Basque population, are undergoing a dramatic change. Among the population born before 1932, 28 percent speak Euskera. Among those born at the height of Franco's repression, when teaching Euskera to your children meant labeling them as "troublemakers," only 21 percent speak it. But since 1972, the percentage of fluent Basque speakers has steadily increased. Bilingual schooling is the common practice, and if trends continue, Vizcaya and Guipúzcoa will soon have a Basque-speaking majority.

The Basque Nationalist Party government of the three provinces has taken over the education system, completely turning around the fate of the Basque language. Once a whispered rarity, Euskera is now commonly heard, not only in rural villages but on the streets of major cities. Even in Bilbao, one of the least Basque-speaking towns, Euskera is regularly heard. Having the language in common usage pressures increasing numbers of Spanish Basques to learn it. Among school-age Basques in Guipúzcoa and Vizcaya, it is the lingua franca.

In the French provinces, or Northern Basqueland, as it is known in the government documents of Southern Basqueland, 37 percent of those born before 1932 speak Basque, but only 11 percent of those born between 1972 and 1980 do. Obviously, a language spoken predominantly by older people has a dubious future. And yet there are a number of reasons for French Basques not to despair. The percentage of Basque speakers in France has been rising recently because Euskera education in schools was legalized under Mitterrand and because, in 1980, volunteers began a program based on the ikastolas to the south.

Spanish Basques have their own Basque governments that run school systems, finance programs, publish materials, and promote Basque culture. It is difficult for French Basques not to gaze covetously at the Basque governments in Spain which share their publishing, radio, and television with the north, where there are not enough public funds to have the equivalent programs.

Since the French Revolution, the Basques of France have had no entity of their own in French administration. They belong to the Département of Pyrénées-Atlantique, which has some 750,000 people, little more than one-fourth of whom live in the Basque provinces.

The government administrative system was designed in Paris with the intention of repressing regional cultures, but the Basques have periodically demanded their own Département. In 1836, the Chamber of Commerce in Bayonne, not an especially radical organization, petitioned the king to create a Basque Département, citing economic reasons. "Bayonne has no interest in common with Béarn," the petition declared. In the 1960s, a growing Basque nationalist movement revived the old demand. In 1981, while campaigning for the presidency, Mitterrand made a list of 110 promises that he intended to fulfill upon taking office, including creation of a Basque Département. Though he surprised cynics by the number of promises he actually did fulfill, a Basque Département was not among them. Once in power, his government discovered, "The situation in Basqueland is very delicate."

The growing cultural movement, the yearnings being felt from watching the Autonomous Community across the border, seemed to worry Mitterrand. In a 1984 speech in Bayonne, he said: "It is time to say to our Basque compatriots, *voilà!* That which you would preserve so that future generations find intact the heritage that you received and even improved upon—if it is thought that this could serve as a clever first step from which to leap further, toward autonomy, toward independence, then I say clearly and eye to eye: not with me, no! I will not let the fabric of France be torn."

In 1900 a Bordeaux physical education instructor, Philippe Tissié, concluded an essay on Basque sports by speculating on whether Basque culture was about to end. He noted that peasants were moving from rural areas, that "electricity now penetrated to even the smallest village. . . . Electricity, telegraph, telephone, automobile, railroad, steam and electric tramways, such are the agents of progress that undermine poetic traditions and turn them into utilitarian prose."

To that formula could be added radio, television, and computers. What Tissié foresaw was the fate of much of European culture, especially those cultures rooted in rural life. Yet the Basques have survived the twentieth century and ended it in some ways stronger than they were in 1900. This is partly because they have never abandoned their rural roots and they have used modern technology to be closer to them. The Carlist reverence for rural life remains. This is as true of the French Basques as of the Spanish. The French provinces have no real urban centers. The largest, Bayonne, would better be described as a large town. Even the Basque cities of the Spanish side, Pamplona, Vitoria, San Sebastián, and Bilbao, are by contemporary standards small and manageable, and much of the Basque population still lives outside them. Nor is urbanization a Basque trend. Modern communications and good roads have meant increased opportunities for Basques to return to their land.

Traditional farm foods are becoming more popular than they have been for two generations. The spread of cider mills is one example. Pacharán, a light-alcohol drink made from sloe berries, a tiny wild plum from the mountains of northern Navarra, used to be a peasant drink in the mountains but has recently started appearing in bars, restaurants, and homes throughout Basqueland. *Bortu gazna*, mountain cheese, long the pride of Basque peasants, has also become fashionable in all seven provinces. Ewe's milk, it seems, like people, develops a stronger character in the face of adversity. The tough grasses and shrubs of the mountaintops produce a more flavorful cheese than that of sheep grazing on lush green valley floors. This cheese can only be produced in May and June, while the valley cheese is made for six months. In a rural society noted for the equal division of labor between sexes, the prestigious mountain cheese is traditionally produced only by men. Part of the mystique of Martikorena, a popular Euskera folk singer and a shepherd from Basse Navarre, is the fact, well known in French Basqueland, that he makes excellent mountain cheese.

Unformed cheese, sheep's milk curdled with rennet, an enzyme found in the stomach of an unweaned lamb, and served as a kind of yogurt with mountain honey, used to be a meager staple of the rural poor. Known as *mamia* or, in Spanish, *cuajada*, it is now the fashionable dessert in fine restaurants in all seven provinces.

Poster from the 1930s by Jean Paul Tillac. (Collection of the Musée Basque, Bayonne)

The Asador Horma-Honda in the village of Bernagoitia, not far from Bilbao, serves modern rural food. Its recipe for *cuajada*, which follows, is a contemporary dessert made with industrially bottled rennet and unusual because it is made with sugar and cinnamon, instead of being served tart and sweetened by adding honey.

### *CUAJADA*

*Boil a liter of sheep's milk with a stick of cinnamon. Let it cool a little, mix in sugar according to taste, and divide it into six cups. Add to each one a spoonful of rennet. Let completely cool and refrigerate.*

During cheese-making season, pigs graze on the slopes with the sheep so that Basques can feed them the whey, the nutritious liquid leftover. There was a uniquely Basque breed of pig in Labourd and Basse Navarre that grazed with the long-legged, hound-eared, white Basque sheep. In the early 1980s, Basques realized that the Basque breed of pig had died out. In the Aldudes Valley, which gets steeper and steeper until farmers along the French-Spanish border are looking into a deep green gorge, it was decided to bring back the Basque pig.

The race was rebred from the few pigs remaining throughout the western Pyrenees who still had the characteristics. What is characteristic of a Basque pig? Appropriately, the most telling feature is extremely large ears, so large in fact that they fall over the pig's face, nearly blinding the animal, resulting in a not typically Basque passive nature.

THERE IS A movement in French Basqueland clearly influenced by events in Spanish Basqueland, and its activists like to call themselves *abertzale,* choosing a word Sabino Arana invented to mean "Basque nationalist," or literally, "patriot." As in Spain, French abertzale emerged in the 1930s, reemerged in the 1960s—a shoot from the Guernica oak was planted by the cherry orchards of Itxassou—and became stronger than ever in the 1980s and 1990s.

A variety of nationalist parties, usually left-wing, began running candidates for local election. Herri Batasuna organized in the French provinces under the name Euskal Batasuna. Abertzale parties have struggled to get more than 10 percent of the vote in the larger towns but have made a significant showing in some rural villages, which is remarkable because a substantial part of the economy of French Basque villages, as much as two-thirds, comes from pensions, farm subsidies, and other social expenditures by the French state.

Some French Basques worry that the abertzale movement will lead to a French ETA. ETA, they remember, started out as a nationalist movement promoting culture and ended up shooting Basque politicians and extorting money from Basque businessmen. For a brief moment, such a group did appear in France. Or did it?

On December 11, 1973, the office of a medical school in a Basse Navarre village was raided, officials were roughed up, and documents were stolen by a group calling itself Iparretarrak, ETArists of the north. In their communique, published ten months later, they wrote: "Our country is in the process of dying, and it will die in a few years, our land will be the paradise of retirees, invalids, and foreigners. . . . If we want our rights, if we want our freedom, we have only one route: fight." Their principal activity was vandalizing the property of the tourism trade, especially in the summer when Parisians flood the coastal region and French campers and hikers take to the mountains. They used slogans such as "Our country is not for sale" and "Euskadi will never be a Riviera." One arrest was made in 1977, but the suspect seemed to be a sympathizer, not an activist, and after 3,500 people signed a petition, he was released.

In March 1980, two would-be Iparretarrak commandos decided to blow up the car of the wife of the *sous-préfet* in its parking place in the middle of the night. But, mishandling the explosives, the two blew themselves up instead. Given the type of devices and the time of night, the evidence indicates that they did not intend to hurt anyone, but many in French Basqueland saw this as evidence that their fears were coming true, that Iparretarrak, like ETA in the 1960s, was turning from vandalism to violence. Faced with violent attacks around the country by a variety of armed groups, both French and Middle Eastern, France started taking Iparretarrak seriously. Voters were demanding that the French police do something about terrorism, and it seemed likely that the French police would do a lot better up against these ETArists of the north than against Abu Nidal of Syria.

French Basqueland found itself with what may be an even

higher number of police per capita than Spanish Basqueland. Officially, the eight officers for every 1,000 inhabitants is almost double the French national ratio. But the police turned up with nothing. In 1982, two officers were killed in Basse Navarre, and the French Basque group was again suspected. Another suspect was the Basque-Spanish Battalion, the forerunner of GAL. The matter was never cleared up, and the Iparretarrak soon vanished.

But the police remained. Unlike in Spain, they try not to let their presence be felt. From the French point of view, le Pays Basque is a tourist destination. Basque nationalism is often re-duced to something folkloric, something nice for the tourists. French travel posters advertise, "Basqueland, land of folklore." The ikurriña, that politically charged symbol that is fought over on the other side of the mountains, is a favorite souvenir of French Basqueland sold in every tourist shop—flags, scarves, earrings, key chains, even scented cardboard ikurriñas to dangle from the rearview mirror of the car.

Efforts to revive folk customs, even when intended as polit-ical acts, get French government support because the tourists like these events. A group in the inland side of Labourd, con-cerned about reviving folk customs, went to Ituren in Navarra to study the *joaldunak*, grim-faced ancestral pagan characters who awaken spring with their giant copper bells and black horsehair whips. They learned how to make the cone-shaped hats and how to wear the big copper bells and perform the dances. They learned enough so that a troop of joaldunak could make an appearance at a carnival festival, although their simple march in and out of town was not nearly as elaborate as the two-day ritual between Ituren and neighboring Zubieta. Joaldunak began appearing for the winter carnival in various Labourdine towns including St.-Jean-de-Luz, where the French always gave them a special round of applause. Joaldunak are characteristic of the residual pagan customs of northern Navarra but had never before appeared in Labourd, which leaves the question of whether a culture is being preserved or created in French Basqueland—what Mitterrand was referring to when he said that the legacy of Basque culture was being "even improved upon." But the joaldunak at the St.-Jean-de-Luz carnival were no more incongruous than the Herri Batasuna campaign for local elections in 1998 in which Basque nationalists rode around San Sebastián with giant plaster joaldunak mounted on the roofs of cars. These joaldunak were not even somber looking. They had broad Howdy-Doody smiles.

OVER THE BORDER, in Ituren, joaldunak arrived one by one at the town plaza, a small paved space surrounded by a town hall and four other stone buildings. Some walked and others came by car, already wearing their laced-up black moccasins, carrying their cone-shaped hats, sheepskins, and bells.

In Ituren they have named the joaldunak Zanpantzar—a name which appears in all seven Basque dialects. In the French provinces, Zanpantzar is a grotesque papier-mâché giant, who is set on fire to burn away evil for the coming year and mark the end of carnival. But in Ituren, the name refers to a group of twenty joaldunak.

Navarra is said to have been pro-Franco, but between the sheer slopes in this isolated narrow valley of the wandering Bidasoa River, there was little sympathy for the invading Fascist regime. At the very beginning of the Spanish Civil War, in September 1936, the Ituren village doctor, a passionate Basque nationalist, was taken out of town and shot by pro-Franco forces. This caused one of Europe's oldest carnivals to disappear. It was not held in the winter of 1937 or for years afterward. The carnival, which predated the Christianization of Basques, had finally faded into history.

But the stubborn people of Ituren remembered their customs and kept speaking their Basque language instead of Spanish, even when it was illegal. As the regime loosened its reign of terror, they slowly resumed their ways. Now every winter, the Monday before Ash Wednesday, once again, the strange events of Ituren awaken the spring in the cold mountain earth.

Since this was not a workday, the few hundred townspeople were sleeping late. They were still in bed at 10:00 A.M. as the sun's rays cleared the rocky ridges, greening the white frosted slopes. The few dozen stone houses that are the town of Ituren emerged from a cold blue shadow.

An older man was in one of Ituren's two bars trying to warm himself up on a mixture of hot coffee, anise liqueur, and sherry. It seemed to work. Although anthropologists say the carnival slowly started up again in the 1940s, he had no memory of any carnival after 1936 until the 1950s. "I think it was 1952 that there was enough so that some priest could denounce it as pagan, un-Christian. Little by little things started again. In the 1960s some general from Elizondo saw it. We thought, oh, trouble. But he liked it and it's been growing ever since, so now it is like before the war."

Slowly the townspeople gathered in the plaza and warmed up in the two bars, playing traditional songs, and teenagers showed off the folk dance steps that under Franco their parents had not been allowed to learn.

Joaldunak are all young men. They start apprenticing at age five, and once they marry they must leave the group. A *joaldun* (the singular of joaldunak) must be young—young and strong. The bells they wear are huge and meticulously crafted of beaten copper, with deep vibrato tones. They are strapped on to each joaldun with a complicated system of lamb's leather cord that is pulled so tight that the bells stand free of their backs.

A rhythmic dirge of bells peeled—a deep, metallic, atavistic rumble. The bells rang by the exaggerated steps of the joaldunak's dance as they maneuvered like a solemn marching band, filing in intricate patterns around the plaza, across the little bridge behind the plaza that leads over a gurgling crook of the Ezcurra, a tributary of the Bidasoa, on to country paths to other parts of town and off to neighboring fields and villages. They never smiled, never joked—even the youngest ones with their smaller bells. Twenty cones in their deliberate stride, copper bells echoing off the rocky ridges of the mountain crests, the joaldunak marched quickly past frosty green fields, leafless forests, and still-barren orchards. Occasionally as they made their way over mountain trails, a leader would trumpet a ram's horn announcing to all the residents of the valley the promise of spring and declaring to the frosted mountain air that they would be Basques in the Basque way forever.

# 16: The Nation

*If you do not teach your children the language of your parents, they will teach you.*
—Sabino Arana, BASSERITARRA, *June 20, 1897*

THE MOST IMPORTANT word in Euskera is *gure*. It means "our"—our people, our home, our village. Cookbooks talk of our soups, our sauces. "Reptiles are not typically included in our meals," wrote the great Guipúzcoan chef José María Busca Isusi. That four-letter word, *gure*, is at the center of Basqueness, the feeling of belonging inalienably to a group. It is what the Basques mean by a nation, why they have remained a nation without a country, even stripped of their laws.

Few Basques have made better use of the new nation than Bernardo Atxaga. Starting in the emerging Euskera publishing industry, and then having his works translated into Spanish and eventually, other languages including English, he has become the most widely read author in the history of the Basque language. His 1988 novel, *Obabakoak*, meaning "Things from Obaba," is a cycle of stories centered on a fictitious Guipúzcoan village. As of 1998, it had sold 45,000 copies in Euskera, a considerable accomplishment in a language with less than 1 million speakers. The Spanish translation sold 70,000 copies, and it has also been translated into fourteen other languages.

Before Atxaga, it was rare for a writer in Euskera to be translated and almost unheard of for them to be translated into languages other than French or Spanish.

Between the first book published in 1545 and 1974, 4,000 books were published in Euskera. In the next twenty years another 12,500 were published. Atxaga said that he started in Euskera by reading Aresti, and three years later he had read every book in Euskera available to him. That would no longer be possible. About 1,000 titles are now published in Euskera every year, including novels, poetry, nonfiction, academic books, children's books, and translations of classics and best-sellers.

For a very long time, publishing a book in Euskera was a purely political act. The first book entirely in Basque was a collection of both religious and secular poems published in Bordeaux in 1545, written by a priest, Bernard Dechepare, who made his intentions clear in the opening paragraph: "Since the Basques are smart, valiant and generous, and since among them are men well educated in all the sciences, I am amazed that no one has attempted in the interest of his own language, to show the entire world, by writing, that this language is as good a written language as any other."

Modern Basque publishing began while Franco was in power. Elkar was created in 1972, established as a French nonprofit company based in Bayonne, with twenty small investors, including some Spanish Basque refugees. The little company produced records of popular music in Euskera that earned money to help finance book publishing. After the death of Franco, some of the refugees returned to Spain and established a second base in San Sebastián. With its twin bases, Elkar became the largest publisher of Euskera, but soon many others appeared. Some were financed by Vizcayan banks, the Basque Nationalist Party, or the governments of the three provinces or of Navarra.

A daily newspaper in Euskera was established, along with several weeklies, magazines, and children's publications. Basque radio and television stations broadcast on both sides of the Pyrenees. The Basque government also supported a young film industry in Euskera.

In addition to the education of Basque youth, 100,000 adult Basques have learned Euskera since Atxaga began his career. The total market is still small. Atxaga recognized that as a great opportunity. "We have the advantage and disadvantage of scale," he said.

"We can do a lot of different things." Not yet fifty, he had published more than eight novels, twenty children's books, poetry, essays, and lyrics for his favorite rock band—all in his once forbidden native language. It is the enviable position of a leading artist in a very small country. The ubiquitous Eduardo Chillida is in a similar position, designing monuments in such defining spaces as the oak tree in Guernica, but also designing the logo for the amnesty movement and the trademark for Guipúzcoa's provincial savings and pension bank.

Jorge de Oteiza, a generation older than the aging Chillida and a founding father of modern Basque abstract sculpture, has not seized these opportunities. The most important collection of his work is stacked on the floor of his studio in the Guipúzcoan coastal town of Zarautz, while he, the five foot tall, white-bearded, nonagenarian enfant terrible of Basque art, shakes his cane and rails against selling art for money. As he sits in his favorite Zarautz restaurant denouncing "the other sculptor's" productivity, a metal plaque shines on the wall from the Kutxo bank, bearing their familiar logo, designed by Chillida.

Atxaga is an elfin man whose work always displays a mischievous humor. His popularity may come from being that old-fashioned kind of Basque who, although rooted in his little country, is an internationalist at heart. His writing makes references to American popular culture, to German politics, to the world at large.

On chance encounters with old friends and former schoolmates from his San Sebastián high school, they often greet him in Euskera, good mother-tongue Guipúzcoan, and for the first time he realizes that they had that language in common all along, though they had never dared to speak it to each other.

Many things have changed since those times. The young woman at Sarriko who invited him to "a cultural meeting" for Maoist indoctrination had left long ago and, in the late 1990s, was still a guerrilla in El Salvador. Another classmate was killed in El Salvador. One of the head Maoists at the university became an important technocrat in the Basque government working on tax policy.

An unpretentious man of simple origins, Atxaga is nevertheless aware of the absurd fact that he may be the Shakespeare of his language. What he does with Batua could well affect generations, possibly even centuries, of writers. Euskera literature is new enough to offer a creative freedom that few other languages could. With that freedom comes difficult choices. There are words in Euskera that are not in common usage, and he worries that they interfere with the narrative flow. Yet he does not want to limit the richness of the vocabulary. "I would say that the first duty of literary language is to be unobtrusive. And that is our weak point, because we lack antecedents."

Ramón Saizarbitoria, though of the same generation with the same early influences, is almost the opposite of Atxaga. Born in 1944 in San Sebastián, he is seven years older. Atxaga's stocky physique, friendly manner, and rumpled appearance suggest his upbringing in rural Guipúzcoa. Saizarbitoria, an urbane native of the most sophisticated Basque city, is tall, thin, impeccably dressed, with a carefully trimmed only slightly graying beard, a slow, careful manner, and a quiet, reflective way of speaking. While Atxaga lives in a village in Alava, Saizarbitoria lives in the heart of San Sebastián, with an office along a wide downtown boulevard that has long been favored for political demonstrations because its many escape routes make it impossible for the police to seal off.

While Atxaga struggled with the local authorities in his village for speaking his native Euskera, Saizarbitoria seldom had occasion to speak it outside of his home. In the San Sebastián of Saizarbitoria's childhood, Euskera was the language of rural people who had immigrated to the big city, people like his parents. Nobody in his school spoke Euskera. "There were not even songs in Euskera. There was no need to prohibit it," said Saizarbitoria. "People who spoke Euskera were suspected of being nationalists.

But also there was a sense of shame in speaking the language of farmers and peasants and poor people."

For years, nationalists struggled with this class image of Euskera as the language of peasants. The lower-class status of the language was often more image than reality. Many educated people spoke Euskera, and in some towns, notably the metal-working center of Eibar, Euskera was the language of both workers and management, a prerequisite for working in a factory even for an inmigrante from Andalusia.

Like Atxaga, Saizarbitoria found his inspiration in the invention of Batua and the works of Gabriel Aresti. Published in 1969, Saizarbitoria's first novel, *Egunero hasten delako* (Because It Begins Every Day), was about abortion, which was legal in the rest of Europe but banned in Spain. The book's subject and lean, carefully crafted prose launched a new genre in Euskera literature— the modern social novel.

His second novel was published after Franco's death, in 1976. Titled *100 metro*, 100 Meter, it relates the thoughts of an ETA suspect in the last moments of his life, chased a final 100 meters, before being shot to death.

Saizarbitoria was never an ETA activist, but he was a sympathizer he said, "like almost everyone." He has remained resolutely political. "I want to defend my culture and my identity, and sometimes nationalism is the only possibility. When I am with nationalists I am against them, but when I am with others I am a nationalist.

José Luis Alvarez Enparantza, known to most Basques as Txillardegi, is a professor of Basque philology, the sociology and linguistics of Euskera, at the San Sebastián campus of the Universidad de País Vasco, University of Basqueland. His baggy corduroys and akimbo hair display stereotypical professorial disorder. On his office wall is a 1914 "ethnographic map of Europe" showing areas where Basque, Irish, and Breton were spoken,

Greek-speaking enclaves in Turkey, all the rebellious niches of European language. By the late 1990s, he had authored some twenty books, including essays on linguistics, a mathematical analysis of linguistics, five respected novels, and lyrical poetry.

Where now stands the icily white, contemporary campus of this disheveled professor, in 1929 was the rural neighborhood where he was born. The rebel is still there. Until 1998, he taught only in Euskera, and when the university insisted that it wanted to offer a course taught in Spanish, he refused, until it threatened to hire a second professor of Basque philology.

The promotion of the Basque language remains the first goal of most nationalists, and although huge strides have been made, there is still much to do. Most of the business of the Basque government is still done in Spanish. Although Euskera is a requirement for nonpolitical government jobs, many elected politicians, even from the Basque Nationalist Party, do not speak it. In 1998, many Basque politicians were angered because the proposed candidate for lehendakari, Juan José Ibarretxe, could not speak Euskera well.

The most visible language fight is over signs on the highway. Slowly, names are changing back to the Basque spelling. Many are easy to understand. Guernica in Euskera is Gernika. Bilbao is Bilbo. But San Sebastián is Donostia, Vitoria is Gasteiz, Pamplona is Iruña, Fuenterrabía is Hondarribia. The only solution that would not lead to thousands of outsiders getting lost on the highway is to do what any small country with an obscure language might do, print names in two languages. But for twenty years, vigilante nationalists have been spray-painting away the Spanish names. The result is exactly what was intended: Anybody who spends any time in Basqueland knows the towns by their Basque names.

"HOPE RISES FROM their hearts to their lips like a song from heaven," wrote José Antonio Aguirre. "That is why the Basques are always singing." Song is the oldest art form in Euskera and the most profitable one. Some of the large choruses founded in nineteenth-century nationalism are in fashion again. Benito Lertxundi's acoustic guitar and protest songs have never fallen out of fashion. Trains, shops, and public buildings pipe in his music, including the old underground songs that teenagers used to whistle at Guardia Civil—daring to think in Euskera in front of them.

As in the 1930s, anything Basque is prospering, and that includes Basque sports. Basques are again attending the goat races and wood-chopping contests, the ports are again hosting ardently contested regattas, and the always popular pelota has more fans than ever before. They are not as drawn to the long-basket jai alai from St. Pée that Basques had popularized in the Americas, but to bare-handed pelota. Appealing to the same old-fashioned machismo as the wood chopping and other tests of strength, this sport uses two or four players, armed with nothing but their bare hands with which to smack a ball somewhat smaller than and just as hard as a baseball. Bare-handed matches have a quality of theater to the way they are played on three walls with the imaginary fourth wall opened to an audience. Since there is no racquet, it is an ambidextrous two-handed game. No athlete ever looked more naked than the bare-handed pelota player with no equipment but carefully placed bandages to protect the two bare hands. It seems the entire body goes into the hand as it slaps the hard little ball.

The many other variations of pelota with baskets and paddles of different sizes were designed to make the ball go faster, making it harder to return, but in a bare-handed match the point is scored by carefully setting up the opponent through the placement of the ball over a series of volleys.

The players used to come from families of players, and many still do. Retegi II, born in 1954, won championships almost every year in the 1980s and 1990s. Tintin III was another leading player. The numbers after their names indicate the number of

Pelota ticket, 1928. (Euskal Arkeologia, Etnografia eta Kondaira
Museoa, Bilbao)

generations of champions. Panpi LaDouche, the greatest champion from the French provinces, was trained by his father in the family court in the village of Ascain in the Nivelle Valley. His legal name is Jean-Pierre, because until recently, parents were not allowed to register their children's birth certificates in France with a non-French first name.

One thing Basques in the 1970s could all agree on was that Panpi LaDouche was beautiful. His surprisingly agile, muscular body played the forward court with merciless precision. Though he was right-handed, his left hand could scoop the ball off the left wall, whip it across his body to the far corner of the front wall and up into the spectators' section before his opponent could touch it. The move is called the *gantxo*. Panpi spent four or five hours a day at home with his father, a former professional, developing the left-handed gantxo. In 1970 he became the first man born on the French side to win both the French and Spanish championship.

The sport has become more popular and more profitable than ever because of television. The game is organized into clubs, *empresas*. Typically, an empresa will control fifty players and arrange matches between them. The empresa earns a percentage of the ticket sales and the betting. But in the 1990s, the empresas, like the players, were earning most of their money from selling broadcast rights to television. With television bringing much more money into the sport, professional bare-handed pelota players are no longer trained by their fathers but hire personal trainers, and, as in other professionals sports, the players are becoming stronger and faster.

But Basques work in families, and one aspect of this sport has remained that way: the balls. When an empresa arranges a match, it also chooses the balls. Down the river from Bilbao, past the shipyards and steel mills and the soot-blackened, crowded apartment buildings where a worker can stand on his cramped balcony and stare out at the smokestacks and grime belching from his factory, is Sestao. Like many blue-collar towns in Vizcaya, the center is marked by three things: a soccer stadium, a fronton, and a cemetery.

At the far end of the fronton, up a set of metal steps, is a six-by-twelve-foot room. This is Cipri, the "factory" where the world's best pelotas, most of the balls chosen for professional matches, are made. Cipri is short for Cipriano. The first Cipriano Ruiz started making the balls in the nineteenth century. His son, also Cipriano Ruiz, began in the 1930s. In the 1990s they were made by the second Cipriano's two sons, Cipriano and Roberto. Cipri never had employees, because the business depends on keeping secrets. When a manager orders balls, he tells them which fronton the match will be in. Each court has different walls and a different floor, and the Ruizes know all of them. The manager might have other requests. Make it fast, make it slow, have it bounce high, keep it low. The managers tell Cipri what kind of a match they want.

When the discovery of America was still new, the first balls were made of rubber. Today they are made of thin, clear, very stretchy latex tape. The tape is wound into hard little balls, which sit in old egg cartons awaiting the next step. Then they are wrapped in pure wool yarn, then in cotton string. When the ball is finished, a goat skin is stitched on in the same way as a horsehide on a baseball. The ball always weighs between 104 and 107 grams. Yet somehow each ball is built for a different performance. This is all the Ruizes will say. Explaining the secretiveness of Cipri, Panpi LaDouche, a native of the Nivelle Valley, said, "It's like a good gâteau Basque."

THE OLD BRITISH freight docks, a huge riverfront operation in the heart of Bilbao that had serviced British industry for more than a century, was closed down in the post-Franco economic restructuring, but soon farmers on the slopes above the city saw a strange new sight below. The metal was whiter and fresher than anything else on the riverfront. And it had the name Guggenheim.

How Bilbao ended up with a Guggenheim museum, paid for by Basque taxpayers, was a demonstration of the inner workings of the Basque Nationalist Party, the PNV. The project was a party dream, with nationalist motives that involved almost every imaginable calculation other than art. Josu Ortuando, mayor of Bilbao, said, "We were able to win out over Salzburg and other cities because city hall, parliament, and the Basque government could act as one." Though it is not clear that the other cities wanted to win, what the mayor was referring to was the fact that all three levels of government were controlled by the PNV.

The Guggenheim Foundation, in financial difficulty, was shopping for a site to build a new Guggenheim, one that would not cost the foundation anything and in fact would generate revenue for it. Tokyo, Osaka, Moscow, Vienna, Graz, and Salzburg were among the cities that had already turned down this financially dubious proposition when the foundation director, Thomas Krens, heard of this curious thing—a Basque government. In the end, the Basque parliament, led by the Basque Nationalist Party, but in coalition with Socialists, approved the project. It was not so much the Basque government or the Basque legislature that was drawn to it as the Basque Nationalist Party. The key figure behind the scenes in the negotiations, the man whose thumb up or down was critical but who held no elected office, was Xabier Arzalluz, the Basque Nationalist Party boss.

The choice of Bilbao was in itself significant. Vitoria, the capital of Euskadi, was too provincial and geographically too removed from the Euskera-speaking heartlands to be considered. The cultural center of the three provinces is San Sebastián. But the headquarters of the Basque Nationalist Party is in Bilbao.

The Basque Nationalist Party, now a century-old institution, is the central and anchoring power in Euskadi. The largest political party, it likes to operate as though it were synonymous with government itself. The ikurriña, the official flag of the Autonomous Basque Community of Euskadi, is also the official flag of the party. Often, the sight of the flag means nothing more than a local party headquarters.

The main headquarters in Bilbao, with its especially large ikurriña, is a modern structure of Stalinist grandeur with two thick, dark, black pillars supporting nothing on either side of a metal detector. It was built in 1993 on the site of Sabino Arana's house, literally Sabin Etxea, and it is where Arzalluz's office is located.

Once you are past the security guards, the metal detectors, and the two pillars—once you are standing on the marble floor of the mausoleumlike lobby, it seems certain that the embalmed corpse of Sabino must be on display nearby. But not even his house is there. Franco, who, like Sabino, understood the importance of symbols, had it destroyed. One of the workers on the demolition seemed to have had nationalist leanings, and he saved a balcony railing, which he kept in his own house during decades of silence. The ornate nineteenth-century ironwork piece now rests above the lobby of the party building, an intentional anachronism.

The Sabino Arana Foundation, also based in this building, gives annual awards, like a nation bestowing its Medal of Freedom. In 1997, the recipient was the Tibetan government-in-exile. The PNV remembers exile. The 1998 recipient was the Saharan Polisario Front, which has been fighting for decades for independence from Morocco.

If the PNV had wanted to improve the museums of Bilbao, the city had another museum, the handsome old Bellas Artes, considered one of the better museums in Spain, which could have been expanded.

But the party leadership had something else in mind. It is what has always been on their minds: nation building. The leadership is well aware that if Euskadi is a nation, it is a tiny nation, and while half the struggle is building the nation, the other half is getting it recognized in the world. The size of their land and their population never seems to moderate Basque ambitions.

To CALCULATE the exact cost to Euskadi taxpayers of the Bilbao Guggenheim is complicated, or perhaps the leadership wants it to be complicated. The figure usually mentioned is $100 million, which is equal to $56 for each citizen. After paying for the building, the Basques also agreed to pay the Guggenheim for using the Guggenheim name on the building. Furthermore, the Guggenheim Foundation chooses the art for the Bilbao museum. The survey of twentieth-century art that made up the initial exhibit seemed like leftovers from the Guggenheim warehouse. The museum, with the exception of a few Chillida pieces, pays no homage to Basque art. Even Picasso's great tribute to Basque suffering, *Guernica*, was not made available for the opening. Officials at the Reina Sofia Museum in Madrid, where it hangs, said that it could not be moved because it was too delicate for the journey. But many speculated that the Madrileños feared the Basques would never give the painting back—a fear rooted in the almost self-evident fact that it belongs in a major museum of twentieth-century art only a few miles from Guernica.

And yet the Basque Nationalist Party got what it wanted out of the project. Arzalluz said, "It was expensive, but it was cheap for what we got. When we decided to do it, everyone was against it. But then, it was argued that in the center of Bilbao would be a center of modern art for Europe. Then we saw the light. It is a great thing for the future. More than we ever thought, it is an important building. Everyone recognizes that it is a great building, greater than what is in it."

Ramón Labayen, who was the Basque government's minister of culture at the time the project was first proposed, said, "It is a great opening up to the world." To bring the world to them was seen as far more important to the Basques than promoting themselves to the world. An internationally prestigious American building would do more to make them a nation than a brilliant display of Basque art.

By the time the museum opened in October 1997, Bilbao was a city with a lot of plans. But they rarely included the word *culture,* except in the phrase *industrial culture.* "From the beginning we wanted something more than culture. It is an investment," said Mayor Ortuando. "It will be easier to attract investments because of the Guggenheim."

This is a city of industry. The hotels here have always offered reduced rates for weekends, because most visitors are Monday-through-Friday business travelers.

The mayor reasoned, "This was an industrial city that was based on iron mines. At the end of the 1980s we started recovering and planning the future. The iron mines were exhausted. Where was the future? How do we use our industrial culture, our traditional work ethic, our human capital? What we could do is use new technology. But this would not be enough. We had a deep harbor, a port with a future, and we could be a service center. We started to develop a postindustrial concept with five points."

Included in the five-point plan were cleaning up the pollution from the old industry, cleaning the river, separating industry from the center city, expanding the subway system and the airport, building more bridges, enhancing technology and managerial programs in the universities, building new industries . . . After looking at the city plans, the $100 million for the museum does not seem as shocking. But only number five of the city's five-point plan mentions anything about cultural attractions.

From the PNV point of view, Frank Gehry was the perfect architect for the project. In his sixties, he had become the international architect of the moment based on several major projects in the U.S. Midwest, the American Center in Paris, and an office building in Prague. He also was smitten with Basque country and expressed a personal affection for things Basque, though this was not necessarily reflected in his work. The last thing the PNV wanted was something uniquely Basque. The party wanted something international. The other appealing thing about Gehry was that he had garnered a reputation as a sculptor. His buildings were said to be works of art in themselves. He told the Basques that if he did a museum, he would regard the building itself as more important than the work in it.

That was what the Basques wanted: an important building. What they got was a fanciful-looking structure of curves and tilts, at the base of the mountains, seen at the end of Iparraguirre Street, the long straight avenue of blackening nineteenth-century architecture named to honor the author of "Tree of Guernica."

The structure has neither the grace nor the originality of Frank Lloyd Wright's Guggenheim in New York but seems to almost subconsciously pay homage to that famous softly tapered spiral. As promised, it is more a sculpture than a building. Though interesting to look at from the outside, it offers no new ideas about museum architecture. Inside, the exhibition space may have the boldness but not the fluidity of the Wright building. As in a French airport, you are never exactly sure where to go. It does not have the sense of humor of the Pompidou Center. Nor does it have the traffic. Contrary to the publicity, it did not seem crowded its first year. About 50 percent of the visitors, according to museum figures, were Basques. Basque families, the men in floppy, dark blue berets, wandered through.

But while the foreign press had predicted huge crowds of international tourists, this had never been the stated goal of the PNV, nor is tourism a priority in the plans for the city. The Basque Nationalist Party got what it wanted when the *New York Times* architecture critic, Herbert Muschamp, called the museum "the most important building yet completed" by Gehry.

The most intriguing side of the Bilbao Guggenheim is the back. Set against a man-made pond, the shiny titanium structures look like a cartoon port, the sort of place where tugboats with big smiles might dock. The traffic speeding over the high, green La Salve Bridge, across the Nervión, appears to be getting swallowed by this titanium monster. Below on the other side is the infamous Cuartel de la Salve, a Guardia Civil station conspicuous for its Spanish flag, a rare sight in Basqueland. Two heavily armed guards stand in front with bulky bulletproof protection, looking unhappy to be there.

When asked for her opinion, a woman who lived in the neighborhood near the Guggenheim said, "I don't know anything about modern art," which is what Arzalluz also said. A law professor at Deusto, the university that is also just across the river from the museum, Arzalluz passes by twice a day and looks at the Guggenheim. "I like it more each time," he said.

Did that mean he did not like it at first?

"No, no, I liked it. But it's not that I wanted a Gehry building. We are not modern architecture experts."

Most of the non-nationalist parties were strongly against the project but lacked the votes to stop it. Once it was built, most criticism ended. One of the building's accomplishments was that it produced newspaper and magazine articles around the world about Basqueland, many of which did not mention terrorism.

But in spite of the publicity, it was still the same old Bilbao, with its ornate, slightly blackened, nineteenth-century architecture, the green Basque mountains showing up surprisingly at the end of streets, and the lentil-brown Nervión River with weirdly colored suds suddenly drifting in the current. The government said the river was being cleaned up and it was smelling better. But hotels still lived off of businessmen, not tourists, and continued to give a discount on weekends.

THE GUGGENHEIM is just the most noticeable part of the plan to change Bilbao. As befitting a Bilbao museum, it has an industrial setting on the Nervión. But the container-loading rail yard next door is slated to be moved elsewhere. The city's problems and the solutions that are being found are very much like those of other nineteenth-century industrial cities, such as Cleveland and Pittsburgh. Except that Clevelanders are not trying to build a country.

One thing about which the PNV has always been extremely clear is the importance of money. Throughout history it was the strength of the Guipúzcoan and Vizcayan economy that guaranteed Basque independence. It is believed that a strong economy will someday win it back again. "Today we have a significant degree of power, and that requires pragmatism," said Arzalluz. "We are not less pro-independence. It is the same line. But to be a David against Goliath requires intelligence. The economy is the first problem. How to build an economy that works within Europe."

The death of Franco was an economic disaster for the Basques, though one few regretted. He had used Basque industry as the engine for a false economy, without exports or foreign markets— an economy that was almost completely within Spain and therefore within his control. Basque industry, the oldest in southern Europe, was archaic. This was true of not only steel but shipbuilding and manufacturing. Only a few of the twenty-two paper mills that operated in Tolosa have survived. Eibar on the Guipúzcoa-Vizcaya border has lost its appliance industry.

Like Bilbao, Eibar was built on the nearby iron fields. In the Middle Ages the town made armor, outfitting the soldiers of the Reconquista. Juan San Martin of the Basque Academy of Language descended from an Eibar armor-making family. Eibar is on a river and its manufacturers learned how to harness water power. By the nineteenth century, it had converted its industry to coffeemakers and other appliances. Later came bicycles, which remain a town specialty. But once Franco died and Spain joined the European Economic Community, Eibar products could not compete with those of more efficient French, Italian, and German industry.

The crisis would have come sooner and more gently had Franco not been there. The Basque iron fields that had once exported ore to feed British blast furnaces had become exhausted and could no longer supply even enough for Basque industry. But of even greater consequence, by the late twentieth century it no longer required a huge labor force to produce steel, and a steel mill that operated with a large number of workers could not sell its products at a competitive price in the world market. Until 1975, Vizcayan steel mills were not trying to sell in the world market, but only in Franco's Spanish market.

In the 1960s and 1970s, Basque industries provided thousands of jobs. In order to carry out his plan of filling Basqueland with non-Basques, Franco had to provide jobs for inmigrantes. But the bloated industries did not die with the Caudillo. In 1975-80, Altos Hornos de Vizcaya was employing 12,000 workers. But for twenty years it had been losing money and the government had been making up the difference. At its height, the steel mill was losing more than $1 billion each year.

Europe made the abandoning of government protection to industry a precondition for Spain's entry into the European Economic Community. In any event, it would have been impossible to have preserved the system in an open economy. The

Spanish market would have been overrun with European goods.

While most so-called rust belt areas have turned to service industries, when the PNV-dominated Basque government took over the management of the Basque economy, it wanted to preserve industry. "The Basque government did not want to lose the industrial spirit of Vizcaya," said Jon Zabalía, a Vizcayan PNV legislator.

The policy was to identify the industries that could be saved, many of which were owned by PNV families, and to look for new industries. Altos Hornos de Vizcaya was remade into Aceria Compacta de Bizkaia, a company that produces steel by using computers but without blast furnaces. Three hundred and sixty workers now produce 800,000 tons a year—more than Altos Hornos de Vizcaya used to produce with 12,000 workers. Shipbuilding has been reduced but maintained. La Naval, the longtime Spanish government shipbuilder, restructured with 1,800 workers instead of 5,000.

A road runs along one bank of the Nervión and a traveler could look across the river, a particularly dramatic sight against a night sky, and see the fiery red glare of exploding blast furnaces, cranes swinging, tall smokestacks releasing dark clouds. Pío Baroja once wrote of this sight, "The river is one of the most evocative things in Spain. I don't think there is anything else on the peninsula that gives such an impression of power, of work, and of energy, as this 14 or 15 kilometers of river front."

Today, it is dark along the Nervión at night. Though there are still a few shipyards and some steelworks, there are no blast furnaces and about 400 industrial buildings have been abandoned. From the death of Franco, for the next fifteen years, Basque jobs were steadily eliminated. Many workers were in their forties and fifties and hard to retrain. They are being permanently supported by Spanish government pensions if they were in the public sector and by the Basque government if they were in private-sector jobs. Thousands from other parts of Spain have gone back to their regions. By 1990, unemployment had reached 26 percent. Since then it has steadily improved. By 1998, it was 20 percent, slightly better than the Spanish average. The per capita income in the Basque provinces is still one of the highest in Spain. But among young people between the ages of eighteen and twenty-five, the ages that Herri Batasuna and ETA are most successful at attracting, unemployment has stayed at 50 percent.

The Basques have remained leaders in banking. In 1988,

Detail from the cover of a 1930 catalogue for the Euskalduna, the now defunct Bilbao shipyard that was founded on the Nervión in 1900 and became a victim of post-Franco economic restructuring. (Untzi Museoa-Maritime Museum, San Sebastían)

Banco de Bilbao and Banco de Vizcaya merged into one of Europe's largest banks. This marked the beginning of a trend in mergers and consolidation of banks all over Spain. Despite these new pan-Iberian giants, the Vizcayan bank created by the 1988 merger, Banco Bilbao Vizcaya, is still the second largest bank in Spain.

Like the nineteenth-century Basques who wanted to use rail links to open up their industry, today's Basque want to build rail links between Basque cities and Europe. A Basque government-built commuter railroad already runs from Bilbao to Hendaye, linking Vizcaya, Guipúzcoa, and Labourd. It is the first local train to connect France and Spain's Atlantic coast. Spain, like Russia, had intentionally built its railroad tracks with a non-standard measurement to protect against invasion by rail.

In 1867, a group of writers in France, including George Sand, Alexandre Dumas, and Victor Hugo, wrote a guide to Paris in preparation for a world's fair. Hugo's introduction to the guide, titled "The Future," began: "In the 20th century, there will be an extraordinary nation. This nation will be large, but that will not prevent it from being free. It will be illustrious, rich, thoughtful, pacifist and cordial to the rest of humanity. It will have the gentle seriousness of an elder.... A battle between Italians and Germans, between English and Russians, between Prussians and French, will seem like a battle between Picards and Burgundians would seem to us."

Only a few years after Hugo wrote these words, the future brought a bitter war with Germany. Two more would follow, leaving Europe all but destroyed. A hundred years after Hugo wrote "The Future," a broad consensus among European leaders would end borders, end tariffs, and issue a common European passport. The process culminated with the 1992 Maastricht Treaty, which was to change the European Economic Community into the European Union, an entity with one currency and one central bank. The agreement was that all of the members had to ratify the treaty or it would be rejected. But when Danish voters turned it down, Denmark was told that it would be ejected from the community if it did not reverse its decision, which it did by a narrow margin. The voters in other member nations also ratified, in many countries, including France, by the narrowest of margins. Only Spain ratified without consulting its voters, saying that it was unnecessary.

Until recently, one of the central characteristics of Basqueland had been that a border runs through it. The Basques had a border culture. Smugglers and border crossers were folk heroes. Sometimes smugglers would cross the Bidasoa on rafts made of planks. Or a "band of smugglers," comprising as many as twelve men, would carry goods through the mountains on the darkest nights, undeterred by customs officials who waited in hiding and sometimes shot at them.

### SALMÍ DE PALOMA

*In the fall, armed men hide in the pine woods by Ibañeta where warriors once waited to pounce on Roland. But they are waiting to shoot the gray-and-white wild pigeons that fly through the pass. The birds are cooked in wine and brandy, which used to be made by monks for the pilgrims. This hunt is at least old enough to be regulated in the 1590 Fuero of Navarra.*

*The following recipe comes from Julia Perez Subiza of Valcarlos, whose mother-in-law started the Hostal Maitena across from the fronton in Valcarlos in 1920.*

*Ingredients for one pigeon*
*1 onion*
*2 garlic cloves*
*1 leek*
*1 carrot*

*1 sprig of thyme*
*a little parsley and black pepper*
*1 glass of brandy*
*1/2 liter red wine*

*Cover the bird in flour and sauté it slowly. Chop the vegetables*
*finely and add warm wine to the ingredients, with the excep-*
*tion of the brandy, which is added at the end. Bring the sauce*
*to a boil and then cook gently.*

Basques love border stories: In the nineteenth century there
was a famous story in Hendaye of French customs officials seiz-
ing thirty barrels of wine, but when they triumphantly brought
them back to Hendaye, they discovered nothing but water in
the barrels. It had been a decoy. In a twentieth-century story, a
man crossed the Behobie Bridge over the Bidasoa from Irún,
Spain, to Hendaye, France, every day. He would ride his bicycle
over the bridge past the Guardia Civil and the gendarmes and
would disappear into Hendaye. Later in the day, he would bicycle back with a sack of flour. The Guardia Civil stopped him
every day and made him open the sack so they could carefully
sift through the flour. But they never found any contraband in
it. And they never noticed that he always biked into Hendaye
on an old bicycle and rode back to Irún on a new one.

An even greater irritant than the duty on commercial goods
was the duty on personal items. Many individual Basques were
small-time smugglers, sneaking across items for their own use.
In the nineteenth century, well-dressed women would arrive in
Hendaye in the morning with flowers in their hair and leave in
the evening wearing the latest French bonnet.

In 1986, Spain joined the European Community, and by the
1990s the border had disappeared. The Pont St. Jacques, or
Puente Santiago, where caped gendarmes in cylindrical hats faced
caped Guardia Civil in three-cornered patent leather, where young

Ramón Labayen and many other Basque prisoners were exchanged, was now largely a truck parking lot. A tattered Spanish flag remained. The French one was gone. The shops on the French

French and Spanish customs at Behobie Bridge in the early twentieth century.

side, which sold foie gras, chocolates, and champagne, were only open in the summer and had few customers. Without tariffs, French products could be bought for the same price on either side, just as in the days of the Fueros, when the customs began at the Ebro.

What had once been guard stations now were papered over with advertising and a few posters for wanted Basques, torn edges flapping in the breeze. The correct way through, around all the parked trucks, seemed anyone's guess. Everyone kept more or less to the right of wherever the trucks parked. But if any rules did exist, there were no police or officials of any kind watching anyway.

Behobie offered a similar scene. It was as though the truck drivers, missing their stop with the customs officials, just stopped there anyway.

At the Roncesvalles pass, France becomes Spain at the little stone bridge over the Nive in the village of Arnéguy. Arnéguy is centered on a church and a fronton. A 1920 photograph shows fans from Spain gathered on their side of the bridge to watch a pelote match in the Arnéguy fronton on the other side. There is also a customs house and a shop that sells products from all over France. Until a few years ago, a French flag flew on the little stone bridge, where gendarmes inspected papers and packages. After crossing the bridge and leaving Arnéguy, the traveler climbed along the edge of a mountain to another Basque village, Valcarlos. In Valcarlos was a store selling goods from all over Spain, and a Spanish flag flying, and the Guardia Civil, waiting to inspect papers and packages. Like Arnéguy, Valcarlos has a church and a fronton court. The two villages are much the same except that Arnéguy is at the bottom of a valley and Valcarlos up on the slopes. Both have the same red-trimmed whitewashed architecture. The people of both villages speak Basque.

The customs house in Arnéguy is now closed, the gendarmes and Guardia Civil have left their stations, and the flags are gone.

The stores are still there, but without tariffs there is no advantage to buying in one town or the other. A traveler who does not remember from before can drive from Arnéguy, through the pass to the heights of Ibañeta where Roland died, and never know where France has changed into Spain. No one is going to send an army through to fight over the difference anymore.

Jeanine Pereuil said with her customary nostalgia, "You used to hide a little bottle of Pernod in your clothes and nervously smile at the customs official. Now, it's not any fun at all to go across."

WHATEVER THE FEELINGS in the rest of Spain, a united Europe is an idea that resonates with the Basques. They are not always happy with the way this new giant Europe is run. To the left, it seems too friendly to corporations and not open to individuals and small business. The dichotomy between large and free, which Hugo promised would not exist, sometimes seems a reality.

But the idea of not having a border through their middle, of Europeans being borderless and tariffless partners, seems to many Basques to be what they call "a natural idea." "If Europe works, our natural region will be reinforced," said Daniel Landart. Ramón Labayen said, "The European Union represses artificial barriers." Asked what was meant by an artificial barrier, he said, "Cultures are not barriers. Borders are barriers." The borders around Basqueland endure because they are cultural, not political.

When Europeans decolonized Africa, they left it with unnatural borders, lines that did not take into account cultures. This is often stated as the central problem of modern Africa. But they did the same in Europe. The Pyrenees may look like a natural border, but the same people live on both sides.

Arzalluz said, "The concept of a state is changing. They have given up their borders, are giving up their money. We are not fighting for a Basque state but to be a new European state." A 1998 poll in Spanish Basqueland showed that 88 percent wanted to circumvent Madrid and have direct relations with the European Union.

In the idealized new Europe, economies are merged, citizenship is merged. But those who support the idea deny that countries will be eliminated. There will simply be a new idea of a nation—a nation that maintains its own culture and identity while being economically linked and politically loyal to a larger state. Some 1,800 years ago, the Basques told the Roman Empire that this was what they wanted. Four centuries ago, they told it to Ferdinand of Aragon. They have told it to François Mitterrand and Felipe González and King Juan Carlos.

They watch Europe unfolding and wonder what has happened to their old adversaries. Most of the political leaders endorse the new Europe whether their citizens do or not. Mitterrand, Jacques Chirac, González, and Aznar were all strong backers of this new Europe. The Basques watch the French and Spanish give up their borders and their currency and wonder why it is so easy for them. Why didn't Mitterrand worry about the "fabric of the nation being torn"? Why does Madrid not worry about losing its sovereignty? And if they do not worry about these things, why do they feel threatened by the Basques?

The Basques are not isolationists. They never wanted to leave Europe. They only wanted to be Basque. Perhaps it is the French and the Spanish, relative newcomers, who will disappear in another 1,000 years. But the Basques will still be there, playing strange sports, speaking a language of *ks* and *xs* that no one else understands, naming their houses and facing them toward the eastern sunrise in a land of legends, on steep green mountains by a cobalt sea—still surviving, enduring by the grace of what Juan San Martin called *Euskaldun bizi nahia,* the will to live like a Basque.

# Postscript: The Death of a Basque Pig

*A property in the valley*
*A house on the property*
*And in the house, bread and love*
*Jesus what happiness!*
—Antonio de Trueba, "The Basques," 1870

IT IS CALLED a *txarriboda*, and the whelping dog, straining at his chain a distance from the house, knew this was not going to be good.

The pig, purchased the previous spring for almost $80, was named Pepe. He was only slightly more than ten months old, and yet after six months of overeating corn, he weighed 290 pounds, an enormous, rounded, awkward, pinkish white squealing beast that it took seven men to drag out and hold down.

He was an unlucky pig, a castrated male who had been a last-minute replacement for a female who shortly before her planned execution had gone into heat and was saved for breeding.

*Txarriboda* is the Basque name for the annual family slaughter of a pig, generally done during the winter when it is cold. Neighbors take turns helping out at each other's txarriboda. In the village of Muxica, three miles from Guernica, it was Felisa Madariaga and Julián Gabikaetxebarria's turn.

Theirs is a small and struggling farm. Julián, in addition to working the farm with his wife, holds a job in a factory in Guernica. Felisa sells their products every Monday morning in the Guernica market, the same weekly event that the Condor Legion had chosen for a target in 1937. On the farm, they have a few dairy cows and some chickens. They also grow lettuce and are one of the principal producers in the area of choricero peppers. A Vizcayan sweet pepper that ripens to a brilliant red and is then dried, the choricero is used in a number of dishes such as the stuffing for chorizo sausages. It is also used in *bacalao Vizcaína*, the salt cod dish that is the most internationally renowned of all Basque dishes, though most foreign imitations are inauthentic because the choricero is hard to find outside Vizcaya and is almost never to be found outside Basqueland. Choricero peppers ripen in the summer and are tied together on strings like garlands of large, deep red blossoms, then hung to dry for two months.

Julián and Felisa hang the peppers on the front of their traditional farmhouse of oaken beams and massive stone. Their house is named Igertu, which in old Vizcayan dialect means "drying," but this appears to be a coincidence since the house predates the sixteenth-century arrival of peppers. Carvings on a stone windowsill in the front of the house, a Christian cross with Basque solar stars on either side, have been dated back to Roman times. Julián has received offers from people who want to buy the house because of its archaeological significance, but it has always been in his family and he will not sell. It is the etxea of his fathers.

In the fall, Igertu turns bright as a New England hillside, because the choriceros are hung on the house to dry. They are also hung from pipes in the white tile kitchen, forming red drapery that completely covers the ceiling. The peppers that are dried outside keep their brightness, but almost half are lost to rot. The indoor ones are not as colorful, but the losses are only 10 percent. The next year the dried seeds are replanted in the fields across the road.

THE SEVEN MEN held Pepe down on his side across a wooden bench, and one of them placed a green plastic basin on the ground under the pig's neck. The knife went into the neck as the pig squealed even louder and struggled harder. But the men held him. Slowly the squeals turned into growls and then descending grunts. As the wound was worked with the knife and the blood poured out, one man kept the basin stirring to avoid clotting. After five minutes, the pig was only making low grunts and sighs and the blood was still pouring.

An ancient belief of Hebrews and some other cultures that an animal that dies an agonizing death is less edible has been upheld by modern science, and so commercial slaughterhouses avoid this kind of killing. In industrial pig slaughter, the animal is stunned and then the unconscious animal is bled. But these farmers insisted that the industrial way of killing was "not as beautiful." They explained that the blood was darker and not as good. This blood was brilliant red.

The pig was then dragged to the edge of the field, for the long process of burning off the hairs by covering the carcass with pitchforks full of dried ferns and grasses and setting it on fire. It took more than an hour of turning and burning before the skin was completely blackened and hairless. Then the pig was washed and scraped with a knife. It now seemed like a huge, jellylike brownish object.

Meanwhile, the women were chopping guindillas, the slightly hot, thinner red peppers, cutting out the stems, opening the peppers with scissors, carefully removing the seeds and saving them, and chopping only the shiny red skin. They also chopped parsley. During this entire day of working and talking, there was never a moment of discussion about who would do what. There were the men's jobs and the women's jobs and no mixing of them.

They joked as they worked, speaking in Euskera and Spanish, mostly in Euskera. They talked about a recent soccer match. The referee had not been a Basque speaker and angrily told the players to speak in Spanish. Finally, he gave a yellow card, a penalty warning, to the Basque speakers. The team later protested. Some of the pig scrapers thought they should have protested; others thought that since the referee asked them to speak Spanish, they should have spoken Spanish.

With a long steel hook, the toenails were yanked off, and then the four feet were cut off and saved to make pigs' feet. Julián worked with surgical precision, opening the stomach with

Etching by Jean Paul Tillac, 1937. (Collection of the Musée Basque, Bayonne)

long, sure knife strokes, cutting through larger bones with a hatchet.

Julian was born in 1931 and was seventeen years old the first time he butchered a pig. As he chopped, he talked about what he had seen when Guernica was bombed. "Planes buzzed overhead and you could hear the bombs," he said, laying aside the bloody hatchet and working close to the bone with his knife, "but what I remember more was over there." He pointed to the wooded hills beyond the harvested pepper fields. "By the next town, there were German soldiers in tanks, and the reds and the Fascists were fighting, and a lot of people were killed."

Felisa also remembered. She was only three but recalls standing on a mountain watching the planes. "Then my Grandmother took us to the soldiers and they took us away."

The lard from around the kidney was carefully removed, the lacy lining, the caul, was set aside, as was the liver, and the heart. The lungs were hung on a hook by the esophagus, eventually to be fed to the dog who had by now lost all interest in the former Pepe because he no longer detected the scent of fear or death— or Pepe; there was only food.

The intestines were taken out and handed to the women, who received them with unhappy smiles. After Julián removed all of the organs, he opened the back and the men hoisted the legless carcass on a chain and hung it from a beam. While Julián carefully carved the fillet into thin medallions, the women were working on the intestines: emptying them, washing them over and over, soaking them in salted vinegar.

Then they went to the kitchen, where only a single row of last fall's choricero still hung from the ceiling. The men sat at the long table, where crusty bread and bottles of Rioja wine had been placed. The kitchen had both an electric and a wood-burning stove, but only the wood burner was used. First, *por-rusalda*, a hot leek and potato soup, was served, followed by salt cod and red pepper salad with slices of garlic in olive oil. Then came slices of Pepe's grilled liver, followed by grilled sliced fillet of victim, and then *brazo gitano*, a custard-filled sponge cake. Then coffee, brandy, Cuban cigars.

They laughed and joked in Euskera and in Spanish. One of the neighbors complained that he could not understand "these Euskaldunberri and their Batua." He could understand Guipúzcoan or any of the other dialects, "but this Batua, maybe if I listen to something twice I could get it."

The neighbor's son, Igor, with his dark hair and black eyes, his long straight nose, his thin face, strong chin, and thick eyebrows, looked like a portrait of a Basque by a romantic painter. Igor had no intention of a life on the farm. He worked in a factory where he made as much money in a month as he could in three months of farm work. But he learned his part at the txarribodas. Julián worried about preparing someone to take his own place so he could be certain that a time would not come when there would be no more txarribodas in the community.

After lunch, the women chopped the greens off twenty leeks, then cooked the chopped whites over a slow fire so that they poached in their own juices. They did the same with five chopped onions. Then they cooked three and a third pounds of rice until it was overboiled porridge. They diced the lard and put it in a basin, mixing it with the cooked and drained ingredients, a pound of chopped parsley, a dozen chopped guindillas, two large handfuls of coarse salt, and they slowly added the pig's blood until the basin was filled with a bright red mush.

Then the women crossed themselves. They say this is the only insurance against the intestine skins breaking. With the help of an aluminum funnel, they stuffed the skins and tied them off into sausages. They then cooked them for twenty minutes in a pot with the leek greens, which help protect the blood sausage from breaking. Cold water was constantly added to keep the boiling down, since a strong boil also would break the skins.

Meanwhile, with the skillful use of Julián's knife, the men reduced the former farmyard animal into a series of cuts of meat. The head was removed, and the ears and cheeks were cut off for eating. They had slabs of fatback, slabs of bacon, legs ready to cure into ham, chops, loins. The meat for the chorizo would soak for a day, and then the sausages would dry for another week by wood-burning fires.

They had a week of continuous pork feasting ahead of them. To sell any of this would be a violation of health laws. The entire txarriboda might be illegal; it's not certain. But they just eat among themselves with their neighbors once a year.

The blood sausages were grilled on a wood-burning hearth in the living room, and when they were done, it was time to sit once again at the long table in the kitchen where the choriceros were drying overhead. The Rioja and bread were distributed again. They joked in Basque about the large behind of Felisa's sister, Estafanía, who was plump and round and had a contagious laugh.

Estafanía's husband presented his theory that all Basques go to heaven because they don't know how to curse, a hypothesis that met with snickers. There are no swear words in Euskera. The only one anyone could come up with was *madarikátue*, which means "damned." The others thought you could still get to heaven if all you said was madarikátue. But Estafanía said, "No. It won't work. We Basques swear all the time. It's just that the words we use are maketos."

They all laughed. After chorizo, there was the blood sausage, which had a fresh vegetable taste unlike any commercial blood sausage. Next came slices from a cut just above the leg.

Well fed and contented, Estafanía sighed and said, "You see, the best times in life are the first year of marriage and the week you kill the pig."

THE SIXTEENTH-CENTURY Guipúzcoan Esteban de Garibay, the first scholar of Basque history and the first to attempt to trace the origin of the Basque people and language, told the Castilian crown in the clear simplicity of the ancient language, that which Basques have been saying ever since: *"Garean gareana legez,"* Let us be what we are.

# The Basque Thank You

I AM THAT rare and fortunate writer, completely convinced that I work with the best people in publishing: my agent, Charlotte Sheedy, who makes me smile while she persuades me, along with everyone else; George Gibson, still my ideal of what a publisher should be; and most especially Nancy Miller, whose skill and wisdom are always there both as an editor and as a most wonderful friend in good and bad times.

I also want to thank the talented and helpful people at Walker & Company who make it the great house it is; Kristine Puopolo for her interest and advice; Matt Spetalnick for his help in Madrid; and Virginia Peters, who a long time ago came with me to fish beautiful streams and bravely stared down back-alley thugs in patent leather hats.

So many great Basques enriched this book with their generosity, interest, knowledge, and experience. I especially want to thank Joseba Zulaika, who did much to improve this book and has been far too helpful to list alphabetically; Teresa Barrenechea for so much generosity and enthusiasm, for sharing her friends, for being a one-woman public relations force in Vizcaya, and for improving my pil pil backhand; Miel Elvstondo for answering so many of my endless questions; Eva Forest for much valuable advice and assistance, and all the great books; Ramón and Clotilde Labayen for their friendship, hospitality, and advice.

Thanks also go to Jose Allendesalazar for his help and interest; Begoña Aretxaga for her thoughts and advice; the Aranzadi Zientzi Elkartea for help with the Elkain cave drawings; Arautza Barandiaran for her help at the San Telmo Museum in San Sebastián; Amaia Basterretxea for her patient assistance at the Euskal Arkeologia, Etnografia eta Kondaira Museum in Bilbao; Itxaro Borda for her help in Mauléon; José Juan Castillo, the great chef, for his kindness and advice; Maïte Faure for her help in Mauléon; Charles-Paul Gaudin for sharing his photo collection; José Gorrotxategi Pikasarri, the great pastry maker of Tolosa, for his thoughts and advice; Maite Idirin for her thoughts and advice; José Luis Iturrieta for his help and many kindnesses; Felisa Madariaga and Julián Gabikaetxebarria for their friendship, hospitality, and advice; Luis Núñez Astrain for his help at Egin; Olivier Ribeton for help at the Basque Museum in Bayonne, Soko Romano Aguirre for her help at the San Sebastián Maritime Museum; Amaia Zabalo for her help at the Kutxa Fototeka.

And to Josefina Aguirre and the late Kattalin Aguirre for first speaking Basque in front of me, for their hospitality, and for teaching and inspiring so many with courage and kindness.

To all the kind and tough people of Euskadi who have helped me through the years: *eskerrik asko,* thank you.

# Bibliography

## DICTIONARIES

Aulestia, Gorka, and Linda White. *Basque-English/English-Basque Dictionary.* Reno and Las Vegas: University of Nevada Press, 1992.

Egaña, Iñaki. *Diccionario histórico-político de Euskal Herria.* Tafalla, Navarra: Txalaparta, 1996.

*Euskera-Frantsesa/Frantsesa-Euskera.* Bayonne and San Sebastián: Elkar, 1997.

King, Alan R., and Begotxu Olaizola Elordi. *Colloquial Basque.* London and New York: Routledge, 1996.

Narbarte Iraola, N. *Diccionario de apellidos Vascos.* San Sebastián: Editorial Txertoa, 1989.

## GENERAL SPANISH HISTORY

Callahan, William James. *Church, Politics, and Society in Spain, 1750-1874.* Cambridge: Harvard University Press, 1984.

Carr, Raymond. *Modern Spain, 1875–1980.* Oxford and New York: Oxford University Press, 1980.

Clough, Arthur Hugh, ed. *Plutarch's Lives.* Trans. John Dryden. New York: Modern Library, 1992.

Jane, Ceci, ed. *The Four Voyages of Columbus.* New York: Dover, 1988.

Kamen, Henry Arthur. *The Spanish Inquisition: A Historical Revision.* New Haven: Yale University Press, 1998.

Preston, Paul. *Franco.* New York: Basic Books, 1994. (A thorough and unflinching treatment.)

Thomas, Hugh. *The Spanish Civil War.* New York, Harper and Row, 1977. (The indispensable source on the war.)

# BIBLIOGRAPHY

## *IGNATIUS LOYOLA*

Lacouture, Jean. *Jesuits: A multibiography.* Washington, D.C.: Counterpoint, 1995.

Meissner, W. W. *Ignatius of Loyola: The Psychology of a Saint.* New Haven and London: Yale University Press, 1992.

Olin, John C., ed. *The Autobiography of St. Ignatius Loyola.* New York: Fordham University Press, 1992.

Tellechea Idígoras, José Ignacio. *Ignatius of Loyola: The Pilgrim Saint.* Chicago: Loyola University Press, 1994.

## *SABINO ARANA*

Arana Goiri, Sabino. *Bizkaya por su independencia.* Bilbao: Editorial GEU Argitaldaria, 1980.

Basaldua, Pedro. *El Libertador Vasco: Sabino Arana Goiri.* Bilbao: Editorial GEU Argitaldaria, 1977.

Elorza, Antonio, ed. *Sabino Arana Goiri: La Patria de los Vascos: Antología de escritos políticos.* San Sebastián: R & B Ediciones, 1995.

Jemein y Lanbari, Ceferino. *Biografía de Arana-Goiri'Tar̄ Sabin: E Historia gráfica del nacionalismo.* Bilbao: Editorial Vasca, 1935.

## *ETA AND BASQUE NATIONALISM*

Calleja, José María. *Contra la barbarie: Un Alegato en favor de las victimas de ETA.* Madrid: Ediciones Tema de Hoy, 1997.

Cassan, Patrick. *Le Pouvoir Français et la question Basque (1981–1993).* Paris and Montreal, L'Harmattan, 1997.

Clark, Robert P. *Negotiating with ETA: Obstacles to Peace in the Basque Country, 1975–1988.* Reno and Las Vegas: University of Nevada Press, 1990.

Corcuera Atienza, Javier. *Orígenes, ideología y organización del nacionalismo Vasco: 1876–1904.* Madrid: Siglo Veintiuno de

*363*

España, 1979. (A valuable detailed study of the roots of modern Basque nationalism.)

Douglass, William A., ed. *Basque Politics: A Case Study in Ethnic Nationalism.* Reno: Associated Faculty Press and Basque Studies Program, 1985.

Forest, Eva (Julen Agirre). *Operación Ogro: Como y por qué ejecutemos a Carrero Blanco.* Hendaye: Ediciones Mugalde, 1974. (The original underground publication, republished by Eva Forest in 1993 under her own name.)

Garmendia, Vincente. *La Ideología Carlista (1868–1876): En los orígenes del nacionalismo Vasco.* Zarautz: Diputación Foral de Guipúzcoa, 1985.

Granja Sainz, José Luis de la. *El Nacionalismo Vasco: Un Siglo de historia.* Madrid: Editoriales Tecnos, 1995.

Letamendia Belzunce, Francisco. *Historia del nacionalismo Vasco y de E.T.A..* 3 vols. Vol. 1, *E.T.A. en el Franquismo (1951–1976),* vol. 2, *E.T.A. en la transicion (1976–1982),* vol. 3, E.T.A. y el gobierno de PSOE (1982–1992). San Sebastián: R & B Ediciones, 1994.

Morán, Gregorio. *Los Españoles que dejaron de serlo: Euskadi, 1937–1981.* Barcelona: Planeta, 1982. (Still one of the best discussions of the issues.)

Rubio, Antonio, and Manuel Cerdan. *El Origen del GAL.* Madrid: Ediciones Tema de Hoy, 1997.

Zulaika, Joseba, and William A. Douglas. *Terror and Taboo: The Follies, Fables, and Faces of Terrorism.* New York and London: Routledge, 1996.

### HUMAN RIGHTS

Amnesty International. *Spain, the Question of Torture: Documents Exchanged by Amnesty International and the Government of Spain.* 1985.

——. International Reports: 1975–1998.

BIBLIOGRAPHY

———. "Report of an Amnesty International Mission to Spain." July 1975.

———. "Report of an Amnesty International Mission to Spain." October 3–28, 1979.

———. "Torture in the Eighties: Global Survey." 1984.

———. "Spain: AI Calls for Safeguards Against Torture," Amnesty International Newsletter 15, no. 7 (9 July 1985).

———. "Spain: Allegations of Torture and Ill-Treatment." March 1987.

———. "Summary of Amnesty International's Concerns Related to the Torture and Ill-Treatment of Detainees in Spain." April 1990.

———. "Spain: Torture and Ill-Treatment: Summary of Amnesty International's Concerns." March 1993.

———. "Comments by Amnesty International on the Government's Fourth Periodic Report to the Human Rights Committee (UN). April 1996.

———. "Spain: A Brief Summary of Amnesty International's Concerns." January–October 1997.

Arana, Begoña. *Senideak: El largo viaje de la solidaridad.* Hondarrabia: Hiru Argitaletxea, 1996.

Forest, Eva. *Diario y Cartas desde la Carcel.* Hondarrabia: Hiru Argitaletxea, 1995.

———. *Diez Años se Tortura y Democracia.* Hondarrabia: Eva Forest, 1987.

*Proceso al Jurado?: Conversaciones con Miguel Castells.* Hondarrabia: Hiru Argitaletxea, 1997.

Moraza, Lurdes, and Mertxe Basterra. *La Columna infame.* Tafalla, Navarra: Txalaparta, 1994.

Senideak. "Informe anual, 1997," Euskal Herria, January 1998.

———. "La Politica de dispersion Penitenciaria vulnera los Derechos Humanos," Euskal Herria, November 1997.

TAT–Group Against Torture in the Basque Country. Report on torture, with appendixes, November 1997.

## BASQUE HISTORY

Aguirre, José Antonio. *Escape via Berlin: Eluding Franco in Hitler's Europe.* Reno and Las Vegas: University of Nevada Press, 1991.
——. *De Guernica a Nueva York pasando por Berlin.* St.-Jean-de-Luz: Editorial Axular, 1976. (There are interesting differences between the European and the American editions.)

Altube, Gregorio. *El Excelentismo Señor: D. Xabier Maria de Munibe, Conde de Peñaflorida.* San Sebastián: Nueva Editorial, 1932.

Anasagasti, Iñaki, ed. *Conversaciones sobre Antonio Aguirre.* Bilbao: Idatz Ekintza, 1983. (Interviews with those who knew the lehendakari.)

Arrinda Albishu, Anastasio. *Los Vascos de la Caida de Roma al Cristianismo: S V–X.* Bilbao: Instituto Labayru, 1997.

Bard, Rachel. *Navarra: The Durable Kingdom.* Reno and Las Vegas: University of Nevada Press, 1982.

Baroja, Serafín. *Crónica de la Guerra Carlista: Enero y Febrero de 1876.* San Sebastián: Editorial Txertoa, 1986. (Pío Baroja's father, a war correspondent, describes a brutal winter in the Second Carlist War.)

Bost, Jean, Gilbert Desport, Mikel Epalza, Jean-Pierre Espilondo, Guy Lalanne, Charles Martin-Ochoade Alda, Raymond Paget, Georges Pialloux, and Monique Salaber. *Saint-Jean-de-Luz.* Vol 1. Ekaina, 1992.

Caro Baroja, Julio. *Las Brujas y su Mundo.* Madrid, 1961.
——. *Brujeria Vasca.* San Sebastián: Editorial Txertoa, 1992. (By the great Basque ethnologist, nephew of Pío.)

Charpentier, Louis. *Le Mystère Basque.* Paris: Robert Laffont, 1975. (Proof that even the wildest speculation about the Basques never fades from fashion.)

Collins, Roger. *The Basques.* Oxford: Basil Blackwell, 1986. (Ancient Basque history up to the sixteenth century.)

Cuzacq, René. *Histoire du béret Basque.* Mont-de-Marsan: Editions Jean-Lacoste, 1985.

## BIBLIOGRAPHY

*Ernaroa. La Siderurgia Vasca: De la ferrería a la fábrica y a las modernas acerías.* Revista de historia de Euskal Herria, no. 12. Bilbao, 1985.

Estévez, Xosé. *Historia de Euskal Herria. Vol. 2, Del Hierro al Roble.* Tafalla, Navarra: Txalaparta, 1997.

Fundacion BBV. *La Real Sociedad Bascongada y América.* Bilbao, 1992.

Garate Ojanguren, Montserrat. *La Real Compañia Guipuzcoana de Caracas.* San Sebastián: Sociedad Guipúzcoana de Ediciones y Publicaciones, 1990.

Garcia de Cortázar, Fernando and José M. Lorenzo Espinosa. *Historia del País Vasco.* San Sebastián: Editorial Txertoa, 1996.

Glas, Eduardo Jorge. *Bilbao's Modern Business Elite.* Reno and Las Vegas: University of Nevada Press, 1996.

Henningsen, Gustav. *The Witches' Advocate: Basque Witchcraft and the Spanish Inquisition.* Reno and Las Vegas: University of Nevada Press, 1980.

Jiménez de Aberasturi, Juan Carlos. En passant La Bidassoa: Le Réseau "Comète" au Pays Basque (1941–1944). Biarritz: J & D Editions, 1996.

Jimeno Jurío, José María. *Donde Fue La Batalla "De Roncesvalles?"* Pamplona: Diputación Foral de Navarra, 1974.

——. *Navarra: História del Euskera.* Tafalla, Navarra: Txalaparta, 1997.

Lamant-Duhart, Hubért. *Saint-Jean-de-Luz: Histoire d'une cité Corsaire.* St.-Jean-de-Luz, Ekoldia, 1992.

Larronde, Jean-Claude. *Le Bataillon Gernika: Les Combats de la Pointe-de-Grave (April 1945).*

Lorenzo Espinosa, José María. *Historia de Euskal Herria. Vol. 3, El Nacimiento de una nación.* Tafalla, Navarra: Txalaparta, 1997.

Montero, Manuel. *Cronicas de Bilbao y Vizcaya: Vol. 1, El Progreso de Bilbao: Los Lugares y las fiestas. Vol. 2, Acontecimientos decisivos en la historia del País Vasco. Vol. 3, Vida cotidiana en los Siglos XIX y XX. Vol. 4, Los Negocios de Bilbao.* San Sebastián: Editorial Txertoa, 1997.

Orella, José Luis. *Historia de Euskal Herria. Vol. 1, Los Vascos de ayer.* Tafalla, Navarra: Txalaparta, 1997.

Ramirez, Txema. *Ertzantza: Heroes o villanos?* Tafalla, Navarra: Txalaparta, 1992.

Real Cuesta, Javier. *El Carlismo Vasco 1876–1900.* Madrid: Siglo Veintiuno de España, 1985.

Romaña Arteaga, J. M. *La Segunda Guerra Mundial y Los Vascos.* Bilbao: Ediciones Mensajero, 1988.

Sada, Javier Y Asier. *Historia de San Sebastián.* San Sebastián: Editorial Txertoa, 1997.

Steer, G. L. *The Tree of Gernika: A Field Study of Modern War.* London: Hodder and Stoughton LTD, 1938.

## BASQUE MARITIME HISTORY

Azkarate, Agustín, José Antonio Hernández, and Julio Núñez. *Balleneros Vascos del siglo XVI: Estudio arcqueológico y contexto histórico (Chateau Bay, Labrador, Canada).* Vitoria: Servicio Central de Publicaciones del Gobierno Vasco, 1992.

Belanger, René. *Los Vascos en el estuario del San Lorenzo, 1535–1635.* San Sebastián: Editorial Auñamendi, 1980.

Casado Soto, José Luis, Montserrat Gárate Ojanguren, José Ignacio Tellechea Idígoras, and Juan Pardo S. Gil. *Itsas aurrean El País Vasco y el mar a través de la historia.* San Sebastián: Museo Naval, 1995.

Ciriquiain Gaiztarro, Mariano. *Los Vascos en la pesca de la ballena.* San Sebastián: Biblioteca Vascongada de los Amigos del País, 1961.

Huxley Barkham, Selma. "The Basque Coast of Newfoundland." Newfoundland: Great Northern Peninsula Development Corporation, 1989.

# BIBLIOGRAPHY

Laburu, Miguel. *Ballenas Vascos y America,* Camera Oficial de Comercio, Industria y Navegación de Gupúzcoa.

Michelet, Jules. *Le Mer.* Paris: Gallimard, 1983.

Soraluce y Zubizarreta, Nicolás. *Introduccion, Capitulo I y Otras Descripciones de la memoria acerca del origin y curso de las pescas y pesquerias de ballenas y bacalaos, asi como sobre el des cubrimiento de los bancos e isla se terranova.* Vitoria: Imprenta se los Hijos de Mantel, 1878.

## BASQUE CULTURE

Allaux, Jean-Pierre. *La Pelote Basque: De la paume au gant.* Biarritz: J & D Editions, 1993.

Barañano, Kosme M. de, Javier González de Durana, and Jon Juaristi. *Arte en el País Vasco.* Madrid: Caudernos Arte Cátedra, 1987.

Barandiaran, José Miguel. *Dictionnaire illustré de mythologie Basque.* Trans. Michel Duvert. Bayonne and San Sebastián: Elkar, 1993.

Basque World Congress, Second. *Los Derechos historicos Vascos.* Oñati: Haee-IVAP, 1988.

Caro Baroja, Julio. *Los Vascos.* Madrid: Ediciones Istmo, 1971. (Classic and indispensable.)

D'Abartiague, Lewy. *De l'origine des Basques.* Paris: Librarie de La Nouvelle Revue, 1896.

"Enquête sociolinguistique au pays Basque." Gobierno Vasco, Gobierno de Navarra, and Institut Culturel Basque, 1996.

Eskutik. *Guide de la pelote Basque.* San Sebastián and Bayonne: Elkar, 1990.

Espagnolle, J. *L'Origine des Basques.* Pau, 1900.

Francisque, Michel. *Le Pays Basque, sa population, sa langue, ses moeurs, sa littérature, et sa musique.* Bayonne: Elkar, 1994. (Originally published in 1857.)

Garmendia Larrañaga, Jaun. *Iñauteria: El Carnaval Vasco.* San Sebastián: Kutxa, 1992.

Juaristi, Jon. *El Boucle melancólico: Historias de nacionalistas Vascas.* Madrid: Espasa, 1997.

Morvan, Michel. *Les Origines linguistiques du Basque.* Bordeaux: Presses Universitaires de Bordeaux, 1996.

Ott, Sandra. *The Circle of Mountains: A Basque Shepherding Community.* Reno and Las Vegas: University of Nevada Press, 1981.

Tissié, Philippe. *Les Basques et leurs jeux en plein air.* Bordeaux, 1900.

Zulaika, Joseba. *Crónica de una seducción.* Madrid: Nerea, 1997. (An amusing and insightful study of how the Bilbao Guggenheim came into being.)

Zintzo-Garmendia, B. *Jeux et sports Basques.* Biarritz: J & D Editions, 1997.

## *BASQUE LITERATURE*

Aldekoa, Iñaki, ed. *Euskal poesiaren antologia.* Madrid: Visor, 1993. (Basque poetry anthology in Euskera and Spanish.)

*Anthologie poésie Basque contemporaine.* Bayonne: Centre Culturel du Pays Basque. (Bilingual Euskera and French.)

Aresti, Gabriel. *Euskal Harria.* Hernani: Egin, 1995.

Atxaga, Bernardo. *Obabakoak.* London: Vintage, 1989.

Baroja, Pío. *La Dama de Urtubi.* Madrid: Alianza Editorial, 1993.

Chaho, Agustin. *Voyage en Navarre pendant l'insurrection des Basque (1835).* Bayonne: Harriet, 1989.

Dechepare, Bernat. *Olerkiak.* San Sebastián, Txertoa.

Intxausti, Joseba. *Euskera, la langue des Basques.* San Sebastián: Elkar, 1992.

Lasagabaster, Jesús María. *Contemporary Basque Fiction.* Reno and Las Vegas: University of Nevada Press, 1990.

Laxalt, Robert. *Sweet Promised Land.* Reno and Las Vegas: University of Nevada Press, 1997. (Beautifully written 1957 account of an Amerikanuak's return to Soale after forty-seven years.)

Loti, Pierre. *Le Pays Basque: Récits et impressions de L'Euskal-Herria*. Bordeaux: Aubéron, 1992.

———. *Ramuntcho*. Bordeaux: Aubéron, 1994.

Maeztu, Ramiro. *Hacia otra España*. Madrid: Biblioteca Nueva, 1997.

Muñoz-Alonso López, Agustín, ed. *Antología de la Generación del 98*. Madrid: Santillana, 1997.

Orpustan, Jean-Baptiste. *Précis d'histoire littéraire Basque, 1545–1950*. Biagorri: Editions Izpegi, 1996.

Sarrionaindia, Joseba. *No soy de aqui*. Hondarrabia: Hiru Argitaletxea, 1991.

Unamuno, Miguel de. *Abel Sanchez and Other Stories*. Washington, D.C.: Regnery Publishing, 1996.

———. *Diario Intimo*. Madrid: Alianza Editorial, 1994.

———. *Paisajes del alma*. Madrid: Alianza Editorial, 1995.

———. *Paz en la guerra*. Madrid: Alianza Editorial, 1988.

———. *Poesías*. Madrid: Catedra, 1997.

———. *La Raza Vasca y El Vascuence*. Madrid: Colleción Austral, 1974.

———. *Del Sentimiento trágico de la vida*. Madrid: Colección Austral, 1997.

———. *Three Exemplary Novels*. New York: Grove Press, 1930.

### BASQUE FOOD

Azcaray y Eguileor, Ursula, Sira and Vincenta. *El Amparo*. Bilbao, 1930.

Beleak, Ymanol. *El Libro del Pescado*. San Sebastián: Kriselu, 1989. (Reprint of a 1933 book.)

Boletin de la Cofradia Vasca de Gastronomia. Año I Cuaderno 1, San Sebastián, 1963.

———. Año II Cuaderno 1, San Sebastián, 1964.

———. Años III y IV Caudernos 1 y 2, San Sebastián, 1967.

———. Año VI núm 6, San Sebastián, 1972.

Busca Isusi, José María. *Antologia Gastronómica.* Hondarrabia: Academia Vasca de Gastonomia, 1993.

———. *La Cocina Vasca de los pescados y mariscos.* San Sebastián: Editorial Txertoa, 1990.

———. *Traditional Basque Cooking: History and Preparation.* Reno and Las Vegas, University of Nevada Press, 1987.

Castillo, José. *Recetas de cocina de abuelas Vascas: Alava-Navarra.* San Sebastián: Ttarttalo, 1995.

———. *Recetas de cocina de abuelas Vascas: Gipuzkoa-Bizkaia.* San Sebastián: Ttarttalo, 1998.

———. *Recetas de 200 cocineros de sociedades Vascas.* San Sebastián: Ttarttalo, 1995.

Conférences de Bayonne. *Chocolat: Bayonne.* Biarritz: J & D Editions, 1997.

Conseil Nationale des Arts Culinaires. *Aquitaine: Produits du terroir et recettes traditionelles.* Paris: Albin Michel, 1997.

Constant, Christian. *Le Chocolat: Le goût de la vie.* Paris: Nathan, 1988.

Foster, Nelson, and Linda S. Cordell, ed. *Chilies to Chocolate: Food the Americas Gave the World.* Tuscon: University of Arizona Press, 1996.

Gorrotxategi Pikasarri, José María. *Historia de la confiteria y repositeria Vasca.* 2 vols. Sendoa, 1987.

Pradera, Nicolasa. *La Cocina de Nicolasa.* San Sebastián: Editorial Txertoa, 1979.

Roule, Louis. *Fishes, Their Journeys and Migrations.* New York, Tokyo, London: Kodansha International, 1996.

# Index of Proper Nouns